The Flight of Ikaros

The Flight of Ikaros

Travels in Greece During the Civil War

KEVIN ANDREWS

Foreword by J. C. Douglas Marshall

PAUL DRY BOOKS
Philadelphia 2010

First Paul Dry Books Edition, 2010

Paul Dry Books, Inc.
Philadelphia, Pennsylvania
www.pauldrybooks.com

Photographs: Kevin Andrews, *Castles of the Morea* (Gennadeion Monographs
IV), rev. ed., with an introduction by G. R. Bugh (Princeton, 2006), figs. 23,
25, 162, 188. Courtesy of the Trustees of the American School of Classical
Studies at Athens.

Typefaces: Fairfield and Optima families
Designed and composed by P. M. Gordon Associates

1 3 5 7 9 8 6 4 2
Printed in the United States of America

Library of Congress Cataloging-in-Publication Data
Andrews, Kevin, 1924–1989.
  The flight of Ikaros : travels in Greece during the civil war / Kevin Andrews ;
foreword by J. C. Douglas Marshall.
    p. cm.
  Originally published: Boston : Houghton Mifflin, 1959, with title The flight
of Ikaros : a journey into Greece.
  ISBN 978-1-58988-064-1 (alk. paper)
  1. Greece—Description and travel. 2. Greece—History—Civil War,
1944–1949. 3. Andrews, Kevin, 1924–1989—Travel—Greece.
4. Greece—Social conditions—20th century. I. Title.
  DF726.A73 2010
  949.507'4—dc22
                                                              2010030677

Contents

Foreword

BY J. C. DOUGLAS MARSHALL

GREECE HAS ALWAYS BEEN a place of contrasts. Homer tells us that on Achilles' shield Hephaestus juxtaposed scenes of treachery and suffering with ones of joy and the celebration of the mundane tasks that sustain life. When Kevin Andrews arrived in Greece as a young graduate student in 1947, he found himself in a world of contrasts reminiscent of those scenes.

Since *The Flight of Ikaros* is a story of Kevin Andrews and of Greece during a troubled period, some background about both is warranted. Andrews was born in the city then known as Peking on January 20, 1924.[1] After attending schools in England, Andrews graduated from St. Paul's School in Concord, New Hampshire, in 1941. He entered Harvard the following fall, but interrupted his studies to enlist in the United States Army, where he saw combat in northern Italy as a member of the Tenth Mountain Division. Returning to Harvard after the war, he received his A.B. degree in 1947 and was awarded a fellowship for graduate study at the American School of Classical Studies at Athens. The narrative of *The Flight of Ikaros* begins at this point and continues until Andrews's return to America four years later.

---

1. For the following summary of Kevin Andrews's life, I am indebted to Glenn R. Bugh's foreword to the 2006 edition of Andrews's *Castles of the Morea* and to Roger Jinkinson's *American Ikaros: The Search for Kevin Andrews.*

In early September 1947, when Andrews arrived in Greece for the first time, the country was gripped by a civil war, which had its beginnings even before the conclusion of World War II. The Greeks had heroically defended their nation from Italian invasion, but in 1941 they and their British allies were overwhelmed by the German forces that conquered the Greek mainland. German occupation was a three-year nightmare. The conquerors seized the food supplies while a significant percentage of the Greek population faced starvation. The Jewish communities in Athens and Thessalonica were nearly annihilated. Some Greeks collaborated, either out of conviction or simply as a means of keeping themselves and their families alive. Others allied themselves with the resistance. EAM (National Liberation Front) and its military wing ELAS (National People's Liberation Army) were the vanguard of this resistance. Politically leftist, ELAS/EAM engaged in guerrilla warfare—a style of combat the Greeks had developed during centuries of Ottoman rule. In these efforts, the British actively aided and abetted them as well as their rival EDES (National Republican Greek League).

By 1944, the Nazi grip on Greece was failing, and the Greek resistance began to position itself for power in a post-war government. ELAS/EAM had strong claims to power because they were well armed and controlled much of the territory outside the major cities. However, with Soviet troops already deployed near the Balkans, Britain feared that the guerrilla resistance might cooperate in a Communist takeover of Greece. In October 1944, Churchill and Stalin met in Moscow and agreed that, in exchange for the Soviet Union's "ninety percent predominance" in Romania and Bulgaria, Britain would have a "ninety percent predominance" in Greece. Numerous stories in the *Iliad* tell of mortals unaware that their fates have already been sealed by the gods; similarly, the Greek resistance fighters found themselves pawns in the chess game of the powerful as the German occupation ended in the closing months of 1944.

Eventually, what had been agreed to covertly in Moscow became evident to the Greek resistance. Fighting then broke out between them and their erstwhile allies, the British, who struggled
to prop up a center-right government that had spent the war years
in Cairo. Andrews's narrative touches on these events as well as
the subsequent reprisals by the Right for atrocities committed by
ELAS/EAM during the years of occupation. By early 1947, the
United States had replaced Britain as the primary guarantor of a
non-communist Greece. President Truman persuaded Congress
to grant emergency aid to "free peoples" whose governments were
facing subversion from within. Greece was a recipient of such aid,
and it proved to be an important factor in providing the military
muscle that ultimately defeated the communist resistance during the summer of 1949. This American initiative, which became
known as the Truman Doctrine, was a subject of discussion and
debate in the cafes described in *The Flight of Ikaros*.

As these tumultuous events unfolded, the newly arrived Kevin
Andrews found himself cloistered in the safe and serene com-
pound of the American School of Classical Studies. His under-
graduate thesis had been entitled "Prometheus and Ahab, a Study
in Clarity and Chaos," but the world of the American School
offered no arena for such flights of literary imagination. Its mission was to instruct students in the craft of archaeology: the anal-
ysis of potsherds, an understanding of technical aspects of Greek
architecture, and the interpretation of the evidence furnished by
coins and inscriptions. Faced with this rigorous program which
was intended to equip its students for academic careers, Andrews
rebelled. "I was a pain in the neck," he writes, "and I was finally
told so."[2] His first year in Greece was further complicated by the
onset of an illness eventually diagnosed as a mild form of epilepsy, a condition that would plague him for the rest of his life.

2. *Flight of Ikaros* (Penguin, 1984), p. 28.

Andrews's independent spirit did not keep the American School from recognizing his talents. Shortly before the outbreak of World War II, the Gennadius Library had acquired a portfolio of plans of fortifications drawn for Francesco Grimani, the early-eighteenth-century Venetian governor of the Peloponnesus, which was then called the Morea. Andrews was asked to produce an edition of these plans.

Fellowship grants enabled him to remain in Greece for two more years as he visited the remains of structures built between the twelfth and eighteenth centuries by Byzantines, Greeks, Franks, Turks, and Venetians. This project provided Andrews the opportunity to leave Athens and the constraints of the American School and to wander in a country traumatized by the memories of its recent past and still in the midst of civil war. The fortresses that Andrews visited were intended to provide security and protection to Greece's conquerors; among their ruins, Andrews encountered Greeks seeking protection from their fellow countrymen. This contradictory world in which warmth and spontaneous generosity were the companions of suspicion and danger is the setting of *The Flight of Ikaros*.

Kevin Andrews returned to the United States in 1951. The fruit of his research, *Castles of the Morea*, was published the following year as part of the Gennadeion Monograph series. For over fifty years it has remained an indispensable resource for students interested in the massive fortresses that punctuate the hilltops and coasts of the Peloponnesus. In 2006, the American School of Classical Studies published a revised edition which retains Andrews's original text.

The production of such a significant piece of scholarship at age twenty-nine might well have launched Kevin Andrews on a distinguished academic career. This was not to be. The people and the land that Andrews encountered as he measured walls and photographed gateways had changed him. Greece had become his passion. In 1954, Andrews married Nancy Thayer, and two years later, the couple left America for Greece where he would spend the rest of his life. It was a country that Andrews loved and that he hoped would be a congenial setting in which to complete *The Flight of Ikaros*, which was first published in 1959. It is this edition that we have chosen to reissue.

The 1967 coup, which brought a right-wing junta to power in Greece, was a watershed for Andrews. Relations between him and his wife were already strained. Against the ominous prospect of life under a military dictatorship, Nancy Andrews left for England with their children. Although they never divorced, they were never reconciled. Andrews's writings during the period of the junta (1967–74) reflect the anger that he felt both about the state of Greece and about his marriage. Frustrated by what he regarded as U.S. support for the Greek right, Andrews renounced America and became a Greek citizen.

In 1984, Andrews produced a second edition of *The Flight of Ikaros*. In his preface to the new edition he asserts, "The present reissue has given me the chance to divest the narrator of some clattering adornments and a whiff of certain attitudes for which, in actual fact, there was neither time nor occasion during the events in question." Why, then, have we chosen to reissue the 1959 edition and not its younger sibling?

Writing about one's past is an exercise in imaginative recreation. The 1959 and 1984 editions of *The Flight of Ikaros* are subtly different in style and tone—differences that tell us more about the author than about the events he portrays. During the turbulent 1970s, Kevin Andrews embraced "the resistance." He led the anxious and furtive life of a polemicist who, if exposed, might face serious consequences. In the rioting that took place outside the Athens Polytechnic in 1973, Andrews was beaten by the police. The trauma of these years left lasting scars.

Reviewing Andrews's *Athens Alive* for the *Times Literary Supplement* in 1980, Patrick Leigh Fermor observed that "recent years have filled the author with feelings which are hot and partisan." Leigh Fermor regarded this partisan tone as a flaw: "Yes, but what about the book's message, the author might ask: the full dessert spoon every half hour? Well, I think the bottle should be given a good shake and the dose drastically reduced."[3] The 1984 edition of *The Flight of Ikaros* was published a decade after the collapse of the junta; it was through the lens of those distressing years that Andrews viewed his early time in Greece. Although he claims to have rid his work of "clattering adornments and a whiff of certain attitudes," other adornments and attitudes take their place. The civil war of the 1984 edition is a struggle between principled leftists betrayed by their erstwhile allies, and a villainous right tainted by a collaborationist past and propped up by the West for its own interests. The 1959 edition tells the story of a young American among good people caught up in horrific events beyond their control. If children are murdered and a village destroyed, the perpetrators are enemies and revenge is demanded. The politics in question fade into insignificance.

A careful comparison of the 1959 edition with its successor reveals that Andrews corrected some proper names as well as place names. We have incorporated those corrections into our edition. We have also recognized the scholarly mission that drew a young graduate student into the battlefields of a civil war. Photographs are included from the recent reissue of *Castles of the Morea*. They portray some of the settings of the human dramas in which Andrews played a part. In essence, you have in your hands the original work with corrections from the later edition.

Bolstered by the fall of the junta and the success of *The Flight of Ikaros*, Kevin Andrews continued to live in Athens throughout the 1980s. He was an acerbic commentator on Greek politics, a masterful craftsman of jewelry, and an accomplished player of several Greek folk instruments. While visiting the island of Kythira in 1989, the 65-year-old set out on a long swim in rough

---

3. *Times Literary Supplement*, 13 June 1980, reprinted in *Words of Mercury* by Patrick Leigh Fermor (London: John Murray, 2003), pp. 239, 240.

seas. His body was found a day later. Like Ikaros, his delight in the intoxicating thrill of danger led to his death beneath the unforgiving waves of Greek seas.

MONTENEGRO
SERBIA
MACEDONIA
BULGARIA
ALBANIA
BLACK
SEA
SEA
OF
MARMARA
MT. OLYMPOS
IONIAN
SEA
G R E E C E
AEGEAN
SEA
TURKEY
Megara
Athens
MAKRONISOS
YERANIA
MOUNTAIN
RANGE
TAÏGETOS MTS
PARNON MTS
PÁROS
Kalamata
Zarnata Castle
Sparta
Mistra
Yeroliména
Cape
Tainaron
M E D I T E R R A N E A N   S E A
CRETE

0   50   100 Miles
0   50   100 Kilometers

The Flight of Ikaros

CHAPTER 1

The Day of Returning

DAYLIGHT BURNED RED on the eyelids—in my nostrils the smell of tar, hot from the deck-boards throbbing under my head. Through the railings, grey-brown rocks sped between a race of water and a heaven deep with sun. I sprang to my feet as masts and cranes listed and the deck thrust up against my soles and knee-joints; then the inky waves foaming out from the ship's side, and the sun and the rocks and the rising and falling spokes of windmills tipped with pointed sails all turned one way as we passed the jetty and with a roar of anchor chains glided into a round, blue harbour. Among bundles and passengers we tumbled into the row-boats rocking under the starboard side, and barefooted men with white sashes round their waists, pushing the oars before them, moved us away from the steamer while it backed swiftly out into the open sea, bound for other islands off the coast of Asia Minor.

We glided in between massive caiques with painted prows floating in the rippling glaze of their reflections. Phrangisko threw his knapsack on to the embankment and steadied me up the water steps—his stern brows and black moustache contrasting oddly with the woolly bulk of the British uniform worn by the Greek Army after the Liberation. He was on leave from the fighting in the Macedonian sector, and we were going together to the house of his cousins from America, a farm in the middle of the island.

Passing under whitewashed arcades, blue in the shadow of six o'clock in the morning, we entered a wineshop where a thin, sweet, pungent smoke mingled with the smell of the sea. "Anything to eat?" Phrangisko called. A man swinging his heels among the empty tables dropped his eyelids and both corners of his mouth, with a slight click of the tongue as he tipped his head back. This was the answer No—a gesture so absolute in its denial as to allow no subsequent appeal except (as in the present case when the man indicated two chairs) the mute appeal of patience. A boy ran in with a handful of red mullets wriggling between his fingers. He poured on them a yellow jet of oil and set them to fry over some embers in a grate, then brought the crusty pink fish and a cylindrical copper cup of bitter wine: "Good appetite," he murmured.

Later, seated sideways on the flat, square wooden saddle of a tiny donkey plying its accurate hoofs over the cobblestones— "you are not accustomed to our roads," said Phrangisko—I saw the narrow walls give way to a path paved in rough, sugary marble, through a brown land rising on either side to naked limestone heights and a massive mountain, dotted all over its lower slopes with the tiny white squares of farms and churches. Sometimes we crossed a stream-bed where thickets of rattling calamus reeds sprouted out of the dry boulders.

On the edge of a gully where egg-plants, ochre, beans and gourds grew in shallow terraces, Phrangisko pointed to a little flat-roofed house with an empty doorway and no windows: "That is where my grandmother has come to be close to my cousins: it's the first time she has ever seen them." From a house on the other side a girl came out to meet us: "My sister," he said. Leaving the beast where it stood, the three of us went to the front where a round pear tree cast its black shadow on a terrace open over the wide valley beyond.

The room into which I stepped was as clean as if the sea had washed it, with a pattern of curly waves in indigo and saffron under the ceiling of glossy, jointed poles of calamus. On the walls huge daguerreotypes of expressionless faces with black headkerchiefs or pointed handlebar moustaches stared out of their oval vignettes, while the salt breeze—though the sea was an hour away to east and west—stirred the lace curtains in the windows and the cloth on a table where a blue and white paper flag sat stiffly in a little vase.

"Be seated," said the young woman, her bare feet arched across the sill. "You have come in time for the wedding of my aunt Evyenía tomorrow night. Forty years she has waited to make her choice, poor burning soul! With her dowry she could have married anyone on the island, but"—with a flexible gesture of the wrist and a roll of her eyes—"such a one as she has chosen! He comes from the mainland, where there is no sea, only mountains. They say the people from there are bad. Here on the islands one is quiet, glory be to God. . . ."

She brought me a tin tray with a small glass of colourless spirit, a glass of water and a saucer of some kind of fruit rind boiled and sugared. I ate the sweet, sticky spoonful and gulped a fiery draught of raki, while the young woman said, "You are welcome." I remembered the formal answer out of my phrase-book: "I have found you well," as I drank my water, and she murmured, "With your good health."

"Do you make this sweet yourselves?" I asked.

She nodded.

"And our own raki," Phrangisko called from a back room where he was changing his clothes, since hospitality was only for strangers. "Every household makes its own."

"And our cousins go from house to house to learn who makes the best," his sister added crisply.

A sharp note of bells carried across the fields. "Now they will come; aunt and cousins, mother and father, brothers, sisters-in-law, nephews, nieces, uncles. In Greece you find big families."

Out on the terrace we could see them coming across the fields from a chapel with a blue dome. I recognized a figure in shorts and T-shirt with a sailor's cap on the back of his head. It was Tom Condor, christened Athanasios Kondarini in the Greek church in Brooklyn Heights, recently employed in an airlines office in Akron, Ohio, whom I had met at boat-drill two hours out of New York harbour. His sisters, on leave from a New York department store, their bobbed hair and pretty painted faces visible among so many heads swathed in kerchiefs, took long strides in their plaid trousers through the other slowly-moving women.

"Poor Ann and Zoe," said Phrangisko at my side. "It seems already half the island has asked to marry them. The other half considers them—you will excuse the word—*tsóules*, because they paint themselves and go about in trousers. They don't deserve it, but people here are narrow in the head."

Mrs Condor, deep in conversation with some other women, bore no resemblance to the grizzled, warm-hearted immigrant I had known on the liner, with her smile of affection for young people cooked into the lines of her big plain face; now she had the look of hard concentration of farmers who talk about crops or the value of their beasts, and she was also darting scowls of fury at her daughters.

A crowd of people stood round me, asking how I had come to Greece, whether I had parents, how I fed myself as a student and where I lived. Mrs Condor called, "Eh, Andrew, what you doing talking to all these bums? You come inside. My brother and sister want to meet you."

All through a day of meetings, greetings and words of friendship and appreciation, I learned the names and relationships of this island clan while the afternoon changed from white to blue and then from gold to violet; then in a tiny kitchen we sat on wooden boxes round a low table, reaching out to the plates of fish and bread and cheese and the wineglasses in our midst. No one drank alone, but raised his glass and everyone touched theirs together, saying, "To health, to the health of us all." Phrangisko's leave, they said, had come in good time since the grape harvest was just beginning; they explained how the bread oven was heated with dry thyme bushes; how there was little to do in winter after the fields were sown until the spring harvest; how stains on the tablecloth were wine stains and these were good luck.

VERY EARLY NEXT MORNING, lying fully dressed and wrapped in a blanket on the little forecourt, I looked up into an oyster sky and heard inside the house Mrs Condor's voice growl, "Zoe, Annoula, God-damn' lazy *tsóules*, get up!"

"Jesus Christ, what's there to get up for?"

"I hear you say Jesus Christ again, I slap your face."

"Hey, fella." Tom was tapping my shoulder. "Come and have breakfast."

Inside, her grey hair falling down her back, his mother crouched beside a tiny hearth cooking Turkish coffee over some glowing twigs. At the far end Zoe and Ann still huddled on a matting of long calamus poles across trestles. Mrs Condor picked up a boulder-shaped loaf: "Those two, all day holler-holler for the Post Toasties and the ice-cream sodas. My kids been working ever since they were little children. Now I bring them home. I just want them to have a nice time."

Two resentful voices drawled at the end of the room, "Goodbye Brooklyn."

Mrs Condor stared at the hearth with a look of incomprehension. A shadow fell along the bar of sunlight on the floor.

"Ooooooh, welcome to the Yannaki!" she cried to a small child holding a dish covered with an embroidered napkin which he placed on the table. He went without a word.

"That's my nephew," said Mrs Condor. "You know, Andrea, I got thirty-two nephew-and-nieces on this island." She sighed. "I don't know why we ever leave this place, honest to God! Long ago my husband had big fleet of *kaíkia* but all the time he has to go away and fight with the *Toúrkous* and *Voúlgarous*; so one day he sells his boats and we go away . . . Thirty whole years we work like the mules, we make the children, we buy the grocery store, we make the money slowly-slowly—and now my husband goes off to Jersey City with some God-damn' *Ispána*. For that I spend my life behind the counter! Ever since I leave my brothers and sisters use my fields and now they want us to stay as long as we like— one year, maybe two. But it would be nice if my husband was here too, eh? Just before he goes away I tell him, I say, 'You listen to me, Zakharia. That woman, she nothing but *skatá*.'"

"Mother, such language!" said Zoe.

"Get out of here, you two God-damns. I'm talking to Andrea."

Tom said, "Let's see what Yannaki has brought us."

His mother lifted the cloth off a plate of honey and sesame seeds. "Nice, eh? Every day the same thing happens: just like that, somebody brings something. I've never been so happy in all my life," she murmured warmly. "You stay here, Andrew, just as long as you want, I tell you." Then she looked at her son in his shorts, bare to the waist, and suddenly snapped out, "I tell you I get mad if I see you go out of the house like that, naked."

"Hell, Ma, it's hot," said Tom.

"Panagia!" Mrs Condor invoked the All-Holy Mother of God. "For what I bring my kids here to make me ashamed in front of my people!"

Voices called to us, "We shall go up into the hills." A train of donkeys halted outside and the grandmother came out of her lit- tle house leaning on a stick, with long skirts about her ankles and a black kerchief over her head and bowed shoulders. Age had worn her face down to a type that could belong to any race on any continent; as one of her grandsons lifted her lightly on to a sad- dle, she might have been some ancient empress; we moved for- ward, fifteen or twenty of us all round her on the path.

We climbed up to the flat top of a hill and saw the blue-grey mountains of the Cyclades and the pale rocks of the deserted shore. Once some Turkish pirates came to the top of this same hill, which "opened up and swallowed them," and the cousins led us to a deep fissure which had never closed again. Mrs Condor said, "Often I think of this place when I'm trying to sell frozen vegetables to the lousy customers."

Passing through a ravine planted with fruit trees, bending low to avoid the spiky branches and the red-crusted pomegranates that bumped our heads and shoulders, we came to a deep spring festooned with ferns and ivy. This place belonged to the old grandmother; with a covert glance at her brothers and sisters Mrs Condor whispered to me, "They're afraid she'll leave the place to me. They're good people but jealous . . . so help me God!"

The rest of the day was given over to preparations for the wedding of her younger sister. Towards sundown the women came wearing clean headcloths and the men with their moustaches trimmed, their chins shiny and the back of their necks clipped white. In the back room a table had been set with a new cloth and candles. The priest, the lower half of his face hidden under a curly beard and his long hair tied up and knotted under a cylindrical hat, swung a brass censer on the end of three clanking chains and chanted the wedding rite while Aunt Evyenía stood on the other side of the table in a short dress, her face a stiff mask, beside the man she had chosen from the mainland. Clouds of incense stinging the nostrils floated beneath the low ceiling and as the priest administered Communion in a long-handled spoon, Ann and Zoe beside me muttered, "Couple of spring chickens!"

Then plates of food were carried in and the room filled with voices talking all at once and a sharp smell of wine, while a loaf of dark, heavy bread which the priest had consecrated was cut up into little squares and given out. Candles and chalice were cleared off the table to make way for a gramophone with a vast, pink amplifier the shape of a morning glory; out of it a voice brayed full, nasal and pitched high over the jangling, syncopated rhythm. Young men danced with their arms on one another's shoulders in an open circle, or men and women followed each other with downcast eyes in endless mimicry of escape. Long after midnight, as we made our way through the beds of gourds and melons in the moonlight, Tom translated for me the song they were singing behind us:

Now all the birds, now the swallows,
Now the partridges softly sing, Awake,
My Master, good Master, awake to embrace
Her body like a cypress tree
And her white neck.

Mrs Condor said, "That's the song people sing when they gather round the house and the bride takes the sheet off her bed with her blood on it and hangs it out of the window, so the neighbours can see no man ever messed her up before."

NEXT MORNING THE TABLES in Phrangisko's house were set end to end under the pear tree. Many of the relatives forgathered once again for the wedding breakfast in the early sunlight. No one went to the winepress that day. In the shade of a wall Phrangisko busied himself making a wineskin from the goat slaughtered for the feast. He sewed together the holes of its severed limbs with a heavy needle and long gut thread, drawing the whole skin through the hole where the neck had been, with the hair inside and the malodorous, wet, fleshy side out. One of his younger brothers brought me a piece of calamus and made a flute out of it with a few strokes of his knife. He cut off one piece below the joint, pierced the joint inside, bevelled the rim of the opposite end into a plain open mouthpiece and bored six holes down one side with a red-hot nail from the kitchen. He held it to his mouth at an angle and blew; each note was clear and sweet and round. His mother stood with a distaff under one elbow, slowly twisting thread from a cloud of brilliant, snowy wool. Through the day we went on eating and drinking while Evyenía sat inside with her husband in his undershirt lolling against her shoulder and rolling his black eyes up at her weatherbeaten face. The two of them left next morning to catch the boat for Piraeus and the cousins went to work in the winepress before daylight.

Tom and I joined them at the quadrangle of plastered walls, with a bottom sunk several feet lower than the surrounding field where Phrangisko and his brothers, their trousers rolled up to their knees and straw hats shadowing their faces, were trampling about on the mound of grapes. We took off our shoes and hopped over the wall.

The sun climbed. We plunged in with purple shins and ankles, lifting our knees slowly and squeezing our toes into the clusters of hot, bursting globes, while the mound sank slowly around us and the juice gurgled out of a hole at the bottom into a deep, plastered pit. A thyme branch stuck into the hole kept back the skins and seeds, to be boiled up for raki and jelly and cakes at a different season. During the morning others of the family came with cartloads of grapes from the outlying fields and dumped them into the press. Sometimes we would step out and lying flat on the ground reach into the pit to bring up a gourd full of the warm, sweet juice we had been treading; it was too sticky to quench our thirst, too sweet to stop drinking. Then under the great silence of the Mediterranean noon we climbed out and went to wait for our meal under the pear tree. Beyond the vineyards stretched a broad, open country with secrets of its own—the sunken paths, the calamus thickets in the torrent beds, here and there stands of cypresses, small caves, hidden springs, the orchards and olive yards of a monastery, and from every high place a different view of the steep, calcareous shore. Yet everything close by was somehow at noonday painful—the bruise of bedrock under one's bare feet and the prick of spiny plants dead since winter; everywhere the vine leaves wilted and unpicked grapes lay hot and juicy over the parched clods.

Ann and Zoe passed below the terrace in their plaid trousers. "We've ate already; we're going over to Naoussa. Maybe we can stir up some trouble."

Their uncle shuffled up from the fields; a woollen sash wound round and round his waist held up trousers that trailed about his bare ankles. Under his straw hat his eyes gleamed out of lean bones ornamented with a long, grey, curled moustache. For a moment he watched the figures of the two girls teetering slightly down the uneven path, then turned to his wife at the kitchen door; they exchanged glances. "They have eaten already," she said—her slow words were uttered out of a face habitually stiff with reserve—"and now they go to pay their calls in Naoussa."

In the kitchen she set before us plates of beans and mullets cooked in oil, wedges of bread, thick white cheese with one or two goat's hairs stuck to it, and a gourd of acrid wine. She stood in the back of the room while her husband and sons, her American nephew and I ate in silence, and two of her daughters sat on the terrace, grinding lentils. Flies buzzed and looped under the low ceiling. The grumbling millstone stopped. The uncle drank the last of his wine, made the sign of the cross three times, yawned to the ceiling, then lifted his wiry frame on to a bed over a grain bin by the oven and fell asleep with his straw hat over his face.

I had been here four days—long enough to be able to wander off when I wished, leaving the others now to their midday rest. I sought my own by crossing the field in the intolerable sunlight to an enormous fig tree that grew beyond the winepress and lay down on the sharp, flinty ground beneath it. This was the hour when all life withdrew into small, shady places, as if sound or motion might somehow affront the immense stillness of the sun at its height; all I heard was the occasional dry rasp, like a goat's tongue, of the heavy leaves of the fig tree scraping.

To wake up two hours later into a world where the light had changed and the landscape was beginning to shape itself anew with shadows was like journeying back a long distance from a state where thighs and shoulder-blades were rooted in the stony earth. I looked up to see Phrangisko standing in the cool darkness under the tree.

"Let us go and drink water before the others come down," he said, and he led the way to three old and bristly pomegranate trees round the mouth of a well. "This is the best we have," he said, pushing a bucket over the edge. "We have six other wells, but they run dry by autumn. Water is all." He yawned and drew the bucket up again. "Do you have the flute?"

I took the piece of calamus out of my pocket and handed it to him.

"You must hold it like this, off to one side." He blew across the hole and a tumult of ear-splitting trills poured up into the leaves that quivered like pointed tongues.

It was four o'clock and the vineyards were receiving the first caress of slanting sun—as if the island were beginning to breathe again—when the rest of the family arrived at the winepress. A scum of foam and bubbles floated on the dark surface of the pit. Sounds began all over the island: goat-bells, donkeys braying, bells of distant churches, mingling in the softer air with our long afternoon's clamour as we dipped the juice up out of the pit with broken gourds and petrol cans and poured it into the goatskin bags like the one I had watched Phrangisko making the day before; the stumpy protuberances of their severed legs and necks bulged into shape and they lay about on the ground and lolled against one another, obscene and lifelike. We lifted them up on to donkeys struggling under their weight, and lashed them four to a saddle. Later we rode to Naoussa on its blue bay, where the eldest brother, who had come back from the Albanian war in 1940 with one leg amputated, kept a wineshop for the fishermen; then home again on the dusty, brittle-stepping donkeys, past shepherds with their flocks, the path melodious with their bells, through a warm wind that sighed in the osiers along the beach where light, swift waves ran in out of the purple sea.

Days passed. The fierce brilliance of morning followed the amber sunrise, and after the blue air of afternoon the moonlight lay warm and honey-coloured on the paving-stones of the forecourt where I slept. We worked all day in the winepress and sometimes went to the sea at night, walking out into the water and drawing in nets full of fish for the evening meal. One night we visited Phrangisko's married brother; two men came with instruments, a little goatskin drum and a tiny bagpipe of a kidskin with two reeds sticking out of it, embedded side by side in wax in a split piece of wider calamus, with a section of cow's horn tied to the end for resonance. The two of them sat down on the parapet, and to the drum's soft urgent thudding and the hysterical shriek of the pipes the others danced with their fingers intertwined, the moon shining on their ankles as they lifted and whirled and stamped. Near me in the darkness Mrs Condor said, "Nice, old-fashioned evening, eh, Andrew?"

PHRANGISKO LEFT ONE MORNING, wearing his army uniform. No one said anything and I was struck by the sudden, soundless finality of Greek departures, as of waters closing over someone's head. A week later I myself walked across the island, then watched the windmills and the rocky shoreline draw farther and farther back across the steamer's widening wake. In the early afternoon we put into the port of Syra, backing in alongside a Swedish freighter unloading tons of American grain. Beyond the girders of the covered after-deck the harbour was like a painted stage: the wave-lapped walls with its flat coping-stones and cobbled area extending round us in a semicircle and on the other side the green- and pink-washed fronts of coffee-shops and restaurants named after the islands of their proprietors, each with its row of chairs and tables outside, crowded with passengers for Piraeus and street-vendors ready to swarm on board with their boxes of *loukoumia* and baskets of tin icons. On the embankment stood a line of men with shaven heads, each with a bundle at his feet. I asked one of the ship-hands who they were.

He answered in English, "Good people. Democratic people— exiles, prisoners. We got rotten government." He was off before I could ask him another question but I caught the words in Greek, "Our countrymen, our brothers."

Then we were all cleared off the stern as about two hundred men were led by armed guards to the foredeck. I squeezed my way past a group of smartly trousered women wearing silk scarves and broad sun-glasses talking French to a Greek Catholic priest; one of them, casting a glance over the rail, said in the throaty, masculine voice of Athenian women of the richer class, "Where would they be taking the goat-thieves now!" Finding no barrier, I walked straight on to the foredeck through the prisoners' midst and sat down with my back to a stanchion, where I read my Greek dictionary in hopes that somebody might notice.

A young man with grave eyes and a sickly, brownish-yellow face leaned forward on one knee and, looking over my shoulder, said, "Are you English?"

"American," I replied.

Three others drew closer. A boy who could not have been older than fifteen, though his shaved and bony head gave him an expression of mature savagery, said to me in broken English, "Better you be American. Churchill God-damn' son of a bitch."

The man with the yellow face said, "It is thanks to him we find ourselves where we are now."

"Thousands of us sacrificed our lives and all we had, fighting the Germans while they occupied our country," said another. "Churchill wanted to show us his gratitude; so he gave orders that we should all be disarmed as soon as our liberators landed in Greece. They mowed us down with their machine-guns as we marched into Athens without weapons. And now to please the British, the politicians send us into exile on islands where there is no water."

"Where?" I asked.

"Youra, an island off Syra, where the sun is strong in the quarries and we break stone all day with one bowl of soup for nourishment; where the beds are of rock and the barracks are made of tar paper which blows in and out with the wind in winter. If you are American, you should see it. What do you do?"

"I am a student," I said.

"In that case you are a *confrère*," he said. "I am a student too." He took my dictionary, then asked for my fountain-pen and wrote his name on the last page, adding beneath the signature: "Law student. A souvenir."

Then a guard with a revolver clanking briskly on his hip barked at everyone to stand up. The prisoners rose to their feet; I remained seated on the deck.

"Eh, you!" the guard shouted. "Get up!"

I pointed at my hair and there was quiet laughter. The guard ordered them to move away.

I moved to another stanchion. More prisoners gathered round me; seated high in their midst, I asked one man who spoke French, why they were in prison.

"Parce que nous voulons une politique populaire."

Another man, glaring at me, said, "Tell this man . . . Ask him why . . ." and one by one the accusations were translated for me. Did I say America was prosperous, and if so why were there two million unemployed? I had never thought about it and asked him where he got his information. In the newspapers, he said, and I protested it must be an exaggeration. Did I say America was a democracy? Then why had the former Vice-President been forbidden to address a university in the Middle West? I said if that came from the papers it was probably untrue as well. The man insisted that thousands of students went to hear Henry Wallace speak in an open field after he had been denied access to the university hall; was that democracy? *"Eh bien, nous aussi, nous sommes des étudiants,"* he repeated as the guard came by to disperse them all again. I had never seen people who looked less like students, but with their shaved heads and their thinness it was hard to tell their age.

After that a man told me he was being set free because he had signed a paper renouncing his Communist affiliations. The others had refused to sign and were being taken now to a detention camp on Makronisos, off the eastern coast of Attica.

The light was fading out of the sky and a cold wind blew. Some one pointed to the mountains of the mainland rising smooth and velvety against the crimson sky, and said, "General Markos is up there, in mountains higher than those—he and others who are still free. They fight for us who are captives, but what happens to individuals is of no importance." I could see he was grinning.

A few feet away some other prisoners were having an argument with a man whose immaculate collar and saddle shoes showing through the dusk proclaimed him for one of the first-class passengers. I watched his beseeching Levantine gestures, and feeling I had no business here, returned to the little deck where the Athenian women and the Catholic priest were still talking in the language they preferred to their own. The moon rose while we sailed into the Saronic Gulf and the shores of Attica and the Argolid drew closer on either side. Once the priest extended an arm out over the sea and said, *"Quel spectacle merveilleux que les rayons de la lune sur les ondes!"* and one of the women murmured hoarsely, *"N'est-ce pas que notre Grèce est belle, mon Père?"*

CHAPTER 2

Taygetos—The Shadow

IN THE AUTUMN OF 1947 the rains fell early, hindering slightly the activities of the students at the American Academy. Travelling by daylight it was possible to reach Corinth, Olympia, Thebes and sites in the Boeotian plain; in every village there was a curfew at sundown, for the Greek state hardly existed outside Athens and Salonika, the islands, a few ports and supply lines by sea or air to certain heavily guarded provincial towns. A week after our trip to Mycenae an English newspaper correspondent was captured by the Andartes, the Communist guerrillas, who led him across the mountains of the northern Morea and set him free on the outskirts of Patras. Less fortunate was the American reporter, bound for the headquarters of General Markos in the mountains of Northern Greece; his corpse was washed ashore on the beach near Salonika. It was a bad winter. The drachma was devalued from five to ten thousand the dollar, and the price of bread rose steadily. North and south, roads, railways, villages and provinces were abandoned for the season to the elusive, impenetrable dominion which had held them since the Germans entered the country seven years before. Sometimes we tuned in to Radio Free Greece, as it was called, and heard the broadcasts from the mountains of Epiros and Macedonia where the nation had once possesed frontiers. The Government proclaimed to all guerrillas under arms a month's amnesty, which went by unnoticed while the Andartes infiltrated into the defiles of Parnes not fifteen miles from Athens.

I fell ill with an obscure nervous disorder and spent most of that winter in a room with brown steel furniture and a window that rattled against the wads of hundred-drachmae notes stuffed into the sash. The plume of a cypress tree in a courtyard down the hill swept silently across the sky, while from the pavements below rose the angry yell, like the cry of an animal maddened by the wind, of a street-vendor calling, "Vinegar . . . Firewood . . . Oranges, five for a thousand!" From my window I could see the army installations springing up along the spurs and ridges of Hymettos. Its forests had been cut during the winters of the Occupation, leaving the mountain a wilderness of bluish marble, washed clean of soil. A new law now banished the herds of goats to the other side, and on rainy Sundays from December to March teams of boy scouts went out to plant seedlings on its flanks. In pot-holes dug between the rocks the tiny pines and junipers took root under the sporadic cloudbursts of the Attic winter, and were dead by spring.

Early in the new year the members of the foreign archaeological schools were allowed into three halls of the National Museum, which had been closed for nearly ten years. In the director's office, moist from long burial, the head, shoulders and outstretched arm of the Charioteer of Delphi reposed in a single piece on a desk littered with potsherds awaiting classification; in a corner stood the green bronze legs up to the waist, straight and slender like a young tree sheared off below the branches. Out in the galleries where we stood about, whispering under the shiny bellies of huge grave amphorae, three cold women with covered heads, bending to the floor, moved in measure with their brooms between the booming walls.

In the Kolonaki district shop windows were full, and expensive little blocks of flats were going up on the slopes of Lykavitós. On windy afternoons on the Acropolis one sometimes saw a party of Congressmen, grim-mouthed under their broad-brimmed hats, being shown the Parthenon. The rains came to an end during a brilliant month when the hills round the city were covered in a film of green, and thousands of flowers blew among the rocks. On Easter Day the Minister of Justice was assassinated in a street behind the Grande Bretagne Hotel. For weeks the papers published details of a Communist plot against the Government, and I heard of people deported to camps on certain islands. In the suburbs buses would halt and squads of heavily armed police mount and make their way slowly down the aisle, checking identity cards; sometimes a passenger was made to descend. Travel restrictions tightened and permits had to be obtained for any trip outside a few miles' radius of the capital.

Greece seemed most disappointing when I began to make my preparations for leaving it. Then, when the other students were already sending home their trunks, I was offered a fellowship to stay and study the fortresses built by Byzantine Greeks, Frankish Crusaders, Turks and Venetian traders between the Dark Ages and the eighteenth century to guard the harbour towns and mountain passes of the Peloponnese, sometimes on foundations of forts dating from Roman, Macedonian or Mycenaean times. I saw the work stretching indefinitely into the future; hardly anything had been written on the subject, and I would be able to travel unobserved and in my own good time. I took the opportunity with delight, and in July, 1948, the Ministry of Public Safety issued me a travel permit "valid for many journeys through all Hellas." At the height of summer I set off on my own with a rucksack and sleeping-bag and money to last me several weeks, for any destination I could reach beyond the Isthmus of Cointh.

Argos was where the bus line ended, and at the railroad station I learned that a train to Tripolis would pass through in the afternoon. It was now one o'clock. I asked the station-master what time it would arrive.

"Now," he replied, from which I could only believe that a train might eventually come.

The platform was already crowded with people, most of them soldiers sitting hunched over their knees or lying fast asleep over their duffle bags. A man silhouetted in the shadow of the corrugated iron roof moved out into the fierce sunlight and lay down, pillowing his head upon the rails. I took my place in the shade and waited, occasionally looking at my watch to see if the noonday torpor had stopped the second hand. After an hour the station-master carried out two chairs and settled himself into them, propped and tilted on the ties. It was well into the afternoon before the waiting crowds woke out of sleep and wandered off to wash their heads and drink from the fountain at the far end of the platform, and the station-master collapsing out of his Casseiopeia's Chair, rose to his feet at last beneath the slow advance of a huge, black, roaring engine. The cars came in, with passengers hanging on the steps, the crowds on the platform pressing against the sooty walls, trying to climb on. Then very slowly the train, half-filled, half-emptied, with people still surging round its doors, began to heave with a steaming, loud plunge of pistons and the howl of its whistle through thick, white smoke down the fiery track, halted again, then rolled as slowly and inexorably backwards.

I was in a car as hot as an oven. All around me men in dusty clothes pressed and shouted; women with black kerchiefs wrapped across their mouths stood with feet pinned down under great baskets, and crop-headed boys dragging their baggage after them struggled along the aisle. A violent shudder all the way down the train made everyone stumble as it started forward again, and then the collective energy of noise and motion spent itself. Quite suddenly there was room for all to sink down on to the wooden seats, room for legs to be fitted in between the packages, while small groups faced each other in closed rings of private speech murmuring above the rumble of the train. Melons were taken out of baskets, sliced open with long knives and eaten like huge, red moons dripping over the floor. The shadows of eucalyptus trees ribboned along the sides of the train, and below the glimmering, grey mountains leafy grape-fields passed like a series of re-volving turntables all crisp in the evening light. Among the strips of planted land blindfolded mules trod their somnolent circles at the wells, drawing the well sweep round and round while water brimmed and travelled down the furrows, and farmers stood up from hoeing to wave as the train went by.

At the far end of the car the door opened and closed on the roar of the wheels. A man came down the aisle unsteadily, a big tray strapped to his waist and shoulders, calling, "I have ciga-rettes, caramels, and the Chiclets of America good for the teeth, the jaws, the mouth, the brain, the stomach, fever, fainting, sea-sickness, lunacy, love-passion . . ." and a wave of laughter followed him out on to the gusty, rattling platform. The door slammed shut; once again the brief crowd-murmur subsided and people's gaze reverted centrifugally to the quiet land gliding past each sep-arate window. Again each group seemed closed within itself, all communication reduced to a minimum by the lulling tempo of the train swaying, rattling, rumbling along the rails, yet I remained constantly aware of a sword-dance of bright eyebeams crossing, the hot wires of curiosity and evasion shifting and quickening round me in the rich sunlight pouring through the windows.

The track began to climb. The flat land slid away behind us, and soon there was no longer sunlight inside the carriages; the shallow hills of the Arkadian plateau closed us in on every side under a smaller sky. The train moved slower between the grey slopes and halted—not long, but long enough for a question, for looks to be exchanged inside the gathering darkness of the car, answered here and there by a lift of eyebrows signifying, one might have said, acceptance; again the train moved on. There was light enough to see green fields fitted in terraces between the slopes where a few men and women stood with their hoes at the irrigation. Inside the car conversations were resumed. We began to climb again and the noise of the train grew louder. When the tracks curved one could hear the soldiers singing in the for-ward cars.

It was seven in the evening when we stopped at a small station called Akhladhókámbos, high on a mountainside above a round, sunken valley. Soldiers poured out of the box cars to fill their canteens at the fountain. I asked the man opposite me what time we would reach Tripolis.

"Do I know?" he said, spreading his hands.

The windows showed a circle of sky still bright above the naked mountain-tops bathing in the last light of day, where Pan once ran beside Pheidippides to Sparta. We were travelling more slowly now, hugging the side of a ravine where four steel pillars rose below us like dead tree-trunks; I could just see to read in my guide-book that traces of a sanctuary of Pan could still be found near one of the pylons of the railroad bridge, now ruined. I asked the man in front of me if it had been blown up during the German occupation or more recently, but he did not answer. New tracks had been laid all the way into the innermost fold of the mountain. One could see the forward cars curving out along the farther flank; an open freight car, which had not been there when the train left Argos, was attached to the front of the engine.

The man opposite me nudged his neighbour and said, "Now it begins."

"Now, do you say? When for seven years every train in the country—"

"But now it's empty. Look," he indicated the freight car. "In 1942—"

"I know," replied the other, "I was a hostage."

The train stopped for five minutes. Then the low hum of speech began again with the sound of the wheels.

"The journeys I made that winter . . . Panagia! Lamia to Athens, Athens to Lamia, back and forth. Whole German divisions going to Africa, and sixteen of us protecting them all, standing out there with the engine right behind us. I rode in the cage three months after they blew up the Gorgopótamos. Every time we went down the valley past Graviá I thought of my brother up on Giona with Ares' band. Who knows? He may have laid the mine during the night. The tracks were covered with snow; we saw nothing until we struck it. The freight car went up in the air and came down with all sixteen of us in it. I remember those Germans rushing out of the train. They must have thought me dead; they shot all the others. There was nobody else for them to kill; the ELAS band was already far up on Giona."

"Where no doubt they still are, the animals!" said another man across the aisle, who had been listening.

There was a moment's silence.

Then the one who had been talking went on, "My brother came down during the amnesty last winter, but they took him off to Youra. We have not seen him again."

"*Keratádhes!*" said the man across the aisle. "That's where they'll all go, or somewhere better still by the time we've finished with them." He had a rifle next to him on the seat.

The train crept out of the ravine, then stopped again. Soldiers dropped down out of the troop cars and dragged their kit and weapons up the slope to a dug-out while shadowy figures climbed on board. During the three hours that followed we travelled slightly over twenty miles. Long after night had fallen one could just make out the black silhouette of gun muzzles pointing from both sides of the train as we rode steadily down into the hill-ringed plain of Tripolis.

The shadows of three, four, five, six lamp-posts passed like bars across the windows and the animated figures of passengers rising to their feet inside the car. I followed them out on to the platform and into a narrow street leading to a broad square where tiers of windows blazed like an ocean liner and HOTEL SEMIRAMIS described a tubular, red glow across the night sky. This was not the place for me; I continued with a dwindling crowd into more tunnels of crooked darkness and out at last into another square, teeming with people and jeep-loads of soldiers in white helmets driving round and round under dangling light bulbs strung between the trunks of short, pollarded plane trees. Here, in the heart of the Peloponnese, street lamps remained lit all night, and a town swollen with refugees from the abandoned villages of Arkadia, observed no curfew in the swarming presence of two divisions of the national army. Outside the hotel, where I found a bed in a room with four others, an open-air theatre played a gangster movie with a raucous sound track of the 1930s cackling incomprehensibly and the reflection off its screen flickering through our shadeless window, while one tap in the corner dripped into the basin until dawn.

Next morning's daylight revealed low houses and dusty, gridiron streets; like nearly every town in Greece it was no more than a village before the War of Independence. The place I wanted to reach was Sparta, forty miles across the mountains; there were castles in that region which people in Athens had said I would never get to see. All day I made inquiries. At the station they told me what I already knew, that there were no trains. Gendarmes merely shrugged, and the proprietor of the hotel closed his eyes at my question and pointed with both palms upward in a gesture of resignation at the mountains outside the window; there indeed lay the answer. I went to the headquarters of a detachment of American troops acting as advisers to the Greek Army. The officers were out with units conducting operations in the hills. The major in command welcomed me into his office and called into an adjoining room, "Any news about the convoy, Sergeant?" to which the only reply was "God-damn' lousy Greeks done fucked up my carburettor!" That night I thought I would go to the Semiramis Hotel and talk with the American engineers whose company had been assigned by the Marshall Plan to dredge the Corinth Canal and lay a new motor road between Tripolis and Argos.

Approaching the hotel across the darkened square, the windows of its ground floor shone like enamel plaques revealing a dining-room full of people in Hawaiian shirts and dinnerjackets. I gave up and walked back into the more familiar streets, where from the pavements stairways dropped abruptly into wine dens and lighted cellars where workmen sawed and hammered on barrels and donkey saddles, bright with tufts of coloured cloth and

cowrie shells against the Evil Eye. Yet, though the entire population seemed to be out walking, house windows were all shuttered
tight. Here and there the light of a street lamp slanted across a
whitewashed wall daubed in blue paint with the slogans of the
counter-revolution, mostly dating from the plebiscite of 1946: HE
IS COMING referred to the return of King George II; the middle
letter X, the Greek *khi*, was painted larger than the others like
crossed hockey-sticks upside-down to represent two *gammas*, the
initials of George Glucksburg, King of the Hellenes. One of the
Rightist organizations that came into being at the time of the
plebiscite took its name from that letter *khi*. HE HAS RETURNED
proclaimed their inevitable victory in what had passed for a free
and internationally supervised election. Some writings on the
walls said DEATH TO SERBS, ALBANIANS AND BULGARS. Another
which threatened the same thing, only closer to home, said HEL-
LENES DECIDE. YOU ARE ROYALIST OR COMMUNIST. During the
four days I waited in Tripolis no one of his own accord addressed
a word to me, and this seemed strange in Greece.

One day a train arrived from Argos; on it there were others
bound for Sparta, but we had to wait for more passengers to fill
enough buses to justify a military convoy into Lakonia. Meanwhile no exit was allowed beyond the limits of this overgrown,
army-ridden village where displaced populations waited for a civil
war to end.

The fifth day, very early in the morning, in the open space
outside the station soldiers squatted on the pavement, casting
black shadows on the white walls, while buses, command cars
and fortified vehicles manoeuvred into place along the roadway.
The signal was given, soldiers and civilians took their places and
the column rumbled slowly through the silent town. We drove
out into a sunny haze thickened by the dust of moving wheels,
a bright cloud extending far out ahead of us across stubble fields
gleaming like a lake in the sun. At eight o'clock we entered the
foothills south of Tripolis. Already the light was so strong that
every stone by the wayside had a fiery edge. Roaring in low gear,

the bus lurched over the craters in the road as it wound up and up into an unpeopled wilderness of lumpy hills that looked as if the earth had been arrested in the act of boiling. The hillsides were all raked and stratified into shallow terraces, but the only vegetation was a tangle of charred, black, leafless scrub. Sometimes one could feel the dry wind blowing through the gusts of heat from the engine. Whenever the road turned the convoy halted. Platoons of soldiers from the trucks in front of us fanned out through the twisted stalks and disappeared over the brow of the next hill, or advanced in a slow procession with long, stiff, clumsy instruments held out in front of them like vacuum-cleaners. We drove through little glens, ringed always by the same low hills, where rare ilex or wild fruit trees dropped their black pools of shade, and every now and then passed soldiers standing alone among the rocks. Inside the buses we faced each other on two rows of seats while the noonday lethargy burned on eyes that felt lidless hour after hour through the dust and the grinding of the engine.

It was four in the afternoon when we came to a house, the first since early morning. From the top of one more rise everything fell suddenly away. I did not even notice Sparta lying far below us in the olive-misted plain. Across the empty air, from the central highlands of the Morea to the southernmost cape of Europe, rose a rampart of vast, dazzling massifs and plunging gorges, dark with fir forests sweeping upward to the highest ridge: a wall of rock, striated, smooth and glimmering yellow in the afternoon light, with all its spiny summits lifted up like the wings of a dragon ready to unfold.

DOWN IN THE PLAIN of Lacedaemon there was abundant light from the sky, although the sun had already passed behind Taygetos. Walking out of Sparta, I saw ahead through the light filigree of olive leaves and branches the towers of a castle along the crest of a narrow hill isolated under the mountain by a ravine on either side; one flat, triangular slope hung with pale walls, roofless, vertical and many-windowed—the ruined city of Mistra, my destination. I walked through a village to a few houses ten minutes up the road with mossy steps, high walls and a terrace with a tiled roof on wooden poles, all overshadowed by the branches of a plane tree. A portly man in an apron came out to meet me.

"The Kyrios is a stranger? Welcome," said he. "In what can I be of service?"

I started to say, "If you have food—"

"Anything the Kyrios may wish. Alas, there is no hotel in Mistra and you will have to stay in Sparta the night, but you may certainly eat here before the last bus goes back." He drew a chair out from one of the tables on the terrace.

"As a matter of fact I don't plan to stay in Sparta. I have brought—"

"But there is a very good hotel there!"

"I don't like hotels. I prefer sleeping out. In America—"

"America? But, Kyrie, this is Greece!" he exclaimed. "That is to say, before the war in Greece you could sleep out anywhere you chose, and no one would have touched you; the Hellenes were the most civilized of people, but these are wicked years. No, in Sparta you will be comfortable and in the morning a taxi will bring you out early."

I said nothing. He brought me supper and sat down at the table. Several times he referred to the danger of night outside the safety of one's own locked door. "Unfortunately," he said, "the Archaeological Service chooses to keep Mistra a ruin. They forbid us to build anything new; so there is no hotel here, not even a proper restaurant. Yet whenever the Director of Antiquities comes down, how many times have I not told him, 'Kyrie Professor, behold my house across the road, on this side my terrace and kitchen. Let us cut down this plane tree which does no good to anyone and build here the new hotel.' Instead, you see me condemned to serve wine to the villagers! Once in a while, yes, a meal to some foreign tourist like the Kyrios, but what does that ever bring to me who have four daughters? And why do we in Mistra have to suffer in this way? Because the Spartans are jealous of our antiquities, which are worth more than theirs, and it is here they all come, the tourists, the educated, the rich people from Athens. For me, I confess, it is a particular misfortune. Until recently there was another family who had their cookhouse next to mine; you see that heap of planks through the archway? But what can you expect? They were four brothers; one of them burned it down. . . . And now at last when I have the place to myself—*Ach*, what I could build! I could have electric lights over all the ruins in Mistra, and a radio here playing all night long to the tourists. . . . Would that we had peace!" He rubbed his hands together. "See too what a view I have from here"—he pointed across the plain to where the shadow of Taygetos had covered the mountains on the other side, laced with the faint zigzag of the road from Tripolis. "But you see how dark it gets already. Now the last bus for Sparta will be leaving. Tomorrow a taxi will bring the Kyrios."

"I think, however," said I, "that I'll stay somewhere in the pine wood half-way between here and the village, if I might just fill my canteen at your spring for the night."

"Ah ha ha," the man murmured, getting to his feet. "That does not matter. I myself shall see you down to the bus."

A woman's voice shrilled across the road: "Kleoméni!"

"Come," the man said quietly, "we must be going."

"Kleoméni!"

The man shouted over his shoulder, "Will you burst! Panagia, the shriek of wives!" he exclaimed fervently under his breath. "Sir, I advise you it is getting late."

"Tell the *Englézos* the bus just left."

The man bit his lip. His eyes looked from side to side. Then he said, "I shall take you to a good place to stay. There are numerous families living in the Church of Ay Yanni. There are balconies and a beautiful view. Unfortunately my house is too small, otherwise it would be a pleasure. . . . But you will be well taken care of at Ay Yanni."

"I beg you not to trouble yourself," I said. "I have really decided what to do."

Kleoméni looked at me sharply. "There are houses out in the plain where no one has dared sleep since 1943. They come down at night," he said slowly, "sometimes into the village square. Here on the outskirts families gather in one house while the men stand guard with their guns till sunrise."

"Then the place must be very safe indeed," said I and picked up my rucksack.

My persistence seemed to have triumphed rather easily. "As you wish," he said, clearing the plates off the table. "Good night." Then as I walked away he added, "Of course tomorrow you may eat here."

I learned later that he was not sure who I might be and preferred not to have me on his hands; if it turned out that I chose to circulate at night among the outlying houses of the village, he might as well leave it to the men who stood guard to take care of me in their own way. As for me, physical danger had never touched me closely except during a few months in the Apennines in 1945 and that was so frightening I had forgotten it long since. And so it was that I contrived to spend a fragrant night alone in the pine forest under the steep walls of the ghost-city of Mistra, seven centuries old; and the air was warm on my face when I awoke in my sleeping-bag, in a trough of the silky, needle-covered slope and looked up through the branches into a chasm through whose inky shaft, thousands of feet above, the golden limestone of Taygetos towered into the morning sky.

Kleoméni served me breakfast under the plane tree, which reached out over the road and the glistening tops of orange trees growing just below it in the plain; some of the upper branches brushed against the russet-coloured brickwork of a high, square tower flanking the line of battlements along the lower hillside. At its base, all day in shadow, icy mountain water splashed out of a marble spout into a carved stone basin and trickled down the moss-grown steps to a pipe underneath the road. As I drank my coffee the hot wave of sun flooded in across the olive yards of Lacedaemon which, for a few minutes longer, seemed to draw a last breath before the day. Then plains and mountains faded in the bleaching sun. Beneath the plane tree the fountain splashed and gurgled. Little girls came in and out through the archway in the walls, stepping carefully in bare feet and balancing on one shoulder their huge, moist earthenware jugs. At ten o'clock I heard the bus for Sparta leaving the village square. I stayed where I was and read about the tribes of nomad Slavs who came down through the Balkans and settled in the defiles of Taygetos where for hundreds of years Byzantine military officials never dared to attack them and French crusaders, who ruled as feudal princes in the Morea, built castles to hem them within their impenetrable refuge. It was noon when some straw-hatted farmers came up out of the bright, dusty road and seated themselves at a table, legs stretched out in front of them, immobile in the shade. Their voices hardly disturbed the silence.

"*Englészos*, that one?"

"*Bá*. Swiss."

"Does he come for propaganda?"

"What are you talking about? The Archaeological Service has sent him down to restore the dome at Ay Yanni."

"You speak of the one who came here in the spring."

"Eh, very well, spring. Who is this one, then?"

"He comes from the University of America, I tell you," said one with a leather-edged army beret on one side of his head. "He goes round to the ancient places and writes a book about them, with pictures."

"Bravo," commented a drawling voice, "bravo."

The man with the beret, drawing his legs under his chair, said, "Be quiet. What do you know about education?"

"Education?" drawled the other. "Like this he educates himself—coming to Greece to look at castles? *Po-pó!*"

The man with the beret whispered, "Horned one of a *keratá!*"

"Well, if he's a professor, why doesn't he stay in Sparta like any other foreigner?"

"Because he doesn't want to, the *ánthropos*. Is that enough?"

"Surely, Kostandí, you're not so young you forget what it was here before the war—all the foreign archaeologists travelling round the country with notebooks and cameras? No foreigner ever comes to Greece without a purpose, and you know what I mean, eh Kostandí?"

"I'll pull your eyes out."

Just then Kleoméni emerged from his kitchen with a beaker of wine. They drank in silence, except for one remark by the man with the drawling voice, which also had to do with me, I supposed, though it was more ambiguous: "Has Pavlakos got wind of his being here? What do you say, Kostandí? He had better not go into Sparta if we want to avoid an episode. Remember the fuss in the papers when that reporter got himself murdered in Saloníki."

They got up and went down the steps. Their dark shapes melted into the glare of the road. Only the one with the beret, whom the others called Kostandí, moved with a light stride to the far end of the terrace.

Kleoméni brought a plate of macaroni to my table. With a deprecating smile he murmured, "Poverty . . . what can one do?"

He kept me company again, saying little but occasionally bestowing on me across the table his hotel-keeper's shallow smile; he seemed to expect me to begin the conversation.

I pointed to some columns of smoke dotting the mountainsides across the plain, and said, "Are those brush fires, Kyrie Kleoméni?"

"Eh, fire . . . How do you say it in English?"

"But so many?"

"Those," he said, "are the foothills of Parnon: wild country with no roads through it. Once there were villages, but now they are deserted. Wherever you see fire, the army is burning out the Andartes. The army, that is, and our own people."

"Your own people? Who are they?" I asked.

Kleoméni stood up, smiling demurely as he picked up the empty plate and whisked away the crumbs. "More coffee for the

Kyrios?" he said. Then on his way back to the kitchen I heard
him mutter, "We'll burn the mountains till there's not a shrub for
them to hide in!"

The young man with the beret was sitting all the time astride
the wooden railing of the terrace, his back to a roof-pole, with
desultory vigour swinging one leg over the roadway below. His
hair was brown, though hardly darker than the colour of his face
with its prominent cheek-bones.

Kleoméni returned with a coffee-cup, leading to my table an
old man who had just come up from the road. "Barba Leonídha
has been long in America," he said; "you will be able to come to
an agreement." He put the cup down and hurried off.

"Thirty-nine years," the old man began disconsolately. "I was
an American citizen too. I came back here to see my old mother;
I only planned to stay a couple of months, but my uncles got me
mixed up with a girl and I had to get married. I stayed too long
and lost my citizenship." The story was a familiar one, and Kleoméni was watching us from his kitchen window. The old man
went on: "I got a good house down in the village. I built it when
I came back from the States. You want to come and stay? Won't
cost you nothing. My wife, she cook you good meals and I tell you
about Detroit. How about it?"

Kostandí, still swinging one leg, said quietly from his end of
the terrace, "It's all right, Barba Leonídha; he's staying with me at
Ay Yanni." He gave me a broad wink on one side of his face.

"O.K." The old man walked away, stopping to say something to
Kleoméni inside his kitchen.

Kostandí strolled over from his perch. "You can stay with me if
you like," he said as he went by, and a holster on his belt knocked
against a corner of the table.

Kleoméni poked his head out and called, "That's a very good
idea. There is room even for the Kyrios at Ay Yanni."

"He can stay wherever he likes best," said Kostandí, grinning
at me from half-way down the steps. There was charm in his

smile and his swift movements, but he wore his pistol-belt like d'Artagnan his rapier; it would be unwise to insult him.

After that no one suggested I stay anywhere. Every day I explored the ruins on the hillside where cobbled paths led up over the edge of open rock faces, round fallen vaults and cisterns blocked with stones, through hollow houses rising in terraces up the slope, all honeycombed with empty windows, and in and out of little, brick-encrusted mansions with niches in the walls but no floors or ceilings overhead, and the silent halls of a tall palace open to the sky. Everywhere there were churches—the only points of colour on the hillside were the clusters of their tight, red domes—long since desanctified and burned, but more recently fitted with new doors and roofs to save the frescoes inside, and domes large and small, shallow and steep, with curved-out rims and scalloped edges of tile undulating over the round-topped windows in the lanterns. One morning, searching for shade, I pushed open one of their creaking doors and stepped into a cold, musty darkness where I felt my way along the porphyry columns until I could see, all over walls and arches, the rigid saints and sad-faced, mantled warriors of the Eastern hierarchy erect amid ghostlike Suppers and Transfigurations. High above the empty altar Mother and Child brooded in a livid nimbus, bright slit-eyes in murky faces keeping their long vigil over the fall not of Adam, but of the empires of the earth. Somewhere on this hill, where the bright day shimmered over the grey-green plain, in the year 1460 the Byzantine Despot of the Morea, the heir to Augustus, knelt before a Turkish sultan seven years after the last Emperor of the East had gone to his death on the land walls of Constantinople. Standing in the open, one could hear the faint, dry scratch of lizards darting over the rubble and imagine the still passage of time in such a place: seasons and years measured only by the muffled sound of a roof collapsing, or by mortar, softened in the rains of unrecorded winters, rising up in dust under the summer heat each time a loose stone fell.

Noon was interminable and windless. I used to fall asleep in the pine woods after lunch and go back to work when the sun was off the hillside, filling my notebooks with diagrams of masonry and plans of gateways. My examination led me every day farther up the slope where the ruined walls thinned out among the upper cliffs and there remained above only the crenellated ramparts on the ridge.

One afternoon as I was climbing the rocks towards a curved bastion jutting out like a ship's prow into the air, a voice called, "Eh, down there! What are you doing?" and I saw two men leaning over the battlements.

"I study the antiquities," I called back.

"Do you have a permit to come here?"

"To see the ruins?"

"You can't come into the castle without a pass," said one of the men.

I said, "I have no pass."

He straightened up and slung a rifle over his shoulder. "Eh, it doesn't matter," he said and showed me the way over some rocks to the entrance gate.

It was a square bastion projecting out from the wall, with an archway blocked with masonry except for a hole just big enough to crawl through. Inside, a vaulted passage was piled with boxes of ammunition and stacked rifles. The two men lounged against the parapet of the bastion, where a machine gun like a big, black insect pointed through an embrasure.

"Are you on watch?" I said.

One of the men replied, "What can one do? In '44 most of the village was living within these walls; people got married and babies were born up here. Now we only keep watch, two by day and five at night. With this," he added, stroking the machine gun's muzzle. "Sometimes when they try to come down the mountain—"

"See what they leave behind them," the other interrupted. He handed me several minute and densely printed leaflets.

The two men smoked apathetically while I read:

TO THE PEOPLE OF MESSENIA, LAKONIA, ARKADIA

In the last fifty days 15,000 of the monarcho-fascist army have been killed or wounded in the Grammos Mountains, now flowing with rivers of your children's blood. Brothers, the Provisional Democratic Government of the Mountains mourns with you over this bloodshed. We are therefore offering honourable and democratic terms. Yet the financial sharks of Athens and the lackeys of Truman persist in this slaughter of your sons. It is no concern of theirs if you hunger and your sons are dying, while they fill their trunks with American dollars. Rouse yourselves now, so that the peaceful, patriotic terms of the People's Government may be immediately accepted.

Hellenes, at this moment monarcho-fascism is passing through a fatal crisis. Now in the Grammos the victorious arms of the Democratic Army are digging its grave. Help us bury it one hour faster.

Two other leaflets contained a more definite warning. One was addressed to the troops of the national army:

Brother-soldiers, do not burn villages. Take care not to arouse the people. Think of your own houses, remember your own families. Do not fight as mercenaries of the American gangsters. Kill your officers and join the ranks of the Democratic Army. Whoever aids the American Occupation will pay dearly for it.

The other was a brief message to the rural population of Greece:

Hellenes, beware. The assassins are trying to draw you into their net—into the cities. Once there, they will force you out of hunger to take up arms against us. In that way they will destroy you, so that they may remain safe. Your life is in your own villages. Stay there. In the cities death, dishonour await you.

Over our heads the sky still brimmed with the last light of day, blue, gold, for a few moments yet limitless and inexhaustible, although the plain of Sparta was fast sinking into darkness and the colour draining off the slopes of Parnon. Voices sounded on the hillside below. Then five men with blankets, ammunition-belts and rifles came up into the castle and the two who had been on guard all day took me down with them to Kleoméni's terrace at Kryovrýssi.

In a week's time a convoy would be gathering for a trip south across the mountains to the port of Yítheion on the Lakonian Gulf. I was running out of money and in a week would not have enough to pay my ticket. All I had with me in the way of credit was a cheque-book of a New York bank, which had yielded considerable profits on the sidewalks of Athens but could hardly be expected to do the same in a small town in the southern Peloponnese. However, I went into Sparta on the bus one morning, confident that something could be managed if only one found a convincing and personal way to set about it; ten months in Greece had intensified a natural inclination to improvise. When I got off the bus a voice hailed me and Kostandí dashed across the street, calling, "Where do you go so early in the morning? Come and have a coffee."

We had exchanged few words in Mistra, but that he was already a friend seemed natural. I followed him into a coffee-house, threading my way between the indifferent backs and staring eyes, and out into an alley where there were some empty tables. As we drank our coffee Kostandí said, "Something is on your mind."

"I have no money," I began; "I don't know if there exists a way, with cheques—"

"There does exist," said Kostandí, "since you find yourself with me. Come."

"Where?"

"The bank is closed today, but I take you to the director," he replied.

In the main street, outside a ponderous building that looked like a sarcophagus sealed for eternity, Kostandí pushed a bell, and a man in jacket, necktie and polished shoes opened the door to us.

"Ah," he said, recognizing my companion. "Good day, good day. Come in."

It was cool inside; tall pillars rose to the ceiling; all the grilles and cubby-holes were empty and the frosty little tellers' windows shut. We followed the man into his office where, tieless in my dusty boots, I shoved a stray shirt-tail into my trousers and Kostandí in his rags and tatters seated himself casually on a plush-backed sofa.

The bank manager fussed about his desk and said, "The Kyrios will smoke?"

"This is the American, Kyrie Director," said Kostandí; "he has no money."

"I have cheques," I said, looking from one to the other.

"But of course!" exclaimed the director. "For as much as you like."

He handed me a pen and I wrote out a cheque for thirty dollars payable to cash. He then pulled out of his breast pocket a sheaf of crackling 20,000-drachmae notes and deposited it on my side of the desk. I counted them; he had given me double the official rate of exchange. I started to speak, but he merely said, "Whatever we can do for strangers is a pleasure. Let us call it in the interests of Archaeology," and gave me a well-groomed smile. "Here, you must meet my sons," he added as two boys, fresh and combed in high-school caps, walked into the office. "They are most interested in your profession. We are so pleased to hear the British School expects to continue its excavations in the bed of the Eurotas . . . Leonídha, Periklí, the Kyrios will talk to you about ancient Greece. Take him to the club."

He saw us all to the door. Kostandí walked away before I could say anything to him; I had been transferred to the protection of others.

I DID NOT SEE HIM in Mistra for several days until one night at Kryovrýssi I found him in loud possession of the terrace, roaring drunk.

"Amerika, Brookli," he shouted as I sat down at my usual table. "Health and joy to you, Andriko! What are you doing over there so proud? Come and sit here." He picked up two wineglasses and threw them against the kitchen door. "Stay inside, Kleoméni. If you come out I shall do to you what I shall—Och, Panagitsa! Andriko, come over here . . . Kleoméni," he bellowed again, "come out of there or I shall cut off your head. And bring wine for Kyr Andrea . . . Ach, youth, vitality! Tomorrow it is I—I and my wife—who shall prepare the table for Kyr Andriko."

Kleoméni sidled out of his kitchen with a beaker of wine.

"May I tell you something?" said Kostandí, gazing at him with an expression of grief.

"What?" said Kleoméni anxiously.

"You have been buggered."

Kleoméni murmured, "Ah ha ha," and backed away.

Kostandí leaned forward and gripped him by the arm. "You forget glasses," he said, then released him, raising his right hand with two upright in the sign of benediction. "Go," he said. "Go, with the blessing of the Panagia . . . and bring one for yourself, you bugger," he called after Kleoméni's retreating form. Then he turned to me, muttering, "He has been jealous of our family ever since we had our restaurant here. He has told the police about you. But you don't have to bother about him or them . . . Ah, here he is. Tomorrow night, Andriko," he said, pouring out the wine, "you will come to Ay Yanni and see my children. I shall get the gramophone and we shall eat and drink and dance all night. You will come, eh?"

"Of course," I said, regretting that by morning he would have forgotten all about it. The day after tomorrow I would be leaving and how could I know that we were to meet again long after?

All the same I went, late the following afternoon, to the church of Ayios Ioannis, which I had not yet seen. Walking along a rocky lane between the narrow walls, I looked for a way in, but there was only an arch opening on a courtyard with the three gates of the church walled up with masonry at the far end.

Then a voice called; an old woman leaning over a parapet overhead motioned me to another archway farther down the wall. Inside, a flight of open steps led up the side of the church. She stood at the top, clawing at the air. "Come up, come up. You can't get in the other way. There are no proper stairs inside for us, the evil-fated." She withdrew through a tiny door, mumbling incomprehensibly with toothless gums. I followed.

Coming in out of the light, I slowly began to see figures moving across a vaulted platform littered with piles of bedding and household goods. It was the upper part of the church, originally intended for the use of women who were not allowed to come nearer the ceremonies below. Everywhere a grey halflight hung in the vaulted spaces of the clerestory, filtered down from rings of windows underneath the several domes into a narrow depth of columns and darkly frescoed walls. Through air stale with the after-smell of incense and snuffed-out candles I could just make out the shrouded, icon-bearing encrustations of sanctuary and altar when I stepped on somebody's leg, and a boy with a fat, round face sat up convulsively, then sank back gurgling and slowly jerking on a straw pallet.

The old woman said, "She can't move, poor burning soul. She's paralysed, eh heh, what can you do?"

At my feet the creature was smiling up at me from the floor, trying to utter words that only broke and rattled on the tongue. It was no boy but a girl with hair cut short round the cheekbones.

The old woman mumbled on, "She gets worse in summer. We live close to one another in this church . . . six families. It is not safe in our houses. Here we are all together."

"Is Kostandí here?" I said.

"He will come."

The old woman beckoned me down the open steps again. I was glad to be out in the light, but the sun had gone. We went round through the courtyard I had first seen and passed under four archways into a graceful peristyle of smooth marble columns, open to the east over the plain of Sparta. There was an upper balcony with wooden poles and tiled roof, and in one colonnade paving-stones and the timbers of a fallen stair lay in a heap under a great hole in the gallery above. Through a door to the church on the lower level half-naked children came out and stared at me.

"This way," she called.

Dusk was falling rapidly. I looked at my watch. I had no wish to linger here, waiting for Kostandí who would probably not come; a Greek could promise anything on two glasses of wine.

Just then a dumpy young woman came out of the church and said "Good evening" to me. She was dressed in a tight shift and smelled strongly. "You come to see us?" she asked. "I am the wife of Kostandí."

"Oh, I was just passing by," I said. "I have to go down to Kryovrýssi to pack up my things for tomorrow." She looked up at the balcony where Kostandí stood, gazing down over the rails.

"You are not coming?" he asked. Luckily he must have heard; now I could get away more easily.

"Not tonight, no." For a moment the word stuck in my throat. But nothing was more boring than a party that did not come off; if I stayed, I would have to wait hours while they got things ready, and we could hardly dance in such a place.

"Tonight I can't eat anything; I have an upset stomach," I lied vociferously. "You will excuse me, won't you?"

Neither he nor his wife spoke as I waved to them both and hurried out into the darkening alleyways between a few wretched houses which had grown up among the ruins, but were no longer inhabited.

Next morning I was taking my breakfast at Kryovrýssi when Kostandí came down through the gate and passed across the terrace. I went over to greet him as he reached the steps. "I hope I didn't cause you any inconvenience last night," I said.

He hesitated, then said sombrely, "Dinner was cooked. We had killed the chicken."

I watched him walking down the road. Being a foreigner, I had insulted him without the least difficulty.

Later in the morning as I was getting ready to leave, Kleoméni told me the Andartes had come down that night and cut Sparta's water supply, a few kilometres north at the mouth of the Langádha Pass. All morning a steady procession of wagons and mules and donkeys passed down the road, laden with barrels of water to sell in the streets of Sparta. Kleoméni insisted on treating me to a farewell lunch. It lasted an hour: macaroni following bean soup, and after that noodles on three plates with bread and cheese and wine, which he helped me to consume. Finally a child called to him from his house that the bus was ready to leave.

"Tell him to wait five minutes," he called back. "I have foreigners, tell him . . . Do not worry, Kyr Andrea. There is plenty of time to make your connection."

When there was nothing left to eat, I shouldered my pack, shook his hand and paid him for more than the meals he had given me. He accepted with his demure manner, murmuring: "What can I do . . . ? Four daughters. Good-bye, Kyrie. Go with good fortune. Good-bye. Thank you very much."

I walked off down the road, casting no shadow on the dust that puffed and floated round my ankles. Dazzling, pointed leaves like birds' wings in the orange groves glared in the naked light. I hurried into the village square. It was empty, the bus had left. I ran out into the plain, staggering under the weight of my rucksack; three miles away the convoy would be starting in forty-five minutes. Along the road the water-wagons were returning from Sparta and in the distance the local bus was already on its way back; I could see a figure hanging out of the window. Wildly whirling his beret in the air and with a grin all over his face, Kostandí swept above me, shouting as he receded words of a farewell I could not hear.

CHAPTER 3

Lakonia, 1948—
The Dark Rains

IT WAS A YEAR since I had come to Greece. Now I knew that with the fall of night peril moved in like a tide over the country, up to the outskirts of provincial towns, where order of a certain sort was kept by soldiers and police, and by men with guns but not in uniform who owed allegiance to neither. By the autumn of 1948 when I set forth on my second journey to the Peloponnese, not overland this time but by sea to a fortified rock offshore from Cape Malea, I was ready to be less adventurous.

The Piraeus train rattled out of subterranean Athens into an October day spread high and blue over the plain of Attica; the first rains had fallen and every week the air was getting clearer. In Piraeus, beyond the harbour gate, a little steamer with a graceful hull floated on the oily water and morning shadows slept along the dock, where policemen strolled, and tidy little ship's officers perused the passenger lists beside the gangplank. Tickets for any journey had to be bought a day in advance for the lists to be checked by the authorities. I waited behind the barrier, with thin peasants and mountainous, black priests squatting on their bundles, and the poor countrywomen of Greece with the black head-cloths round their faces, newsboys and sweet-sellers and vendors of tin icons, and soldiers—short, sunburned men with sloppy uniforms and chiselled features—some returning home on leave, others destined for a new theatre of operations; for the war still lay both north and south of Athens.

An hour later from the ship's stern I watched the pale hills of Attica fading into the sunny distance. Someone else was sitting near, and I turned to meet the gaze of a lanky, unclean, ruffianly-looking person, who said with a slight twitch of his mouth, "Where are you from?"

"America."

"That's what I thought the moment I saw you."

"And you?" I asked.

"From Lakonia. From Yítheion."

"What do you do?"

"I'm a fisherman," he answered.

"You've been in Athens?" My Greek had improved during the year and the acquaintances I had made gave me an unfamiliar self-confidence—one of the paradoxes of speaking a foreign language well.

"Ná!" he exclaimed genially, with all ten fingers giving the sign of the Evil Eye over the ship's wake boiling behind us. "I went to Athens to collect a legacy. I stayed a week and spent it all. Girls, you know. . . ." There was a shifty grin on his face. "Whatever you have, in the end they eat it up, the poutánes. They lead only to trouble," he said, indicating a bandaged hand. "What can you do? We all die in the end. Now I go back to my nets—a filthy life, but what does it matter? Do the rich enjoy themselves? Why keep money if you can spend it? We Greeks are fit for the chains; we happily snatch another's money, and then we are just as happy to lose it all ourselves. Like the cicadas we sing till winter." He laughed and a row of silver teeth glinted darkly across his mouth.

"I feel the same as you, though I have been brought up differently," I said. "In my country we are taught to be careful about money, enthusiasm, everything." Having said something I believed, I liked him better: so I told him about my work in the Peloponnese.

"Will you not come and see the castles we have in the Mani? Come to Yítheion," he said.

I could warm to any words remotely resembling an invitation. "Some day I shall come and see you there."

"Ah, I shall have you to stay in my house. I'll show you the boats and how we make our living. . . ."

Some day, I thought, all of Greece would be for me a map not of places but of human relationships, of people known and experiences shared—a kingdom of my own.

Someone else joined us in the stern. He and my companion talked together, addressing each other as *koumbáros*, a word denoting the peculiar relationship existing in the Orthodox Church between godfather and the family of the godchild, and in a marriage between best man and bridal pair, extending in both cases to all the relatives on either side—a tie considered more binding than blood, having to do with personal, irrevocable choice.

Early in the afternoon a wind came up. The three of us remained on deck, while the waves grew big and through the clouds a lurid, silvery light glowed slantwise across the sea. The two sang lustily against the wind the songs from the slums of Athens and Piraeus, rude rhythmic plaints heavy with the sensation of hot city nights full of depravity and craft and yearning.

Night has fallen without a moon,
Darkness is thick,
But there is a young man who can not sleep.

What is it he waits for
Through the night till morning
In that narrow window where a candle burns?

The door opens, closes
With a heavy groaning.
If I too could only know your anguish!

The fisherman from Yítheion explained that the police had forbidden the singing of this song and any other that might be taken to express sympathy with people in prison or in exile. "But what does it matter? Nobody can hear us now," and they went on singing until all one could see was the black jaw of the Lakonian coast across the water.

Their voices sounded close beside me in the darkness: "What do you say, shall we eat, Koumbáre?"

"Not yet, Koumbáre."

"We're getting near Monemvasia, Koumbáre."

"Eh, Niko." The man from Yítheion was talking to me. "Niko."

"What?" I said.

"This is where you're going to get off?"

For a moment I hesitated—my upbringing had not been altogether successful—then said, "I've changed my mind. I'll continue on to Yítheion with you. I have to go to the Mani sooner or later; it's all part of my work."

Already the passengers were gathering on the deck. A cliff loomed blacker than the night itself. I could feel the steamer turning, while the sound of its engines re-echoed from the shore. We sailed close under rocks towering overhead like the side of an ocean liner; when the deck-lights lifted from the darkness red roofs and domes massed up to the brim of steep, crenellated walls, all swallowed up the next second as we steamed on past a causeway to the mainland. Then into the arc of lights cast out over the swell came the row-boats, rocking briskly on the black water. One by one the passengers lowered themselves over the side by ladders and their bundles slid down the ropes behind them. Across the water tavern windows glowed around the port.

"Niko." The man from Yítheion stood next to me. "Just so that no one could say I had brought you under false pretences, I hear there have been bad winds along our coasts. You might find it difficult to get from place to place. I don't want to—"

"I don't mind," I said; "I'm happy to come anyway. It's all right, isn't it?"

His reply was drowned by the groan of the winch as the anchor rose, pouring water, like a monster from the sea.

I shouted, "By the way, my name is—"

He had gone. Already we were moving backwards and away. The ship turned with a shudder of the engines, and again I felt on my face the buffeting night wind.

It was seven more hours to Yítheion round the cape and up to the head of the Lakonian Gulf. I wandered over the deck in search of the others, but when I saw them in the stern, eating a meal out of a large basket, I went off alone to eat the apple and piece of bread in my pocket. Later I came on the two companions bedded down among the life rafts.

"Ah, there you are, Niko. Lie down, why don't you?"

I climbed into my sleeping-bag. The two of them were still singing, but I could barely hear them; it was a night where all sense was darkened, muffled, numbed by the wind roaring louder and louder as we rounded Cape Malea. . . .

There was a whistle from the funnel overhead, then silence; a scalding shower of condensing steam fell on my face. By my watch it was two in the morning and I was alone on deck. Grabbing my things together, I hurried to the rail. From the dark a voice called, "This way, Niko," followed by a burst of laughter.

The waterfront of Yítheion was busy under its street lamps, where little boys with trays of sweets ran in and out between the people sitting at the metal tables in the square. The open boats went in like black hummocks on the water, vanished from sight under the embankment, then disengaged into separate figures climbing up the steps into the yellow fuzz of electricity. Other boats were bringing aboard the passengers for Piraeus. It was another seven hours back to Monemvasia; so I lay down again on one of the benches along the lower deck, resolving ever after to beware of my own expectations, of others' curiosity and too quick acquaintance.

The next I knew we were thudding through white water. The air was wet with spray and fleets of clouds sped by above the dark mountains of a cloven coastline. The first-class passengers filled the little lounge, locked against the wind and any influx from the outer passages, where peasant women huddled and sprawled along the benches, moaning, retching, vomiting over each other's feet, while small children, boxes, baskets, chickens and turkeys with their legs tied lying flat upon their breasts, rolled in the thick puddles on the deck-boards.

Some people ran by me, sliding unsteadily, and called, "Alcohol! Get the steward."

In the stern a woman was having convulsions. Four men crouched round her with her head in their hands; one tried to stuff a wad of cloth dipped in alcohol down into her dress, while another man prised her jaws open, and her fingers gripped the air like bent twigs and her legs threshed violently from side to side with ridiculous, pointed shoes on the end of them, and in her yellow face the eyes were wide and staring as if in accusation.

Two or three others got off with me at Monemvasia. In the little skiff we bobbed in slowly to the shore, squeezing together on the seats as the water lapped the gunwales and hundreds of feet above us the rock island rose up into the mist. We landed on the stony shingle of the port on the mainland, which consisted of a hotel, a shop, two police stations and four coffee houses. That afternoon I crossed the causeway to the steep south talus of the island with the old city inside its quadrangle of walls neatly fitted between cliff and sea, still half-inhabited. A winding path led up into the fortress of the same cliffs that once gave shelter to populations fleeing from the Avars and Huns, and was always the last stronghold left in each invasion when the rest of Greece was overrun. From the summit I looked down on to a ledge once sealed against possible assault by a wall with a ruined bastion at one end; through its fallen floor the water tearing like white fangs along the shoreline. Clouds were blowing up from Cape Malea over the grey water of the Cretan Sea. Birds called and cackled in the cliffs, and wild pigeons dived down the open face of the red rock like darts hurled into the abyss. It began to rain. Over the long summit of the rock thin grasses blew and stalks of asphodel rattled on withered roots and flew up into the air. Four ruined towers rose pale in the swirling mist, and an old woman with bare, bloodstained feet leaped from one rock to another, flinging stones to right and left of a small herd of goats and screaming shrilly above the wind.

At nightfall men were standing guard with rifles at either end of the causeway, and on the mainland I was stopped and taken into a police station to declare my business and identity, a formula I was to learn by heart not many days later.

Another night I found the port thronged with shadowy figures hurrying by in the dark. I pressed past them through the inn door into an effulgence of smoking lights on burnished faces; above the din the voice of the innkeeper shouting into the kitchen where his wife and children dodged each other among the pots and pans, a servant-boy running out with trays and plates and glasses and a lantern in his hand, dripping burnt olive oil behind him as he climbed the ladder to the upper floor. From far away came the whistle of the steamer rounding the island, then the grinding anchor chain, a familiar echo through the shallow ports of the Aegean. Then the door opened and the people off the boat came in with a gust of wind that swept over the lights. There were a few soldiers who dragged their sacks and rifles up the ladder to a platform where I found them improvising beds of coats and matting on the wooden floor, laughing and cuffing each other as they stretched out and rolled their coverings around them. A group of women sat on bundles in a corner.

One of them asked me as I passed what time the boat came back.

"From Yítheion? In the early morning," I said. "Are you going to Athens?"

"Yes." She was only a girl; under her black kerchief her eyes looked straight ahead of her without blinking.

"Is everyone else here going to Athens too?"

"Do I know?" she said.

"Are you going for long?"

She answered enigmatically, "How long?" and pointed at their baggage. "There are six of us."

"Where do you come from?"

"From a village on Parnon, north of Molái. First the men went, some of their own will, some taken. Now the others are coming down and taking the women. So we leave too."

"Do you go to relatives in Athens?"

"We have relatives."

"Do they know you're coming?"

"How would they not expect us?" she answered briefly.

I went to my room. All that night the wind beat against the shuttered window. It was like the hold of a ship where the sleepers tossed, breathing heavily among the blankets in the other beds. A lantern on a chair glowed and fumed beside mine while I watched the shadows on the ceiling. One of the soldiers got up, kicked on his boots and seeing me awake, asked for a cigarette. I gave him one and he sat down on my bed.

Rubbing his eyes, he muttered, "Wounds from grenades. I have a piece in my head. I was five weeks in hospital. Now they tell me to go home for a month."

"Where were you?"

"In the Grammos."

"How was it there?"

He turned away, puffing on his cigarette, with his arms folded inside his khaki sweater. "You shoot," he replied; "sometimes you kill; all the time you try to stay warm—war, what do you think?"

I asked, "Where are you going tomorrow?"

"First to Molái. I have to get a donkey from there to my village. I can't walk more than ten minutes at a time."

"And after that where will you go?"

"After? Who knows? They say it will get better when I stay still in one place. Panagia, today . . . ! On the boat, up and down, from side to side; then tomorrow two hours on the bus, and after that . . . I'm sitting still now and I ask when will it stop!" He put his cigarette out on the floor and stood up, bony, ungainly in his underdrawers and boots, and lay down again on his bed.

THE MORNING DAWNED COLD and wet. The steamer had already passed and picked up the refugees from Parnon. From my window I saw some old automobiles getting ready for the journey to Molái, fifty kilometres north-west. The drivers were cranking up their engines, and those who had spent the night in the inn stood round the cars, lashing luggage, carcasses and live fowl on to their sagging framework, while the rest of the village waited about in the puddles of the street. I could hear the growl of motors far up the road as the first cars disappeared from view.

I travelled light. I had seen in my *Guide bleu* mention of a Frankish fort in Molái, and that was reason enough for me to collect my belongings and rush into the street where I opened the door of the last car and threw myself on to five other passengers in the back seat as it lurched forward.

We drove inland through the orange groves and vineyards of a valley where the dark, ploughed earth rose up towards cliffs that swept like organ pipes into the clouds floating through their defiles. Inside the car a soldier stuffed his kit under his knees and sat forward, gazing to right and left.

"They have no vines in Macedonia," he said. "No fig trees, nothing. From the mountains we look down and see only the plains of tobacco."

At the head of the valley a large white village was spread out over a hillside. As the car wound upward through its streets the soldier began to cry, calling and waving through the window. Shouts followed us into the main square. Then he threw open the door and jumped out into the embrace of four or five men who bore him away, red-faced and struggling.

I stepped into a crowd pressing round the car, and immediately my arm was caught; before me stood a colossal gendarme, balancing himself on a walking-stick. Who was I, what was I, what was I here for? The questions came out fast. When I had answered, he turned and announced: "An American, who has come to see the *kástro*. An archaeologist, a student, a tourist in Molái! We are the antiquities, Kyrie; study us. And if you have come to look at the fortress, this whole town is a fortress. Half the population comes from villages deserted on the mountains. Each of these men here, Kyrie Archaeologist, has a gun and stands guard day and night. Why? Because ten days ago the Andartes came into the town and slaughtered thirty people. We sent out a band of our men and lost nine, all civilians. They, the others, had Russian machine-guns in the hills; we had none, thanks to the Americans. The night before last, two were murdered down there in the fields. So?" he concluded triumphantly, the centre of everyone's attention. He indicated me with his big, ringed hand, saying, "Eh, we have made him dizzy, the poor *phoukará!*" and walked away.

I went to announce my arrival at the police station immediately. The police chief surprised me with a courteous reception and told me about some unidentified ruins several kilometres away at a place called Eliá; he would try to get a car to take me there in the afternoon. Meanwhile a gendarme was assigned to show me the castle.

It was an insignificant little fort on a pepper-pot hill just above the town. The gendarme and I climbed up a steep rock by a fixed rope and hauled ourselves over the crumbling walls. There were machine-guns at either end, one pointing into a gully of the hillside, one trained upon the square. Two gendarmes were keeping the day's watch. They mentioned a total of fifteen policemen in Molái.

"Is that all?" I asked.

"We have help from other sources," they replied.

I made some notes and drawings, but there was little to see; so my gendarme accompanied me down again and sat with me while I had lunch in a taverna. I asked him the distance to Eliá by foot.

"Two hours."

"It's quite early still," I said. "I think I'll go and see those ruins your chief was talking about."

"Don't be in a hurry." He was a dark-skinned Cretan with a curled moustache and chilly, brown eye. "Slowly-slowly. He will drive you down."

"Oho, procrastination *à la grecque!*" I produced an ill-timed laugh. "Actually, I'd prefer to walk."

"No," said the policeman, and we sat there for an hour. At last he got up from the table: "I have work. Sit here, the officer will come."

I decided to go as soon as he was out of sight, but when I caught a glimpse of him watching me from a window across the square, I remained where I was.

Soon the chief of police came by. Seeing me, he exclaimed, "Ah, the Kyrios!" in such a heart-warming Greek manner that I ceased to wonder whether or not he wished me any good. I longed to believe these people felt genuine pleasure in seeing foreigners. He took me to a coffee-house with a better view over the square. An armed man stood at every corner; the inhabitants walked back and forth like animals sauntering in a cage. We had a second cup of coffee. From time to time he would call to a passer-by, "Kyrie Schoolmaster, Kyrie Lawyer, come and meet a visitor." And so most of the afternoon was whiled away in conversation with the gentry of Molái, until the police chief finally said, "We had hoped to find a car to take you to Eliá. However, it makes no difference; the antiquities there are not worth mentioning." He rose, bowed, excused himself and so loosed me from his casual custody. Apparently it was now late enough to leave me to my own devices.

Alone at last, I walked through the town into olive orchards and ploughed squares of land, wet from the late autumn rains, stretching away in the silence of the afternoon. Voices sounded from far off and the church bells in the town were ringing. People were coming down the path, with a priest in front, boys chanting behind him, and a long line of farmers all dressed in suits with buttoned jackets. I hopped to one side to let them go by: four men with a coffin on their shoulders and others holding between them a very old woman whose feet waved helplessly over the rough stones, her upturned face rolling from side to side, her eyes shut and mouth wide open, wailing. I saw through the olives the grave-yard in the distance.

I was ready to leave Molái next morning, only to learn there were no cars back to Monemvasia. This was the price of impulsiveness. All morning and afternoon I watched the people in the square and noted the discontent which day after day sharpened the babble of their voices, hardened the glint in their eyes and pared down the bones in the faces of those who sat about in the public places, waiting. Towards evening I was approached by an elderly man who had spent the greater part of his life in a candy store in Minneapolis. Thankful to have someone to talk with, I begged him to join me inside a crowded coffeehouse.

"You came to see the fortress. Did you see much?" he asked in English.

"No."

"Your coming up here makes it embarrassing for the police—." He checked himself. "They don't like it." He leaned down to pick up a box of matches from the floor and murmured: "They want Americans to have a good impression, but if they come to a place like this, they won't get it."

"Why is that?"

"Too many murders," he replied in the same low, casual voice, as if to deflect the many-eyed scrutiny all round us in the coffeehouse.

"But it does no harm for us to see what's going on," I said. "On the contrary—"

"You should only see what makes you send more aid to Greece."

"We have to help you finish your civil war!" I protested.

"It doesn't do to see too much," he said. "I've seen people driven from their houses, driven from their work, and murders . . ." Again he paused, looked round us, then smiled disconcertingly. "Reign of terror, you know. . . . Listen, you think it's all right to travel around the country and gather impressions. But the people sitting here at these tables have nothing to do. Months go by, then when a stranger appears, they start talking. Today I heard about some fellow who has come here with forged American identity. You want to be careful; ideas catch fire."

The coffee-shop was emptying and through the window I saw people leaving the square; the light was going out of the sky. The man left me and I stood outside alone, wondering whether there was still time to get a meal before withdrawing from the forbidden night into my room at the hotel. However, my uncertain steps lingering in the dusky square were watched, and there appeared at my side the taciturn gendarme who had been with me the day before.

"Come with me," he said, "and eat your supper."

"What about the curfew?"

"That doesn't matter; you're with us." He led me to a restaurant and kicked open the door. "Inside." It closed behind me, and I felt my way round the corners of tables on which the muzzles of shotguns, carbines and rifles projecting from under a heap of overcoats caught the glow of a kerosene lamp masked by the humped shoulders of some men sitting at the far end, near the kitchen.

One of them rose as I approached. "So the foreigner comes here!" and I saw a stout, black, bristling-bearded warrior standing in the passage with his legs apart, hands stuck into his belt, and bandoliers slung across his chest. "Come in here," he said; behind the beard his teeth flashed like ice.

I followed him into a dark kitchen, where he picked a knife off the table and running one finger down its edge exclaimed, "To think I was once a lawyer! Eh, cook, wake up and cut off some of this for the American." He jabbed the knife into the carcass of a goat that hung from the low ceiling.

Back in the huge, murky room he told me to sit down. He pulled up a chair next to mine, seated himself and pushing it backwards with his heels, tilted up his face and looked at me across his beard. "So? What do you think of Molái? What do you think of Hellas?"

"At the moment—"

"*Bá*, don't answer," he said, then looked at the gendarme. "What does he think he knows, this man?"

The gendarme made no reply. Three other men sat by, who looked old, though it was hard to see their faces between their coat collars and the caps pulled down over their ears.

The man with the beard turned to me again and said, "So you have been in Greece one year. You go to a school in Athens. You are writing a book on castles. You travel round the Peloponnese and try to see everything, am I right?"

"You talk too much, Photi," said the Cretan gendarme. "Let him eat his supper."

But there was no food yet on the table, and the other man went on, "It was you who wanted to go down to Eliá yesterday afternoon. I would have taken you myself if it hadn't been for—"

"Photi." The Cretan flicked an eyelid at him. He paused while the Cretan spread his hand out underneath the table and moved it, palm downward, from side to side.

The man muttered something impatiently under his breath, then drew some pictures out of his pocket: one was of a girl with a baby in her arms, another of the same girl holding flowers and standing beside a heavy young man in a tight-fitting suit with a slack and lazy jaw. "That's me four years ago at my wedding," he said.

I ventured to say, "Better with the beard."

"A thousand times!" he answered heartily. "Look at this one," and he handed me a postcard of a man bearded and strapped and armed exactly like himself. "Do you recognize him? That's the leader of EDES. I was with him all through Epiros in '42 and '43. He made me bodyguard to his English friends. It was we in EDES, with British help, who beat down the Communists when they tried to seize power in '44. If it hadn't been for us, *amán* . . . !" He was referring to the British team which parachuted on to Mount Giona in October, 1942, made contact with the two rival resistance groups and enlisted their help to blow up the railroad bridge over the Gorgopótamos ravine, at a crucial moment cutting the Germans' supply line through the Balkans to Rommel's army in Tunisia; after that the same Britishers had stayed on in the mountains with the avowed purpose of healing the rift between EAM/ELAS, dominated by the Communist Party, and the Rightist resistance group called EDES.

I said, "I thought the British came to pull the Resistance together and make it into a single fighting unit."

"Bá, they tried," said the man with a shrug of his capacious shoulders, "but we had other things to do."

"What about the Germans and Italians who were occupying the country?"

"They left us mostly alone," he said.

The cook came out with a plate of fried goat, but the bearded man had something else to show me before I began to eat it: a form of identity card with the letter X, or Khi, at the head.

"That," he said, "is my membership in a volunteer force now recognized by the government. Ach, the things I could show you if they would only let me!" he exclaimed. "Shall I tell you first how the Communists killed my father and brother? Would you like to see one of the villages they held till not so long ago, which I burned down with these two hands? I suppose you've seen a slaughter-house?"

The Cretan cut him short, pointing to the window. "The others, Photi—they're waiting for you."

The man stood up and with his eyes still fixed on me as he adjusted his bandoliers, gave himself a shake and went out, heaving a gun off the table at the farther end.

Another gendarme, the corporal of the night's guard, came in, threw his rifle and blanket on the floor and strode towards our table.

The Cretan said to him, "It's the American who came here yesterday."

"American!" he exclaimed, sitting down across the table. He looked at me for a few seconds and then said in a very clear young voice—he looked hardly over twenty: "Tell me whom you consider to blame for what is happening now in Greece. Do you say Russia? You are wrong. It is you, England and America, who have betrayed us."

Through the fibres of a mouthful of goat I mumbled my surprise.

"It's good that you should hear me say it. Yes, you, the Great Powers, should know what you have done to Greece."

"Done to Greece?" I echoed. "In the famine of 1942 we sent you from America enough flour to keep you from starvation and—"

"Keep us from starvation! *Pó-po-po-po-po*, you kept us from total extinction—here indeed are several of us still alive to prove it—but not from starvation. No, Kyrie, and you have not done so yet."

"What about the Marshall Plan and all the aid we're sending you?"

He tossed his head back. "Aid—measured out with a nose-dropper!"

"American aid comes into Greece at the rate of I don't know how many hundred thousand dollars a day," I retorted.

"Where? Where? Show it to us. Where shall we look for it?"

"In the roads and bridges we're rebuilding, in the canals and ports we're dredging, in the contracts we give out to Greek industry."

"*Amán!*" he exclaimed softly. "Roads—for your own strategic uses. Bridges—you rebuild them and the next night the Andartes come down and blow them up again. Harbours—all for your own ships. Contracts with our industry! You mean the contracts you have directly with the pockets of the rich in Athens. Do you think we ever see that money or anything that's done with it? Ask these old men here if they have ever seen American money coming into Greece. Ask those who are starving now what they think of your philanthropy."

"Whatever is done with it, it's money paid out by ordinary taxpaying Americans," I said.

"And to us it comes with a label: charity. Forgive us if it seems more to us like window-dressing."

"Then forget money," I said. "Consider instead the number of Americans in Greece—several thousand—working for the good of your country."

"And with those salaries you pay them to do it, salaries that could feed whole provinces—out of the money which is meant for Greece! Oh no, it's not only the rich Greeks who eat it up." He made a gesture of stuffing something into an inside pocket. "No: you're learning from us. As for all those Americans in Athens, do they ever leave the capital?"

I said, "Think of the specialists we send to help you with agriculture and teach you farming methods you have never heard of, and the labour missions to help you organize your unions, and the sums granted for educational purposes to—"

"How much those sums mean to people who can't read or write!" he interrupted. "Committees on agriculture—who, do you think, has any opportunity now for agriculture? No, no, no, you are letting us be wiped out, because you know that if Greece were a great power she could crush you all. Long ago we were an empire and ruled all the nations of the Near East; now our people have to sail abroad to earn a living washing plates in restaurants! It served the interests of France and England when we fought for our independence from the Turks in 1821—until we had one of our own race for president. He was a friend of the Czar and the Eastern Church, and would not have been the puppet of the English. They were content to see him assassinated, so that they could prove to the outside world that we couldn't govern ourselves; after that they sent foreign kings to rule over us. And in 1920 they urged us to take our army into Asia Minor to punish the Turks for fighting on the German side. Do you remember how they promised to support us until we surrounded Constantinople and got to within fifty kilometres of Ankara? It was only when we were being driven back into the sea, with fellow-Greeks being massacred in Smyrna by the thousands, that we found out the English were no longer helping us, and all the time the French had been selling arms to the Turks! Panagia, we have seen enough these last years to know what your good intentions mean. One day guns and dynamite for Zervas, another day guns and dynamite for EAM and ELAS."

"Who is to blame for the civil war you choose to fight among yourselves?"

"Oh, nobody but the Germans and the Italians and the English and now the Americans."

"You have been fighting civil wars in Greece since the beginning of history," I said. "There's a nice description in Thucydides—"

"Because we are poor!" he said explosively. "Poverty drives us always to depend on someone stronger than ourselves. How can a rich nation understand us? Only when you too have fallen low—"

"It is you who choose your allies," I cut in. "Don't blame us if some of you choose Russia and others of you choose America and England."

"You belong to a nation that has suffered nothing. Nevertheless yours is the country we Greeks have had to choose; therefore—"

"Some of you, not all," I said.

"Eh, then, since we have, why is it you do nothing to help us but merely sit and wait for us to be blotted off the earth!"

I said, "Don't you know every gun, tank, plane, ship, shell and bullet in your armed forces comes from us?"

"Does America want us to defeat the Communists in this civil war?"

"Well, what do you think?" I said impatiently.

"Then why do you limit the size of our army? By your orders it is kept down to a minimum, while we," his voice rose, "die like flies in the Grammos and all over the country. Have you not seen, at least in Athens, men coming out of hospital with their legs cut off, pushing themselves along the street on wheels, selling oranges and matchboxes to keep their families alive? The blame is on you."

Sitting far back in his chair, the Cretan said to me, "This one has been to high school. He has therefore a big head, full of ideas."

The other gendarme hastened on. "Why don't you send your own troops over here instead of paying us to do your fighting for you?"

"I suppose you know what that would mean?"

"Yes," he answered swiftly. "War. Eh, why not? You have the power. What have you to lose?"

"What power?" I said.

"The bomb."

"And nothing to lose? Does a bomb solve problems?"

"It can wipe out an enemy."

"Other problems remain," I said.

"It can solve them by solving the problem of existence once and for all."

"Is that what you prefer?"

His voice rang out, "What is worse than this? In Greece we have come to an end, we can go no further. Look at these people sitting beside you. They are old and all day they work in their fields in the rain—they are lucky, they have fields—and all night they must stand guard round the town with guns. They are grandfathers; their sons are soldiers fighting; to their grandchildren what will happen? Ask them if they think anything can be worse. Look at this man's white hair," and he pulled the cap off the head of one of the old men. All evening the three had sat there, saying nothing.

"Ask him," the young man persisted. His clear voice echoed in that shadowy room where the others slumped in their chairs and the one with his hair rumpled still said nothing; and I saw in their half-closed eyes the apathy born of interminable weariness and fear.

The young man cried out, "What way do you propose for us?"

I said, "The way of moderation."

His eye glinted at me across the table. "Do you think moderation is enough in an age like this? Have not most men of moderation already committed suicide?"

"You are alive; can't you hope for anything?"

"Yes, for one thing—that you should drop your bombs over all the world."

I got to my feet, saying, "Do you wish for a Third World War?"

Then they all sprang up and pressed their faces close to mine like blind men, and one of them said, "What have we to live for? Let there be war tomorrow!"

It was cold outside in the square. The silent policeman walked beside me to the hotel up a street behind the gendarmerie.

"It's late," he said. "Time for sleep. It's not good when people open their mouths too much."

We parted, and I went upstairs to a room where a tiny wick, the downy calyx of some dried plant, floating in a saucer of oil, produced the smallest of all lights. Down in the street I could hear voices and the movement of vehicles and the sound of preparations all night long.

CHAPTER 4

Athens—
The Shortness of Hope

A T THE BEGINNING of my second year in Greece a neurologist sent me for two months' observation to a small hospital
beyond the last stop of the suburban tramline.

It was a rest from travel, also from the much greater exertion
of settling down to a winter of intense study and three meals a
day with my compatriots at the Academy; a place where the only
noise was the muted screech of trams as they started back on
the long trip into Athens, and below the windows little rocky,
unpaved streets led away into the olive groves and market gardens
of the plain. My two months were extremely happy in a third-class
ward which was big and clean, all windows and light, with only
four beds, and views out over cypresses in the courtyard and tiled
roofs beyond, and the naked, baked, brown mass of Tourkovóuni
across the nearest avenue with a white chapel on its ridge; in the
distance the gleaming rock summit of Lykavitós, and the fragile shapes of the Erechtheum and the Parthenon amply framed
in one of the window-panes. From the first moment, dressing
myself in hospital pyjamas, I put away from me, as I believed, all
outward semblance of a foreigner and rejoiced to think that here
at last I would find companionship, anonymity and self-forget-

fulness. I found all three, though the reality proved in the end uncomfortable like any other.

I would even have chosen a fourth-class ward if I had known about them; my first evening in the hospital I visited one, and fifteen or twenty patients on army cots set close together gave me a noisy welcome. However, in these wards the hospital supplied no meals, and so the patients' families came in the afternoons with baskets of bread and fruit and hot food in tin containers. Here too the floors were swept by those who were able to get out of bed. Yet it made little difference where I was; in the evenings there were parliaments of grey-robed, shuffling figures up and down the corridors and stairwells like the crowds one sees thronging the squares of any Greek town after a certain hour of the day; in its lulled and dreamlike tempo the hospital was like a coffee-house in eternity.

Many here had illnesses dating from the German occupation, yet from their manner it was hard to tell which of them awaited recovery and which did not; they all behaved as if they were on holiday. I have since seen Greeks going off to war or exile, sitting in prison, or on the benches of a judgment hall, waiting for the death sentence, and all behaved in the same way. Now, however, it was still new to me to hear no one complain: not the Cretan peasant who lay with a club foot recently opened up and re-set in a plaster cast suspended over his cot, nor the seventeen-year-old boy from Andros who had been brought here after a factory accident and had his leg cut off the week before I came, who gaily wheeled and whirled himself along the passages, singing. The day he left I saw him putting on his trousers; while he hopped and hobbled about he said, "See the mess we're in, Andrea?" and in his voice there was as much indifference as finality. The man in the bed next to mine never let out more than a half-strangled imprecation on the Mother of God when the surgeons gathered round to swab his stomach, wide open underneath the sheets, and I would listen with delight to his quarrels with the head nun whom he called Sister Poison because she took away his cigarettes, or with a pasty-faced and thin-haired civil servant in our ward who sat by the hour in the window, crooning sections of the Orthodox liturgy in a soft falsetto while he gazed at the nurses' dormitory across the court. Lying awake at night Stéphanos, my neighbour, would overhear the civil servant recounting in his sleep the calumnies he had used to oust colleagues from their posts, and in the morning would accuse him of a want of honour and denounce him as a *malakisménos rouphiános*, which means masturbated pimp, with eloquent disgust between mouthfuls of rolls and coffee.

My first afternoon, waking up out of the siesta, the sunlight was slanting in long parallelograms across the linoleum floor and the ward was full of people talking in low voices round the other beds. Beside mine lay Stéphanos flat on his back without a pillow, his lids red with sleeplessness, surrounded by a populous family of old and young, all with the same brilliant eyes in their dark peasant faces. They greeted me when they saw I was awake and at once began talking. Stéphanos' mother, dressed in black, said, "I made twelve children. I have seven alive."

"And these are yours?" I said to Stéphanos. In Greece any mention of children must always be accompanied by a formal wish for their welfare since children are believed to be easily subject to the Evil Eye. So I added, "May they live for you."

Stéphanos' wife, sitting between our two beds with her elbows on his mattress, turned in her chair and said, "You should take a Greek to wife if you wish to make many children." She gravely controlled a smile.

"A good idea," said I, a little enviously; "the more the better!"

"That they should live, though," she said, and the laughter went out of her eyes.

Across the room I saw a grey-haired man with thin, bent shoulders, a lanky boy who looked nearly as old, with a cruel jaw of teeth, a stout, dark woman in a tailored suit, and an older woman wearing a straw hat garlanded with artificial fruit and flowers on the front of her head, who spoke in the flat and toneless drawl of Greeks who have come back from America. "I'm flying home to Chicago tomorrow by TWA," she said. "How come you're here?"

Effortlessly I told them what I had seen of Greece during the past year, when the patient in their midst got out of his bed and wandered over to my corner with an abrupt and jerky stride. He said haughtily through a puff of cigarette smoke, "If you want to speak Greek, learn *Katharévousa*, the language of the educated. Talking like us won't help you with your studies."

When the bell rang announcing the end of visiting hours and all the others left, I asked him why he suggested I speak the graceless, archaizing language of official texts and scholarly pub-lications. He replied, "Eh! The nurse told us an American was coming, and when I saw you walk in with all those books I said, 'Surely this is some cauliflower from the University.'" Time in a hospital has its own elisions. Nikiphóros became my compan-ion in less than a day and my best friend the next. He was short and ugly, with a wide forehead, long nose and pointed chin; his skin was too white and dry and furrowed for someone in his early twenties and his way of walking, as we strolled together up and down the corridors, gave an effect of pacing behind bars. He was witty and ironic, eloquent, peppery, not at all easygoing, some-times gentle and sometimes out of temper, never the same two days, two hours running.

One day his father came—the man with the bent shoulders and the weary voice—and addressed me familiarly as *koumbáros*. Pleased to be so accepted, I said, "*Koumbáros?* How nice!"

"Why not?" said the old man. "Since you keep company with my son . . ."

"Cucumbers!" exclaimed Nikiphóros contemptuously.

"And why cucumbers?" said I.

"Because *koumbáros* means *koumbáros* only in a church with the proper mysteries," he replied crossly. "I dislike words that have lost their meaning."

That evening he gave me all the figs his father had brought during visiting hours. I begged him not to, but he only said, "Eh, be quiet. You have no family here."

One night he tied a string of goat-bells underneath my bed and by a cord from his side of the room kept them jangling at half-hourly intervals, to my irritation and everyone else's merriment. Once I got into bed and in the dark found myself sitting on a raw egg. I shouted; a passing nurse turned on the light and I was revealed angrily shaking drops of water from my fingers; Nikiphóros had sucked the shell and filled it from his water glass. Another time he climbed on my shoulders wrapped in his sheets, one of the others pressed the bell and as the nurse opened our door the light from the passage fell on to a tall, white, undulating form inside the room. She fled with a shriek and collided into Sister Poison at the turn of the corridor. "I saw a mouse!" she cried.

The quality of his pranks varied with the amount of mercy he happened to feel at any given time. Unlike other Greeks whom I had met, he had no polite, consuming curiosity. Yet he was capable of asking me one day out of a blue sky, "What sort of person would you like to be, Andriko?" Then he was more than patient while I tried to give tongue to introspection in demotic Greek, pausing here and there to leaf through my pocket lexicon for words like "consciousness," "subjectivity," or "in extremis." Though the inconvenient language persisted in transforming my most abstract thoughts into concrete, ludicrous nonsense, he said nevertheless at the end of my recital, "I think I understand you. You really wish you could act without thinking."

To which I replied, "Amen!"

He came from a village north of the Corinthian Gulf in a mountain range called Ágrapha, which means Unwritten; it was five hours by mule track to the nearest road. During the 1930s when thousands of people migrated to the capital and many villages all over Greece were deserted, he came to Athens as a small boy with his family. For fifteen years his father had made his living hiring himself out to restaurants as a specialist in roasting a delicacy called *kokorétsi*, entrails wrapped round and round a spit. The old man was now out of work and so had time to bring things to his son in hospital. Nikiphóros' mother swept floors at the Athens Telephone Company from six to nine each morning for a salary of 150,000 drachmae a month, then the equivalent of fifteen dollars. Her dowry of a small field on a mountainside had long since been abandoned, and a daughter had died in the famine of 1942, but nothing seemed to have broken her yet; her role was to endure and laugh with as good a grace as possible, and she accepted all that came to her as only the good or the stupid can. Nikiphóros had two younger brothers. The one with the long jaw drove a truck at odd times and played cards through the off-season, while the youngest was attending a course at a mechanics' school; he was their hope, for whom the others sacrificed what separate hopes they had. Nikiphóros himself had left school after learning the alphabet and got a job working on the telephone poles and high-tension wires.

"That was something I liked," he said; "it was high up, there was plenty of air . . . I was sixteen when the Italians invaded Greece. You should have seen Athens then—every day hundreds of men and boys without uniforms or guns or training marching through the streets and singing all the way to the Lárissa station. We used to run out into the crowds, singing too to encourage them. One day my mother sent me out with all our blankets in my arms—I could just carry them—and I gave them to as many as I could. God knows they had nothing else to keep them warm that winter on the Albanian frontier. It was cold for us too at night, what did that matter? I had a stick a shepherd gave me once when I was small; I gave it to a man who had no gun. I remember how he waved it over his head, shouting, 'Thank you, little one, I'll drive the *makaronádhes* into the sea with this.' They did too. They all went north and hurled the Italians back to the coast, and then the Germans came and our men froze in the snow. They say some of the army doctors were pro-German— trained by Metaxas, you know—so they cut off the men's frozen arms and legs to finish the business quicker. Later, during the Occupation, some Italian soldiers caught me writing slogans on a wall one night. They condemned me to death on my eighteenth birthday. But that was in 1943, just when Italy surrendered to the Allies. Then the Germans in Greece put all the Italians in prison and set us free. The day I got out I stood on a street corner and watched the Germans driving before them whole companies of disarmed Italian troops. Imagine, just a week before they had been still parading round the streets as conquerors. There was a woman near me on the sidewalk, who taunted them and shouted, '*Buon viaggio!*' The bystanders struck her down and almost killed her. Even though we despised the Italians, who burned our villages and tortured our people, it was not right to jeer at them when they were defeated. We Greeks are a vile race on the whole, but there are moments when we have honour. . . .''

He told me how he went back then to his father's village where many of its former inhabitants had returned already, no hungrier there than in the streets of Athens where the pavements were littered with the light bodies of the dead. All the mountains of Greece were in the hands of one resistance band or another, and Nikiphóros' village in the Ágrapha was run by the organization called EAM, dominated by the Communist Party. For a year he held the post of town clerk there, and then the German armies retreated from the Balkans and the British landed in Greece in November, 1944. He returned immediately to Athens, but the suburb where his family lived was a stronghold of EAM and ELAS during the December uprising, and it was heavily bombed. Here there was a gap in his account. The next year he went back to work on the telephone poles. He used to fall ill frequently, until at last the civil war broke out all over Greece and he was drafted into the national army. He told us how at the induction camp in Tripolis the new recruits were given either black or brown boots according to what was written on their political records. When his turn came, the quartermaster jeeringly asked him if he were a propagandist, and he was given black boots and put into detention with everyone whose record bore the words EAM/ELAS. But they sent him home when they discovered he had tuberculosis.

At supper he would regale us with the stories he had heard in prison; they were pungently, almost mythically obscene and told with Byzantine grandiloquence, and we missed him whenever he was not there. He was well enough, apparently, to be allowed out after the siesta, but he never said where he went, though once he casually remarked, "I had a good time in someone's bed this afternoon." Another day he brought back an expensive, new radio—"I had a few gold pounds," he said; "why keep them?"

I resented his departures and was on the whole glad when he stayed out till three o'clock one morning and a doctor and two night nurses hurried him into the ward; this was the last time, they said. It took the three of them to talk him down, and in the dead of night he woke up the whole floor with his shouting.

The weather was warm next day and the two of us took a turn in the hospital's vegetable garden. I congratulated him on the vigour of his argument.

"Oh, you must never let them win too fast," he said good-humouredly. "When the authorities attack you, don't defend yourself; attack them, say anything, get them arguing at cross-purposes, only don't give in. That is fatal. They will of course win in the end," he added wearily. Then he suddenly exclaimed, "*Ach*, I hate being in here!"—and looked up at the cypresses and the high walls round the garden.

"Do you really? For the time being I would rather be here than any place in Greece—"

Nikiphóros emitted a soft breath: "For the time being!"

"Believe me, this place is more instructive than sixteen universities," I rejoined. "I am afraid of certain things in my character—hesitation, fright, indecision; all round me I see people overcoming just those things. Most of all I am afraid of never becoming involved in life; yet here I come close to it."

Nikiphóros said, "Between you and me there is an abyss."

I said, "There may be. But I think one can bridge it by talking, by understanding each other."

"Understand yourself first."

I protested, "I understand myself very well! I have just been telling you—"

"As if you knew what you had!" he murmured. "You—with all the treasures of life, and you don't know it."

"What do you mean?"

"You are free, Andrea. You can choose. You can go anywhere in the world, do anything you want. When I leave here, the doctor will suggest that I go to some quiet place in the provinces and rest. Instead, I shall go back to a room in Pangráti four metres square—that is where we live, you know, the five of us."

"Oh? But your village, couldn't you go there?"

"Not," he replied, "as the only inhabitant. The place is deserted now."

"You have no other relatives in the country?"

"I have one uncle on Evvia, who lives low down where it's damp." He pointed into his ribs: "You see, I can't live there."

"When you're well again, will you go back to the same work?"

"Eh, I'll probably find some lighter work," he said gently, for he must have realized then that I knew nothing about him; it was not till much later that I learned that he had nephritis and leukemia. With a comical look he added, "Cheer up, Andriko, the Telephone Company still pays for my hospitalization."

Not long afterwards a representative of the company came to visit him. He looked badly that day, his nose thin and pinched and the temples rather more sunken round his corrugated, wasted brow. It might well be anxiety, I thought to myself as his visitor asked a few questions and jotted something in a notebook. However, he said as he went out the door, "There is no need to worry, you know; your insurance is safe as long as you are employed by us." But the following week three more officials were shown to Nikiphóros' corner. He lay in their midst while they stood like priests around his bed, clicking their brief-cases and shuffling papers as they took his name off their pay-roll. It lasted only a few minutes. Then they departed, bowing to the doctor and the nurse who showed them out. At supper that night Nikiphóros was particularly amusing.

Indeed from that time on he seemed much more at ease, less volatile, less irritable. I admired him for the impression he gave of a person who had seen his own life whole.

We talked often, outside in the vegetable garden and as we strolled in the corridors; time was never heavy. One evening the two of us sat on the stairs, while nurses passed up and down beside us and the white veils of nuns floated across the shiny floors, and he asked if I had ever loved anyone. I told him about my feelings for a girl I had known in Italy during the war, but when I finished he said, "You didn't really love her."

I reluctantly said "No" and then, because my thoughts were bitter on the subject, exclaimed, "I have never loved anyone!"

A little absently he said, "Think of what it must be not to be able physically."

"Yes, I imagine."

"And what would you say if I told you I had been castrated?"

"God knows!" I said with a laugh.

"That is what happened to me," he replied.

I stared at him.

He leaned back against the wall and smiled. "It will be four years this December. It happened during the EAM revolution. There was, you know, a great deal of street fighting in the suburbs. One day during the noon truce I ran out to buy bread, and a mortar shell exploded near me. They operated. I have never spoken of this to anyone. So what do you say?"

Unable to meet his gaze, I said, "I love you more; that's all I can say."

"Yet nothing you can say or do really makes any difference, does it? It's like being in prison, what? Imagine the life sentence."

Just then a nurse called to him, "Kyrie Nikiphóro, we wait for your injection. Come."

He walked away and I sat where I was; I heard the voices of several people I knew greeting me as they passed by. I was still there when he strolled back, munching on an apple.

"Hoo-oo, look at you!" he suddenly burst out laughing. "How you suffer! You really believed me all that time? *Bà*, if such a thing happened to me I'd be dead. And yet it did happen to a friend of mine. I could hardly believe him when he told me; I just sat there like you, saying nothing. Eh, courage, you cauliflower! Cheer up."

What hurt most was that he should care so little for my sympathy. I felt no relief. This was unreasonable if what he had said was only a joke; but that night I began to wonder which was true, the joke or his denial. I never found out.

Finally the day came when the neurologist told me I could leave in the afternoon. So I took off my familiar pyjamas and grey dressing-gown and put on my own clothes once more. We all said good-bye to each other, and then I walked out into the sunny street, and the hospital doors closed behind me with a clang of frosted glass. Somebody called to me from an upper window, but the words were lost in the roar of a tramcar on the avenue, and the next moment I turned the corner.

I walked across Athens in the deep blue afternoon, climbing first the stony heights of Tourkovóuni rising above the northern suburbs like a hill in the desert, where there was a view out over all the mountains round the city. Someone had said to me, "You are free, you can go anywhere you choose," but I hardly remembered him or the place I had just left in the exhilaration of using my legs again in the open air. I walked through long, dusty streets and it was evening by the time I reached Lykavitós and climbed up to its bare rock pinnacle with the infinitesimal, white monastery and blue shadows everywhere trickling down the clefts between edges of limestone, bright, watery and translucent. Descending through the pine trees on the other side, I could see the gleam of the Saronic Gulf tangled in their black branches, and the grey hills of Aigina and the distant Argolid. After a scramble down the gravelly slope I found myself back in the well-paved Kolonaki streets and began to feel in my pocket for my key to a room on the top floor of an institution I had not thought of for the past two months. A year ago it had been a prison, with its spacious library shelves and filing cabinets, its cool linen closets and dark halls with bulletin boards, with all its ease and space and privacy. Now, it was quite true, I was free; and I began making plans for a trip to the Peloponnese the following week.

However, it was necessary to go back to the hospital for an injection a few days later. I shouted up under the window of my old ward, but no one appeared. When I rang the bell, a nurse opened the door and said, "Nikiphóros is ill. Don't stay in there too long."

There was a newcomer in my bed. The others greeted me quietly. My friend lay with the blankets over his head and bending down, I could just see part of his face, all swollen.

I said, "Hey, it's me—Andrea."

His lips moved; it was only a mumble, sounding from far away. With his eyes still closed he muttered, "Good you left. I'm no use any more when this happens . . . hurts too much."

"The day after tomorrow I'm going away," I whispered to him. "You will think of me from time to time, eh?"

Again the voice out of the bedclothes, hardly recognizable, "Go with good fortune."

I remained a few minutes talking with Stéphanos and the others. Three days before I had known them all so well; now I had no business here. I said good-bye to them and left Nikiphóros where he lay, somewhere on the verge of life.

HE HAD GONE HOME by the time I returned to Athens at the beginning of the new year. It was only a fifteen-minute walk from the Academy to his house, down the hill and across the streambed of the Ilissos, a naked gorge half-filled with drainage pipes that runs like a frontier through the heart of Athens, dividing on one side the Palace and Embassies, hotels, Parliament buildings and apartment houses from the bleak wilderness of suburbs that sprang up in 1922 when the refugees came into Greece from Asia Minor.

There, in a two-room shack with flaking plaster walls at the back of someone else's courtyard in Pangriti, Nikiphóros lay bedridden month after month, and from all over the city friends came to see him after their working hours. His father, still out of a job, was always there when I went, and so were the two brothers who could not afford escapades in the evenings. Their mother, Kyra Eleni, would come in, battered and grey and laughing, with her small bag of food for their supper. Then one by one the others would arrive: apprentice boys from next door, who at an earlier age had tended their father's flocks on Helikon and Parnassos; Nikiphóros' uncle, who did good business with a coffee house, at the corner; an old priest from their village in the Ágrapha, whom they called Pappayánni, who had lost his living because he had been in EAM too and now wandered from church to church in Athens, looking for work; and a stout, grave, taciturn woman in her thirties called Kallirhói, whom I had seen frequently in the hospital. She taught home economics in a girls' school. I knew nothing else about her except that she had a small daughter, and knew Nikiphóros better than anyone else.

Food would be cooking on a brazier in the next room, and each of us, as if by ritual, would begin to make his excuses and get up. Then Nikiphóros would leap about on his rickety bed under the window, ordering his brothers to bar the door; nobody could leave before the plates were on the table. Reluctantly Pappayánni would take off his chimney-pot hat and put it down beside him, and with each newly filled bottle of wine would say, "Quick, I must pronounce another blessing." The show of reluctance was something I had not yet mastered, and they teased me for it, saying, "Bravo, Andrea, he admits he wants to stay. Why do we Hellenes always make such a pretence?" In company Nikiphóros was at his best. He always had another story that none of us had heard, and knew how to draw us out until everyone in the room was arguing while more wine was brought on, with Pappayánni shouting above the rest, "I say down with national frontiers, all men are brothers!" Sometimes they sang, and then I would feel the circle of conviviality drawn tight as antiphonally across that shabby room their voices spun the old, interminable laments—a shepherd's mother warning the chieftains not to descend into the valley, a message between bands of klephtic warriors across the Gulf of Corinth, news of a defeat from "black Ioannina" or a Turkish captain's dirge over his slaughtered army. Nikiphóros, who said he could not sing, lay propped on one shoulder, listening carefully, every so often whispering, "Soft . . . softly that verse."

We left late, and I generally took the bus back into Athens with Kallirhói. One night, just before I got off at my stop, I asked her some casual question about Nikiphóros' future, and she answered without any change of expression, "His illness will not be cured."

Nevertheless, as time went on he gradually got better. I found him one afternoon up and busy in his uncle's *kapheneíon*. Across a room filled with people he called, "Andriko, did you see the new sign I've painted? Eh, blind one, come and look." We went out and he pointed above the door to a single word stretching across the whole front of the shop:

KAPHEOINOZYTHOPSITESTIATORION

"I made it up: Coffee-Wine-Beer-Roast-Meat-Restaurant. Our language is like us, elastic, adaptable. Come and see what I do inside."

His uncle had given him a corner of the shop with a window opening on the street; a carpenter was setting up the plywood walls for a small kiosk while someone else fitted a fluorescent light-tube in its roof. Nikiphóros said to me, "Imagine me selling pencils, papers, prophylactics . . . like a wounded soldier, what? I have to do something!" he exclaimed impatiently. "This way it's better than lying in bed all day long. My friends here won't let me

pay for the wood or the lighting, but soon I'll have earned enough
to pay them back. So *ná* to the Telephone Company, I give it the
Evil Eye!" Then he took me down the street to see a tailor who
was cutting him a length of blue-and-white-striped canvas for an
awning. "He too gives it to me free," he said. "So for that he will
have three weeks' free choice of anything he wants as soon as the
kiosk is ready."

Back at the *kapheneíon* I watched him scamper nimbly up the
ladder with hammer and screwdriver in his hand. Swift and pre-
carious, he leaned far out to fix the canvas bit by bit on to the
metal frame already in place above the window.

"You have good balance," I said.

"Oho, you should see me higher than this! Tell me, what shall I
call it? The Kiosk of the Good Heart? *Bá*, I shall call it the Kiosk
of the No-good *keratá*—that's what you call me." All was ready
except for the goods on the shelves, but the work had tired him
out and he had to return to bed.

A week later I passed by on the far side of the street. He was
sitting in the window of his kiosk. Someone stopped, and he sold
a packet of cigarettes. I continued round to his house by a back
way and found Kyria Eleni at home.

"Oh, the Andrea!" she exclaimed. "I go at once to call Nikiphóros."

"Please don't. I went by on purpose so that he shouldn't see
me. I have to go right away, I only brought this; I thought perhaps
he could use it." I put on the table a sweater I had had for years.
"Don't give it to him if he doesn't want it. He's so proud it's hard
to do anything for him, as you probably know yourself, eh Kyria
Eleni?"

She stood, folding and unfolding the sweater on the table.

I said, "Maybe it doesn't do, in which case—"

She folded the sweater, turned it upside down, and unfolded it
again. "It does," she said.

"If he'd rather not accept it, I don't mind," I went on; "it's going
at the elbows."

"No, no," she said, "it does."

It embarrassed me that she was crying.

IT WAS A LONG TIME before I returned to the house, and then I was watching for a change in my friend's manner. We had had no long talks since we left the hospital, and I wondered if he felt as much as I did the abyss he had once spoken of which widened each time I saw him. All the friends were there, just as before. It was raining, and when they left Nikiphóros insisted that I should not go out. I stayed on a little while his mother began to make up the beds; there were only three for the five of them. Then the rain stopped and I made to go, but Kyria Eleni said, "Stay, Andrea. Nikiphóros will go into that bed; the boys will sleep in the other room and you can have this one by the window."

"But what about you and Kyr Niko?"

"Never mind about me and Kyr Niko. I spread the blankets on the floor, and the old man and I sleep like that, full of joy."

Still I protested, but Nikiphóros said, "Do you want to insult us, Andrea? Do as she says."

So I stayed. Before I fell asleep in the bed he had vacated for me, I heard the old woman murmur from the floor, "It's very comfortable. Don't worry . . . full of joy."

I went again to congratulate him on his name day, but only his parents were at home; he had got up and gone into Athens with friends. I never heard from him, and it was with no great sense of expectation that I went again a month later, without even much surprise that I saw the window of his kiosk empty. Half a block farther I climbed the stairs into a windy passage and down into the courtyard where a light shone from the window of the shack. I pushed open the door. Alone, under the glare of a light bulb dangling from the ceiling sat Eleni on the bed, her red hands in her lap.

"Is anybody in?" I said. "What's the matter?"

Her voice struggled to the surface. "Nikiphóros—"

"What is it?"

"They took him."

"What!"

Her head shook. "Back to the hospital."

"When?"

"This afternoon. All the time he shouted, 'Let them kill me!'"

"Where's your husband?"

"He has a job. Go and find him . . . the big restaurant in Klafthmónos Square." She waved to me as I went out.

The March night was cold in the centre of Athens. Across the dark space of Klafthmónos Square I saw the bright windows of the restaurant and old Niko in a white jacket standing on the sidewalk, turning long spits over a bed of coals in the iron tray set up outside the door. People walked past him into the warm, crowded room; others emerged and the loud gaiety of people who have dined well resounded in the street. A little window opened in the wall behind him, and a waiter poked his head through, calling "Two more orders." Slowly Niko sliced off portions of the sizzling meat on to plates and handed them through the window.

When he saw me, the skin round his jaws moved in a stiff smile. He bent down to look through the aperture, then cut off a piece of meat and gave it to me. "Here, Kyr Andrea. Quick, before they see you."

"I've just been to the house," I said.

He answered nothing, only shoved a poker into the coals and carefully turned each of the long, black, dripping rods.

"It's good you got the job," I said.

Niko spat into the street. "Look through this window—that's the proprietor behind the counter, see him? All night long he sits there, taking in the money. When he leaves, he carries it home with him in a bag. But me, the waiters, the boys who sweep up after him—he walks on our corpses. Restaurant owners are always sorry when they lose me, but till then I am nothing to them but (begging your pardon) *skatá*."

"Aren't you glad for the work?" I said.

"Glad to stand here in the cold," he murmured to himself. "That worthless son of mine who sits in the *kapheneíon* all day doing nothing . . . ! I make enough, Kyr Andrea, to buy my family one meal a day."

"Who is going to pay the hospital?" I asked.

"Six orders!" cried the waiter and slammed the window shut. Niko shrugged his thin, bent shoulders.

A few minutes later the window opened and the voice shouted again, "Six orders, old man. The owner says to hurry!"

Niko began waving his arms. "All the time he accuses me: why didn't I send him to school, why didn't I help him more? Eh, what could I do to help him! Was he ever grateful!" His voice rang out over the empty sidewalk, while behind him the meat dripped and sputtered on the coals. "Ah, Nikiphóro, you left a memory . . ."

I WENT OUT to the hospital one day in the spring. He was in a different ward. He seemed in good spirits and had just finished reading *War and Peace*, which Kallirhói had brought him. I gave him a translation of *The Grapes of Wrath*, and he exclaimed, "Oh, but this is nice! Whenever I have a new book, it's as if I had someone to keep me company."

"Tell me about your friends," I said. "Don't they come and see you?"

"I don't have any friends," he replied. "A long time ago I had one or two, but after the Revolution they went over the frontier into Serbia; they took different roads. As for other people, they have no patience with me as I am now. I don't blame them; everyone has his life. Do you know what, Andriko? Everybody wonders why I am so sure I shall get well. Now I can tell them I'll get well for the sake of Andrea who visits me and keeps me company. I look on you as a human being, you know, not just as a foreigner."

He went home a few weeks later, and I found him one afternoon lying in his bed under the window. I asked him if he had been reading, and he replied, "No, I don't read much nowadays." He looked over the sill into the barren little courtyard. "Still only

April. . . . It's as well I don't get the sun in this room. You know, it's the season when one likes to be out of doors."

"You don't get out?"

"For the time being, no. When I left the hospital, the doctor said, 'You will be quite all right, Kyrie Nikiphóro, as long as you stay in bed.' I asked him, 'How long do I have to stay in bed, Kyrie Doctor?' and he replied, 'That depends on how well you are.' It's all a matter of 'it depends.' Eh, why worry? I must do what I can, naturally I don't expect to live many years."

We talked for hours. With other people there his manner towards me was either indifferent or oratorical, when he would say grandly, "Andriko and I have become friends like brothers!" and friendship was the same as everything else, part of the brave show he might have been making for his last appearance. Now, without an audience, he merely knew he was going to die.

I told him I was leaving soon for the Peloponnese and would be in Kalamata at the end of May if he wanted to write me there.

He said, "I never write letters. If I ever began, I would write a whole volume. So don't expect ever to hear from me."

"Why don't you telephone me sometimes?"

"One day you're in Athens, another day you're gone. You know," he said, "where you can always find me."

I was no use to him. I saw him less and less, for my own life filled with interest, with journeys and other friendships and at last one long, reckless and intolerable happiness.

I did not see Nikiphóros again till the following winter, early in 1950, on the day of the national elections. Every public place was closed, the Pangráti streets were empty, and the front of the Coffee-Wine-Beer-Roast-Meat-Restaurant locked tight. But the back door was open, and I pushed my way between the smoking tables where the whole neighbourhood had gathered: the part-time workers, the ones who had no jobs, the hawkers and the shoe-shiners, the displaced peasants, landless migrants, and those who had once fled from mountain villages in Phrygia and Pontos and the burning cities of the Asia Minor coast. Back from the voting booths, they sat here through the day, each a fugitive from the intolerable privacy of home. For only in a coffee-house could their voices, all together, shatter the silence of waiting until night came with its news of whether this was at last the day of reckoning for an angry population in the suburbs. Through the smoke I caught sight of Nikiphóros dressed in a suit and tie, his face quite white and the legs inside his trousers hideously swollen. People pressed round his chair; he gave me his hand, which was weak and puffy in my grasp, shouting all the while to the others sitting near, "I tell you I vote for him because it's only he who will set them free, your relatives, your friends, your own brothers rotting there on Makronisos! Hello, Andrea, come and sit down, I can't get up out of this chair—you'll have to help me home in a few minutes."

A year and a half later we met for the last time. It was summer and he was out of bed, and we sat at a table outside one of the expensive confectioners on Constitution Square at the evening hour when the shops close and the whole square is like a drawing-room with people sauntering up and down. "What are we doing here?" he said suddenly. "Shall we go and listen to some music? Come." We got into the nearest taxi, and he called to the driver, "Take us to Phaliron where we can hear them playing the *bouzóukia*," and we drove off down the long, straight boulevard towards the sea. He opened both windows; the wind blew in on us and I could hear the hanging leaves of the eucalyptus trees whistling past on either side. "Faster!" he shouted. Then, already in sight of the shore-lights along the bay, he suddenly said, "Why are we going here? Driver, turn back!" The car swooped round with a screech of brakes, careened over to the other side and started back along the avenue.

"Faster than ever!" Nikiphóros cried. "Let me have some wind . . . Ah! Now truly it's as if I were going somewhere."

CHAPTER 5

Mani

FROM A DIARY OF 1949

April 21. Left Athens yesterday at mid-morning; the boat journey to Kalamata takes thirty-six hours, but this still remains the
quickest way to get there. I slept like a log past Cape Malea and
all the way up the Lakonian Gulf. At four this afternoon I was to
have been in Kalamata. That was a long time ago.

I'll probably tell myself some day my travels have represented
the famished quest for a knowledge of human beings, that pru-
dence or common sense or indeed any economy not strictly financial only leads away from life, and that the true traveller should
be the world's greatest fool. I would certainly be a fool in the eyes
of the United States Government, which last week issued me my
third fellowship; I expect it to feed me for another two years at
least, though even without it I would have found some means to
stay on here; I can't leave now. Only —— would not think me a
fool, though I have been so happy this spring I couldn't even feel
grief at parting and she doesn't know where I am now or when
I'll be back. But nor do I. Today I cut adrift from my own plans,
which is always delightful, though I now have to pay the price of
my impetuosity with this indescribable sensation in my bowels
and I can't get out of the courtyard door which is locked. I must
be thankful the windows of this bedroom are shuttered tight so

that the light from the lamp does not show to anyone down in the alleyway—nor, I hope, through the floorboards to my reluctant host.

At sunrise today we were riding at anchor and across the water the harbour front of Yítheion slumbered in the early light. Everything was so quiet; many windows were still closed, and the little tables were empty along the embankment. After standing on deck for a good ten minutes I noticed above the rooftops a white tinge showing through the dusty sky—the high snows on Taygetos, floating there with nothing underneath but the warm haze of the early spring morning. Then the ship started south down the coast of Mani. I have never seen anything like it in all Greece, where the wildest scenery is always a background to the lives of people and the highest mountain only casts a longer shadow under the plane tree in the village square, and in the deepest gorges and along the edge of cliffs the tiny paths are travelled over by the feet of donkeys in endless journeyings from one village to another, and there are always goatpens in the rocks. There was no sign of anything human on these yellow slopes rising out of the water, radiant and bare as pyramids. The barbarians must have been a terror for the Spartans, even the Spartans of the *basse époque*, to have fled here for refuge. Kakovóuni, the Evil Mountain, the terror of all ships that sailed round Tainaron, where the Turks never dared to penetrate . . . I looked in vain for some of the villages shown on my map, with the angry-sounding, harshly aspirated names— Skóutari, Kotrónas, Koúrnous, Káyio, Xangía—and then I read what it says about Mani in the guide-book: "One of the most original parts of Greece, both for its scenery and the customs of its inhabitants. It is wise, however, to have a recommendation; they still practise the blood feud, and are fierce and inhospitable, though loyal to the guest once accepted. . . ."

As we drew close to Tainaron, where the last cliff of Taygetos drops into the sea, I saw the first tall stone towers and then the cumbrous, truncated mass of Cape Grosso fissured and streaked with blue-black shadows striking down into the water. A brown bay closed round the ship as it headed in towards a cluster of houses on the shore. I had known all along it would put in at Yeroliména, that this was the last stop but one. Decisions are never sudden; they are only the final stage in the slow maturing of desires; often in the moment one is hardly conscious. Squinting through the glare, I watched the row-boat coming out to meet us, then grabbed hold of my pack and hurried aft in time to drop down with two or three other passengers, and a few minutes later I left the keel grating on the rocks while the steamer vanished round Cape Grosso. Someone helped me out on to the pebbly beach of a port just big enough for a few fishing-boats. People thronged around me in total silence, with swarthy faces close to mine, faces the colour of earth with eye-sockets like black holes under the vertical sun. Here there was no gabble of tongues, none of the glistening, mercurial web of glances avid of perception: all eyes looked straight ahead. Everybody was armed; round the port and up and down the street shot-guns and rifles pointed behind each man's back, with cartridge-belts slung one upon the other across chests and shoulders, holsters slapping and revolver handles sticking out of trouser pockets, while the swarm of intent and speechless men moved like troops in a village just behind the lines.

The castles I must see lay far to the north; I had to think quickly. I felt conspicuous with the rucksack on my back and had no wish for that opaque and smouldering atmosphere to turn into vigilance and direct itself on me. One man standing beside a donkey had several weapons strapped about him and on his head the rough-textured cap of the *Agrophýlakes*, the gendarmes of the countryside who watch over the villagers' fields and recall stray herds off neighbours' property. Because he was standing still I pressed towards him through the crowd and asked the way north to Tsímova. He asked quietly who I was, and I told him I was American; I didn't even have to show him papers.

"My name is Vasíli," he said. "I shall show you the way from my village. Let us go."

He climbed on to the donkey, and out of the crowd an old man with a beard, also mounted, joined us as we proceeded into the country. The path was a narrow trough full of stones like a torrent-bed with high walls on either side thrown up out of what I was slow to realize were tilled fields—fields of stones, completely bare of soil, where the thick spears of wheat grew as by a miracle under the scrawny olive trees.

Gazing to right and left, I lost my balance on a loose boulder in the path and stumbled from stone to stone until Vasíli leaned out from his saddle and caught me by the arm, saying, "Be careful how you walk in Mani."

The old man in front of us said, "Very true. When God finished making the world, all He had left was stones, and He made the Mani last of all. . . . The Germans were careful people; they left the women alone."

"But Greece has never been the same since the Italians were here," said Vasíli. "Ten years ago, if you met a woman on a path and looked into her face, her people would come out and kill you on the spot."

"It is over women that wars are fought," said the old man in the accents of a patriarch. "Now I take this road to my own village. May your hour be good."

He disappeared under the branches of the olive trees. At another crossing several soldiers joined us on the path, and at the next two women who talked with the others in bold, loud, careless voices. When they left us, I confided to Vasíli that I had grown used to hearing women talk quietly in Greece if they talked at all.

"This is Mani," he replied; "women fight together with the men. The Turks were more frightened of our women than of us. A woman can be fearless here because no one is going to touch her. Sometimes when a stranger comes into a house, the father will put his daughter into the same bed with him to sleep, to show his trust. A stranger here is regarded highly. If anyone does him an injury, his host will set about shooting the offender, and then both families fight until no one is left on either side. A war between families only stops when a stranger comes, for it is only he who can pass freely from house to house. But if anything should happen to him, woe betide! The fighting after that will be worse than anything that went before. What can you do? People have to die; there is no room here. . . . Every once in a while at weddings or christenings when many are gathered together, people will let their guns off without looking where they fire, let Charon take whom he will. . . . In the old days whenever a man killed someone, he could escape to America, yet even so some relative of the murdered man would follow him across the sea until he found him out and killed him there."

I said, "Doesn't the race die out?"

Vasíli laughed. "That's why we make children."

"To be killed?"

He exclaimed, "Look around you. How can one expect to live in such a place!"

It was a long, narrow plateau stretching all the way north with the sea on one side and great slabs of mountains rising one behind the other up the eastern edge of the peninsula—brown, grey, black and bare of vegetation as if they had been scorched.

"It doesn't look as if there were many springs up in those hills," I said.

"Springs!" he exclaimed. "South of Tsímova there aren't even springs down in the flat. All of our water we collect in cisterns."

"And if it doesn't rain in winter?"

"That's what I mean when I say there is no room for everyone to stay alive," said he with a shrug. "But those who do—why, there's a woman in the village a hundred and twelve years old and she still carries loads of wood on her back." He paused, then said, "You know, Tsímova is a long way off; you wouldn't reach it tonight. I would like you to come and stay in my village."

If I had gone on to Kalamata I would have missed this; thrilled at the thought, I told him I would love to, and he broke into a smile and said, "It makes one glad to see a stranger! By the way, forgive me for riding on this beast, I was wounded recently in the leg."

The plateau was laced with skeins of walls running half-way up the mountainsides. We were passing under some low branches of a tree and Vasíli ducked his head, when suddenly there was a crash of gunfire and three men leaped over a wall and dashed across the field as a few feathery shapes dropped down out of the soundless air.

"Rock pigeons," said Vasíli. "In the mating season they all come here."

I said, "Doesn't the law forbid shooting during the mating season?"

He replied, "The law, yes." Then with a crooked smile, "But this is Taínaron."

"Yet as guardian of the fields you should be enforcing it?"

"*Bá.*" He reached behind him and pulled out of his saddle-bag two soft, ash-grey birds with long wings and pointed bills; they were still alive. "I got them in my snare this morning," he said and held them up for me to see, then wrung their necks. "Now we come to my village," he said, indicating a group of tall grey towers built close together in the middle of the sloping fields. "It is the strong who built those, but now many towers are destroyed. During the War the Communists burned down our houses while we were away in the Security Battalions. Afterwards, though"— again his furtive smile—"we came back and burned down theirs. Do you see, over there on the hillside? In that village there's not a house left standing. Mine too is gone."

I asked where he lived. He pointed up at the sky and said, "The sun is hot. There was little rain this winter. Which is difficult also, because now there is no water."

The path wound up between the houses—each a slender, vertical fortress with narrow windows on several levels—and up into an open space along one side of a church opposite a wineshop.

In the middle was an ilex tree with a table under it.

"Wait here," he said. "I shall go to my house. It's not a place where I can invite you, Kyr Andrea."

So I sat down with my rucksack at my feet and waited and watched through the afternoon; there was no moving away.

A few yards off, boys lolled and lounged around the wineshop door. They had pimples on their necks and were dressed in heterogeneous pieces of military clothing, heavy boots with white socks rolled over the tops and blunt-shaped German Army caps pushed down over one eye, and their guns, which looked too big for them, clanked whenever they moved about. Small children played in the narrow area with the bodies of live rock pigeons; sprawled over the cobblestones, they pulled the birds' beaks open till they broke, and squeezed the downy heads between their fingers—soft little hands lingering pleasurably over the extinction of life. A tall priest strode out of the church and walked off down the path, his jack-boots showing under his soutane.

At four o'clock I was hungry. Vasíli finally came back, a woman following with plates of food which she deposited on the table.

"My wife," said Vasíli.

Not knowing what to do, I stood up and shook her hand. She turned her head aside and left us.

For me there was a dish of rock pigeons cooked in cheese and macaroni. Vasíli told me to eat and not be ashamed, since I did not keep the fast. He had only macaroni.

Gradually the ilex-shaded square became more animated. A white-haired man came out of the wineshop with a cobbler's kit under his arm, sat down on the ground and began to mend shoes, singing and chattering to himself.

Vasíli murmured in my ear, "His youngest son is up in the hills with Sphakianós."

"Who is that?" I asked.

"The leader of the guerrilla band. This old man has another son who swore long ago to kill his brother, but he was lazy and did nothing about it. Yesterday at last his mother said to him, 'Go out and kill him now; the whole village despises you.' So he went. . . . Look at the old fellow, he doesn't know what to do; the boy hasn't come back yet. Eh, Barba Niko," he called out, "I'm suspicious of you. You're a Communist too, you'd better look out."

The little old man waved his hammer in the air and cried, "*Bá*, I am a Nationalist, la-la-la-la-la-la-la."

The lads outside the wineshop snickered, and one of them drawled in a voice that could only just have broken. "Did you hear, Barba Niko? Vasíli says Barba Niko should look out."

The old man only went on gabbling incoherently.

Oh, the endless afternoon! Experience is nine-tenths boredom. . . . It was almost evening when Vasíli led me out of the village and I followed him as he crept, gun in hand, along the stone wall, sometimes dropping to his haunches and raising the gun to his shoulder, then moving off again, always giving a wide berth to the others who were out on the hillside too, skulking behind walls or squatting poised on the butts of their shot-guns.

Mediterranean dusk falls quickly. Vasíli took me to a wineshop in the lower part of the village—a dingy hovel with an earth floor, lit by an infinitesimal oil-lamp hanging on a wall. He told me to sit down and I waited in the darkness, trying to hear what he and the proprietor were saying in the far corner, but they hardly spoke above a whisper; the dialect, supposed to be particularly close to ancient Greek, is almost incomprehensible. In the doorway two hands appeared, holding a plate. Vasíli took it and brought it to my table, then stepped away again without a word. I fell to devouring another offering of acrid cheese and pigeon; had I eaten less I might be asleep now.

Vasíli in the corner was saying, "What's the matter with you, can't you even give him wine!"

There followed a mumbled altercation. The other man said, "No, no, don't you understand?" They went out of the room and I heard them arguing in raised voices outside the door.

Vasíli's voice hissed, "But he's my friend, I tell you!"

As soon as they came in I went over to them: "If this has anything to do with me, could I—"

Vasíli cut me short. "My house is a ruin, Andrea. There is room only for the four children; I haven't yet put on the roof. This man here, Stamáti, has a house, a good house where I want you to be comfortable."

The other man exclaimed, "How can I have him in it! It's all in disorder, you haven't seen it. . . . How can I tell who he is?" he said, talking faster. "Do you know? And have the others seen him yet? *Ach*, don't wish him on me, for the Christ! My old woman has been plastering the walls, the plaster's fresh—"

Vasíli said, "Anathema on you, *keratá!*" and the man turned to me: "Vasíli suggests you sleep in my house."

"But I don't have to," I said. "I have my own blanket, I can spread it here on the floor."

He gazed at the ground. "No, that doesn't do. This way." But he faltered in the door, turning back towards Vasíli with both palms thrown out in a gesture of despair. "I tell you the old woman has been plastering!"

We stepped outside. There were stars all over the sky. A few paces up the path he stopped under a wall and whispered in the dark. "In there. Look out for the door-sill. Up to your right."

I felt my way up the open stair along the side of the house, while the courtyard door closed behind me and the key turned in the lock. Then I felt Stamáti's hand pressing my back. On the top step he turned me and pushed me through another door. Somewhere close beside me he muttered an obscenity as he tried to light a match. The next moment this large room with the brass bedstead in which I am now lying glowed around us while he lit the lamp and said, "Tomorrow you go to Tsímova."

He went out without another word and I heard his boots crunching heavily down the stairs. I was soon asleep.

It is now three hours since I woke up with all the devils in hell inside my stomach. What can I do? There is no bathroom in Mani. I have been standing in the doorway and have watched the waning moon that signals the approach of Easter shining on the tiles off which last winter's rains poured into the cisterns. Everywhere the silver-sided towers rise between dark plumes of cypress trees; the courtyard is a pool of moonlight. Outside in the alleyway two men are talking in low voices and I hear the click of gunmetal.

I wonder how early it will get light.

April 22. As soon as I heard people moving about downstairs I descended to the courtyard where Stamáti bade me a genial "Good morning" and took me to the wineshop for coffee. Vasíli was already there with a gun over his shoulder. I told them I had no wish to cause disquiet to Kyr Stamáti and would be happy to show my papers to the police authority in the village, at which Stamáti made a deprecating gurgle and Vasíli laughed, "Do you think we need police? Down here the authority is—" He pointed to his own chest.

He told me about a ruined fortress on a point of land an hour distant and took me part of the way. "Come back here afterwards to fetch your pack and I shall put you on the road north. Remember you are my friend." He seemed to like me the more, not being able to offer me hospitality.

Three miles down the hill the village of —— stretched round a bay with the houses set apart from one another, with fewer towers and a broad street leading by the shore. People greeted me as I went by, and a swarthy young soldier ran after me, calling, "Eh, American, let me take you to the fort. They just sent a message from Katránio."

He led me through the village and up the ribbed, white rocks above the sea, where the tight-bunched heather, thyme and sage with roots deep within their cool interstices and soft, brittle stalks that broke under our boots, lifting clouds of powder from furry leaves, and gorse bushes clotted with yellow flowers in the spines, freighted the hot air with the dry, sweet, Mediterranean smells of spring. From the cliff tops of the promontory one could look down into the sea's purple shadows straight below and back over the land at brown hills, brown towers, baking in the crystal light, the humps of Tainaron and Grosso and to the north the knife-like ridges thicker and steeper towards Taygetos. Mani is like the landscape of one planet closer to the sun. I took off my boots and socks to dry the sweat out, then climbed in bare feet around the rocks, scratching and rubbing my soles and heels; and the dry stalks crackled between my toes.

Back at his village an hour later the soldier took me to his house where a cheerful family gathered round us in a room where, coming in out of the full day, it felt almost cold and I had to blink to see anything. Someone said, "This way, wash your hands," and two of the soldier's sisters came close to me on either side and rolled up my sleeves. "Put your hands together, *áide bravo*, splash your face while we pour."

We all sat down at a large table and the soldier's mother brought plates of bitter herbs in olive oil. "Do you like this green plant?" she asked. "We gather it ourselves on the mountainsides."

The others said, "Do you like the Mani?" and something inside me wanted to shout, "Yes, this is a glorious day and I wouldn't have missed it for the world!" but I could only think of them celebrating Easter together in three days' time.

The soldier said, "You must forgive us, this is only slight hospitality we have to offer you. A little brother of mine died last week, and I came down here on leave from Macedonia. It would have been pleasant if you could have stayed with us for Easter. We are in mourning, of course."

The others were laughing and eating all round me. Later, as the soldier and I walked up the street, he said, "My father is president of the village; foreigners sometimes used to come and stay in our house before the war. You too must come and stay with us."

I wondered if he could mean now, but whether or not it made any difference in their lives that a child had died the previous week, there were reasons why I must not accept. I said to him, "I would very much enjoy visiting you. As it happens, I was leaving Katránio today, though I'm not in a hurry to get anywhere. Yesterday Vasíli asked me to his village, but he is—" I was on the point of saying poor, but checked myself. "That is, he was unable to take me to his own house, which is destroyed. It would not look well if I were to leave Katránio to come straight here which is next door, so to speak, now—"

"Bravo," said the soldier.

"One does not want to—"

"Bravo," he said again, and I felt the anticlimax that always comes when one has sacrificed an impulse to scrupulous behaviour.

Up in Katránio I found the pimply boys of yesterday afternoon gathered inside Stamáti's wineshop. Stamáti himself pretended not to notice when I came in. Feeling bolder at the prospect of being on my way, I thanked him all the more vociferously for last night's lodging. He only scowled over his shoulder and muttered, "Eh, good-bye, then."

"But I'm sorry to miss Vasíli," I said. "You'll greet him for me, won't you?"

He shot me a feeble smile and the boys began to turn in their chairs to get a good look at me. I heaved the rucksack on to my back and set off along the only path I could discover leading north, taking long strides to get out of the village fast. I had been walking twenty minutes or so when a voice called my name from the fields. My sudden instinct was to crouch under a wall, then I saw Vasíli hurrying towards me up the slope.

"Vré, I waited for you all morning! I thought you must have run away just like that, but I was mistaken. It would have distressed me not to see you again. Now may your road be good," he said. The European embrace always takes me by surprise; I knocked his temple with a corner of my eyeglasses.

After three hours' walking through the silent afternoon I realized I would never reach Tsímova tonight and decided to sleep out alone under the spring sky. This, however, is not very easy in a narrow strip of plain where the towered villages rise up at intervals of three or four fields. I was about to spread my map to see if there were some less populated area ahead when I saw houses in front of me through the trees; so I climbed out of the path and ran along the edge of a wheatfield, keeping low to the ground so as not to be seen. The map did not show what I wanted and so I had to go back to the path and walk straight on into a broad expanse of grass, bordered by houses round the farther side, towards a fountain where some women stood with their water pots.

A girl called, "Look, here comes the American! *Po-pó*, and I thought he was some malefactor when he ran across that field. Didn't you want to greet us? Eh, give him water, the poor burning one . . . sit on this stone and rest yourself. Why did you want to go and sit among the wheat? We knew there was a stranger in the Mani. Panagia, look at those trousers, you'd think he had been with the goat-thieves in the mountains! I shall mend them for you; Aunt, run and get the ouzo. Would that our men were here! Come with me, don't be shy."

Life makes its strong claim on one at every step in Greece; again there was no escape. So I walked with the girl across the grassy square and up into a tower where lace curtains in the archer-slots filtered the sunlight of the late afternoon.

We went through the liturgy of the Greek welcome. "But what a pity my father isn't here," she said. "Last week he and my mother went to Piraeus where I have three brothers, and they will all have Easter together. Father said Piraeus is no place for me, what can I do? But you have fallen from the sky, American. My aunt and I were saying we would weep this Easter, left alone, our men so far away, but now it is us they will envy since we have a stranger here to entertain. They'll be home next week, though, and you can stay and meet them. Aunt, would they not like to see him?"

She prattled on, while there echoed through my mind the words of Vasíli and the old man on the donkey setting out from Yeroliména yesterday morning: "It is over women that wars are fought . . . The Turks were more frightened of our women than of us . . . Sometimes a father . . ."

But there was no father here. I got up and said I must go.

"And sit in solitude among the wheatfields, no doubt," exclaimed the girl.

It was difficult to get away, they were both so kind. Now I have found a lonely stretch far from houses and spread out my sleeping-bag on grassy ground behind a stone wall. I have eaten some bread and cheese. I don't know what I'll say if someone comes on me during the night. I can hear waves breaking under the cliffs of the western shore a few hundred yards away. A mist is rising in the twilight.

April 23. There was a sound of goat-bells through the pearl-grey mist when I opened my eyes this morning, and all I could see around me were the ghostly stalks of asphodel before the sun rose and burned it all away.

At half past ten I reached a ravine where the path made a long, level curve into the mountainside and out again around the farther spur. I preferred the short cut through the ravine and up the other side, but when I was half-way down someone called to me and I judged it wiser to climb back. A farmer stood on the path with a small revolver in his hand. I told him who I was and about my friendship with Vasíli in Katránio, and he said reflectively, "It is well. But when I saw you climbing down the gorge I said to myself, 'The good man does not leave the level road.'"

The two of us walked to Tsímova, where many of the farmers have blue eyes and straight backs, walk with a springy step and look as if they belonged to the *Almanach de Gotha*. I have found the relatives of —— who left this region as a boy many years ago. They have taken me into their house and we shall spend Easter and St George's Day together. . . .

April 30. Easter is past, and the long night services in the church and the marvellous chant:

> Khristós anésti ek nekrón
> Thanáto thanáton patîsas
> Kyé tis en tis mnímasi zoîn kharisámenos

sung over and over again until the sky began to whiten outside the windows, and also the long day's feast and the afternoon, sleep, and the dancing and singing that went on for days and days after. Life is generous. May I never stop travelling. Unfortunately I had to leave and now I am staying in a village on the sea, where it is an hour's climb up to the Turkish fort of Kelephá.

May 2. Sphakianós was killed this morning in a cave in the mountains. News has just reached the village *kapheneíon*. People speak of him with affection, though he was on the other side, and this means the last of the Andartes in Mani. A man said, laughing, "Ah, Sphakianós the *levéndi!*" (But there's no single word for that in any other language: a man who is strong, careless, handsome, modest, swift of action.) "He had great style. Do you remember the two pistols he always carried in his belt? One of them he called Maria and the other Eleni. Once he came into a village on a Sunday at the hour when everyone was at the *Litourgía.* He walked into the church alone and called to the priest, 'Stop the Cherubic Hymn, *Dhespóti*,' then stepped up into the sanctuary himself and placed his two pistols on the Holy Table and prayed with a loud voice, 'O Panagia, accept Maria and Eleni and inspire all these your servants to join ELAS this instant, other-wise I'll blow their brains out!'"

May 4. At last Kalamata, and a letter waiting for me poste restante.

It's strange after twelve days in a region where there are no roads or railway lines or inns or even water flowing in the earth, to find this city of boulevards and buses to the harbour and unpaved, dun-coloured streets that are almost white at noonday when in the silence and the emptiness a stray passer-by looks as if he were hunted. I have a room in a hotel with cool, broad corridors and a ramshackle bathroom where cold water runs abundantly into a tub. The room is full of green light from the plane trees outside the window where I sit and watch amid the lengthening shadows the leisurely activity under their branches at the hour when a distant hoot and whistle announces the train coming in from the west coast of Elis and Messenia. The fort here is

Medieval castle at Kalamata

small but complicated, dating from the twelfth century at least, set on a rock above the river-bed of the Nedon, which emerges from the high land behind the town and has its source among the cataracts and snow-filled gorges of Taygetos. All morning I work over its walls and gates and all the different kinds of masonry that guard so jealously the secret of their building, until the noonday insects begin to shrill among the pines that grow tall and sinuous inside the ramparts. On the platforms of the bastions the grass has not yet dried into the matted turf of summer nor the dusty little yellow flowers hardened into thistle. Today I was sitting with my back to a parapet and my legs hanging over the edge of the wall, beside me my measuring rod still folded and my notebook with the ants crawling over its blank pages in the grass, while under the tower a pair of gendarmes sauntered in the alley, and on the other side I could see down into a courtyard with sentry-boxes on the walls, where thirty or forty ragged-looking men sat about in the open sun or walked very slowly back and forth all morning and afternoon. Some of them caught sight of me up on the tower and waved. A gendarme in the street below signalled to me to move to another position.

While the shadow of the pines spread over the tiled roofs below, I sometimes looked out through their branches at that steep coastline stretching south with black hills one behind the other and a few towered peaks just visible in the distance; I was there only a few days ago. Experience is freedom: now all of it belongs to me—Tainaron and Mani and this well-watered plain and the brown city where from the castle I can hear the vast, faint murmur of the populace emerging for the evening walk. I am so happy I don't mind being here by myself. I feel no hurry. A man's affections are by nature numerous and I suppose at my age they can all exist side by side without seeming to conflict.

May 6. Loneliness, however, is the spectre of night-time in a foreign city. Sullen, crafty faces materialize suddenly before me among the shadows of the unlit streets; raucous gramophones shriek out from row on row of coffee-shops and restaurants, and the charred smell of roasting entrails floats across the river-bed with its thawing mountain streams and pale banks of sand smelling like a urinal. I am a foreigner and belong to nothing. I can only walk through places, pass by people. Travel is only a substitute for experience, and love itself not necessarily freedom.

Last night I ate slowly at a table on the sidewalk near the station, trying to postpone the moment when I would have to turn the light on in this empty room. At least there was a lighted hall behind me, with waiters moving about and people talking together inside; several blocks away I could hear the sounds from the main boulevard leading to the harbour, where the courtyard cinemas and eating-houses stay open till the early hours of morning. I was breaking my crust of bread into minute fragments over the tablecloth when a little man appeared out of the dark street and dragged off two chairs from the nearest table to the edge of the sidewalk. He placed on one of them a big, trapezoidal *santoûri*, which is an Eastern form of dulcimer, seated himself in front of it and bowed his head with a shock of dusty hair hanging down over his instrument. Forty resounding strings clanged beneath his hammers, then he lifted up his head and a hoarse, chesty voice above the thrumming chords filled the whole street.

> Little bird of mine who has wandered far,
> A foreign country greets you. I too know your sorrow.
> What shall I send you, stranger, what can I offer you?
> If I send apples, they will rot; roses will fade,
> Grapes dry out and quinces wither.
> I'll send you my tears in a golden scarf;
> My tears are burning, they will burn the scarf.
> What else can I send you, stranger, in a foreign land?

> I rise at dawn, for I find no sleep.
> I open the window and watch the people passing.
> Envious, I watch the neighbour-women
> Dancing the babies in their arms,
> Giving the sweet breast.
> I turn my back to the window and go in again
> To shed the black tears of the foreign land.

On the last syllable, the hammers still clattering over the sounding-board, he raised his head and looked straight at me. He got up and quickly as he passed I pressed a handful of money into his palm.

He stopped—hardly taller than the top of my head where I was sitting—and mumbled in my ear, "Foreign people are the only ones who are *endáxi*, I mean *comme il faut.*"

"Will you have some wine?"

With a drowsy, sideways glance he moved into a chair and I called into the restaurant. The waiter stood above us with the usual waiter's look, half-stupefied, half-supercilious.

I cheerfully demanded wine.

The waiter smiled kindly. "A very good man is Yanni," he said, and vanished through the door.

The little man pursed up his lips and spat across the pavement. "What a species!"

We drank, and I offered him a piece of meat on the end of my fork. He placed his hand on my wrist, guided it to his mouth, lips wide apart, closed his teeth on the morsel and drew the fork out with a quick, delicate motion. He confided to me he worked in a barber's shop by day and that his fiancée was earning her dowry in a brothel. "And what's that in your pocket?" he asked.

I looked down into my coat, half-expecting to find my reed flute spirited away.

He drew out his hammers. "Go on," he whispered, leaning down to pick up his dulcimer. He pulled it on to his knees and struck the strings, then jerked his jaw in the direction of my flute and said, "You on the *phloyéra*, I on the *santoûri.*" He struck another chord and I put the hole to my lips and blew. It was the right note.

"Pay up in there," he said, "and come with me."

Until long after midnight Yanni and I played together outside the tavernas up and down the boulevard. Waiters brought wine and ouzo to us where we sat on the sidewalk, and then plates of hot, salty *kokorétsi*, while the passers-by dropped money on the stones beside us. At last when we parted company, he went off with all the oily little thousand-drachmae notes in his pocket. I wandered about the streets alone, singing at the top of my voice. . . .

That was twenty-four hours ago. Now I am once again writing by the light of an oil-lamp in the upper room of a strange house, in a village of Outer Mani.

My first waking thought this morning was: I want to get back to Athens. How rapidly one can reach the most distinct conclusions about the chronology of walls when one is really in a hurry! Three hours this morning were enough for me to finish my work on the castle at Kalamata. I ran half-way across town to catch a bus to Kámbos, the nearest village to the Turkish fortress of Zarnata, which is where the motor road south from Kalamata comes to an end.

In the square where the bus was leaving—I was well on time for once—the other passengers were getting on: dark-browed Maniate peasants and two women in black, one old, one young. When the bus was filled, the driver said I could ride on top. I pulled myself up the ladder at the back and the driver's boy,

Fortress of Zarnata

a lad of eighteen, climbed up after me on to the bulky, stiff tarpaulin tied down over baskets and bundles with ropes lashed back and forth between two thin wooden rails on either side. We braced ourselves among them as the bus started forward.

Beyond the low houses of Kalamata and the ancient olive yards of the plain the road wound and climbed. Underneath us, jolting on its springs from side to side like a rickety cube, the little bus crawled along hot valley walls deeper and deeper into Taygetos. We were going too slowly to feel any breeze or move forward out of the towering dust off the road where ten years' rains had washed away the asphalt. The mountains were all the time growing higher ahead of us, but the road began to drop into a vast ravine. As the vehicle hung out over the first turn I saw the rest of the road falling in long, thick loops down to a bridge that crossed the gorge in a single span. One moment, roaring in low gear, we would pass it—far below—on the left; the next, heading out into the empty air, I saw it move behind us on the right as I clung to the tarpaulin. We reached the head of the bridge and halted. Heat rippled off the engine. Under the bridge the narrow

sides of the ravine converged in a dry bed of white stones plunging from far above to the deeper valleys down the mountainside.
People were getting off, and I saw again the two black women—
the younger, with her face covered, standing at a distance with
her back to the rocks, while the older one came to the corner of
the bus. Piercing eyes stared up at us under the kerchief drawn
tight round her hooked nose and bristly chin, while the boy dislodged from the bundles a spade and mattock and threw them
clanging on to the road. Then he flung down a burlap sack, calling, "Take this too." The women lifted the tools and the sack on
to their shoulders; the other passengers got back into the bus and
we started forward again.

Next to me the boy was talking, but I had difficulty hearing
him above the noise of the motor: ". . . and he was coming back
to his village, for he had given himself up during the amnesty,
but the others were waiting for him and they were all on this
same bus together, travelling to Zarnata. They began to say things
to each other, he and they, and they got into an argument—you
know the way it happens. Then he made some remark, and they
shot him as the bus was crossing the bridge. They threw his body
into the gorge. Now, a year later, his wife and mother go to gather
up the bones and take them back to—"

"I can't hear," I shouted. "What did you say?"

We were across the gorge now, mounting, turning, doubling
on our tracks until the road lay in all its loops beneath us. The
women had vanished.

"They're hiding down there under the bridge," the boy said.
"Eh, they do well to wait till we are out of sight, not to give us the
Evil Eye."

We were nearly at the top when I looked back and saw them,
two black specks moving far down the wall of the ravine in that
windless heat still echoing to the roar of the engine climbing
slowly up towards the sun.

CHAPTER **6**

Unwritten Villages

IN THE AUTUMN, with the Athens government re-established throughout Greece, one saw all over the capital posters proclaiming: 1949 THE YEAR OF VICTORY. It was perhaps significant that it was not called the year of peace, though police, army and the auxiliary bands were in control of the remotest districts, and except on Mount Olympos and along the Bulgarian and Albanian frontiers the guerrillas had vanished off the mountains. A civil war, however, does not end so easily.

I went as usual from village to village wherever there were medieval remains, walking when I could, dressed in old clothes and army boots to resist the wear and tear of rocks and ilex thickets, with everything I needed on my back. In every place I met those barriers of hospitality or suspicion which were familiar to me now, but which make it so hard for any foreigner in Greece to participate, form judgments or indeed do anything more than observe as best he can. Yet the people I met seldom hesitated to tell me their stories as soon as they were satisfied as to my identity, and they were grim tales; people seemed to warm their spirits over them in the telling, much as they sat about in cold, little, earth-floored rooms, slowly turning their wrists and hands over the small warmth of braziers.

One young gendarme told me his family had kept at the back of their house in Pangráti during two and a half years two English soldiers who had not escaped with the rest of the British expeditionary force in 1941. They taught him English and became, he said, like brothers to him. The Germans never found them out. In 1944 when the liberating British troops landed in Greece and the civil war broke out a few weeks later, a band of ELAS Communists came into his house and, because they had sheltered English soldiers, killed his father, mother, brother and four sisters. "Three times I wrote to Jack and Edward," he said, "to tell them what had happened. Neither ever answered me. Some day I should like to go to their country and say to them only this: 'It was not to get money out of you that we saved your lives, but all my family died for it. You can't bring them back to life. I only want to know that you remember us, that you acknowledge I am still alive—for the sake of the Eye, not for anything else. . . .' And now I'm twenty-two; I applied for service last year as soon as I was of age. What was done to my family I have paid back in gold." I asked him what he meant, and he answered gravely, "This is a small village, I am the only gendarme in it. Captured guerrillas are sometimes handed over to me. I kill . . . I don't say this to you for either praise or blame."

For the most part the guardians of this year's victory were men who had no other occupation than to sit about among the coffeehouses of the village squares, wearing discarded sections of a uniform and always a revolver on the belt or rifle slung lazily across the shoulder. There was always one such to follow me around as I went about my business (which could hardly have looked innocent) of scanning walls, taking photographs and measurements, and at every few paces making entries in a notebook. At one large fortress built by the Turks to defend a certain stretch of coast against the fleets of Europe in the sixteenth century, a man used to stroll along the ramparts, sometimes at the opposite end from where I happened to be working, sometimes a little closer, but always in good view, so that as I moved from one position to another he and I would circle round the enclosure like the hands on a clock face. One morning I happened to find the gate to the upper enclosure locked, so I climbed up the wall where the mortar had crumbled away between the stones, leaving good hand- and foot-holds, and began my work on the big gun platforms that ran all the way round the top of it, for once able to forget the presence of another person watching me. It was a windy day; low in the dark sky a fitful sun, now bright, now dim, played nervously over the bare land and the angry little waves, and the rocks of the shore shone white as bone when the loud spray flew upward, while from the direction of the Adriatic a raincloud advanced very slowly like a broad, black broom over the sea. The storm broke on the coast in the middle of the morning, just as a crowd of boys from the high school arrived to do their exercises on the parade ground of the lower enclosure; when the rain met them they scattered back towards the town. I took shelter inside a vaulted casemate, and then came out again to take advantage of the sunlight.

The courtyard below me was divided into sections by several high walls running crosswise inside a ring of vaulted chambers, each with a barred window and an iron door. I was about to take a photograph when the courtyard gate swung open and in walked the man I had seen every day, with a big key swinging from his finger. He climbed up the flight of steps on to the platform and approached me, smiling. He had milky blue eyes and blond hair, and it struck me that fair colouring in a Greek is a form of nakedness, exposing all the cruelty of the sharp, distinct features.

"Well?" he said; he had gold teeth on one side of his mouth and teeth of polished steel on the other.

I murmured "Hello" with the casualness assumed when one has no business in a certain place, then gave him my papers to read.

"I'm the guardian here. This was a prison till last summer," he said, drawing back his shoulders as if in the pleasure of reminiscence. "We had them packed inside those cells down there, fifteen or twenty in each; they had to lie on top of one another."

I asked, "Who were they?"

"Communists," he said. "But there was a time when we had prisoners of every sort, from ELAS, from EDES, from the *Khi*. We used to open the doors of all the cells and let them out into those compartments, Leftists on one side, Rightists over here. We used to stand on the platform and listen to them abusing each other. It was better than a theatre."

"You had Rightist prisoners too! But how so?" I asked.

"Eh, you know that in 1946 we had the plebiscite for the return of the King; anyone who didn't vote the right way—" He paused. "There were killings," he went on casually. "That sort of thing happens. . . . A few were given sentences, but they didn't stay in prison long. They were our brothers, after all; we had served together in the Security Battalions during the Occupation when the condition of the country forced us to take sides with the Germans. After that we had been together in the *Khi*; so a couple of years ago when there was the amnesty we let them out. 'Back to your villages, quick!' we said, and we made as if we didn't see them."

"And your other prisoners?" I asked.

He gave me his gold and silver grin. "That amnesty," he said, "was for the benefit of what newspapers call 'world opinion'—for the Americans chiefly. But it was for us to enforce it—or not. In '44 EAM and ELAS took over this town: in one day they had a public trial of all the educated people—lawyers, merchants, doctors—and they sentenced them to death and killed them in the square. Two years they ruled here; no one's life was safe. But our turn came after the plebiscite. As you can understand, we had no wish then to let the amnesty apply to the Communists. We kept them here another year or two, then sent them to the camps on the islands where foreigners don't interfere with us."

"You weren't in the army, were you?"

"I was here," he said. "It was a good job. When the prisoners' wives and sisters were allowed to visit the men once a week, we used to make it hard for them to get in. As soon as they began to beg us, we would say, 'Enough of that,' and take them into the little room down there beside the gate. They used to be frightened afterwards, thinking we'd tell their men about it. Sometimes we did, just to be able to stand up here and watch their reunions. The men would shout, 'To the devil with you, *poutána*, when I get out of here I'll stab you to death!' After that many of the women went to Athens to earn a different sort of living. Who knows," he said, smiling again, "you may have run into some of them yourself?"

"Now," I said, "you have nothing to do?"

And he replied, "We wait."

Nothing, it seemed, had happened to him personally. He was an extremist now for the same reason that would have made him, in more peaceful times, a petty malefactor or small profiteer: the active cynic who flourishes on the world's disorder, when governments disintegrate and the only law is the law of armed men in small communities, when a nation or a civilization decays.

THOUGH I COULD GO anywhere I chose now without difficulty, travel was becoming a more intricate and devious business the longer I remained in Greece. Yet I had only to leave one place and approach another to feel expectancy outweigh apprehension, as I did one afternoon late in November among the wet, black tree-trunks of an olive yard where with every step illimitable vistas formed in all directions, switched and crossed, dissolved, converged around me as I walked in a rutted track down one of the innumerable avenues all parallel beneath one vast, low ceiling. I was going to stay with the village priest who had been recommended to me by the hotel-keeper in the town I had just left, while I worked on a neighbouring castle—so much I knew, but more exciting was not to know what encounters awaited me among the white walls of the village that began to appear in the grey distance where the olive yard came to an end. The road turned into a muddy alleyway between low houses with whitewash flaking off them and led into a small open space between the desolate crusts of buildings gutted by fire. It was the village square, but no one was in sight under the darkening afternoon.

Then a woman passed with a load of faggots on her back. I called to her, "Where can I find the priest?"

"Do you look for Pappastavrós?" she said, glancing at me sideways from under her burden. "You will find him among the olive trees." She beckoned to a child in an open door: "Go down with the Uncle and show him where to find the Pappouli."

The child trotted off. I followed him as far as a tree where some women were spreading out a canvas sheet and a man stood, beating up into the branches with a long pole, while the stony fruit fell like hailstones on the canvas.

"A stranger to see the Pappouli," said the little boy, who then scampered back up the path.

The women straightened themselves and the man turned round to look at me. A fragile figure with a white beard and long, white hair falling over his shoulders, vigorously beating at the topmost branches, stopped and climbed down a ladder, exclaiming, "*Bá?* I thought it was my son!" He walked towards me across the stubble, saying: "He has blue eyes also. He is just out of the army and I have been expecting him home for days."

I began to go through the elaborate preamble of telling him who I was and what I did, but he cut me short: "But I'm glad you have come," gazing at me with a mild and somehow vacant expression. To the others he said, "Have we not done enough for today?"

Then a donkey was brought, and the old priest lifted up an enormous basket full of olives, while the others lashed it on to the saddle and said, "*Ach*, Pappouli, you tire us out!"

On our way to the village the old man said to me, "I live alone, you know. My wife is dead. My hospitality is nothing." When we arrived at one of the burned-out houses, he pointed up at the charred walls and the empty windows like eye-sockets against the sky: "The plight of the Hellenes!"

"Such things the Germans did to us," said the other man as we halted just below it at a stone shed built into the hillside.

One of the women said, "Indeed, Germans!"

Then they unloaded the basket and went on down the lane with the donkey.

The priest said, "This is where we used to bake our bread. And that ruin was my house. Now I live in here. It distresses me greatly that I'm alone and can't treat you as you deserve."

"But you don't know anything about me," I said. "Nowadays people don't always welcome a stranger."

He pointed impatiently at the sky and said, "There is God; what does one have to know about a stranger?" Then he pushed open the door of the shed, and the two of us stepped down into a windowless room built round a big baking oven with a heavy iron plate against its mouth. The ceiling and walls were black with the pitchy smoke of fires long extinguished; a bed and table, a basket of moist, black olives and a hairy blanket thrown over some boards across two wooden crates were all the signs of an old man's lonely habitation. Indicating these possessions, he said, "Have I anything to lose?" and crossed to a corner of the room where he put on a soutane over his working clothes, gathered his hair into a knot and shoved it up under his chimney-pot hat.

"Let us go and amuse ourselves at least," he said. "It is long since I have had a guest."

Early dusk had fallen over the little square where the villagers who had gathered for the evening looked up with surprise, whispering among themselves as we walked past them. We entered a wineshop and sat down in the corner. By the light of a solitary oil wick fifteen or twenty dark faces ranged against the walls stared at us in silence. The priest asked someone to bring us wine. No one spoke; I counted the minutes going by.

Then I said to the priest, "I don't suppose many foreigners come here these days?" The statement echoed like a stone dropped down a well.

From the other side of the room a voice said, "Where are you from?" and out of the semi-darkness, one by one, came the inevitable questions: Where had I learned the language? Why was I interested in castles? Why did I go about on foot, alone? I answered with laborious candour and finally suggested showing my papers to the gendarmerie. Across the table Pappastavrós made a gesture of negation, but from somewhere in the room another voice said, "Yes." I waited, but no one moved.

Then Pappastavrós said, "Shall we go? My cousins have laid the table for us."

Silence again descended as we got up from our chairs to go out. Much as if he were leading me away from hostile country back through the night behind his own lines the old man took me down an alley where a door was opened and a hand on my wrist guided me up some steps. Then we entered a room bright with candles and oil lights, where a number of young men and women welcomed us and there was a scramble for chairs, and everybody talked at once.

We joined them at the large meal they were all eating together, and one of them told me there were two families living here because next door the house had been burned down.

"Like yours?" I said to the priest. He merely gazed at me and I thought he had not understood; so I said, "In this village how many houses have been destroyed?"

Someone answered "Six."

"What about the people who lived in them?" I asked.

Someone else answered, "Eh, we mostly live together."

"They have mostly gone to prison," said Pappastavrós crisply. "Such as the eldest son of my cousin here, who is on Makronisos." He indicated the mother of several of the young men and women; she was sitting in a corner with a pair of black-rimmed spectacles on her nose.

When we had finished and the plates were being cleared away, the door opened without a knock and two farmers walked in. Conversation stopped. They drew up two chairs next to me and began asking me detailed questions about my work, my habits, my interests. "Why," they asked, "do you come to the Morea rather than, say, the islands? You should go to Kérkyra; all tourists go there. Has the Kyrios never been to Kérkyra?"

"My work doesn't happen to take me there," I replied.

"But these fortresses, and the crusaders you talk about—who exactly were the crusaders?"

"Oh, they came here a long time ago," I said, drawing on my reserves of patience, embarrassed to have to speak of all this in front of Pappastavrós and his relatives. "They came here long before the Turks, when—"

One of the two said, "If you don't mind, we would like to have your papers to show to the authorities."

I gave them my credentials and they went out again. Pappastavrós flung out both his hands with a slight gasp and turned his back to the door. "That they should come to you who are a stranger," he exclaimed, "a stranger and alone in our country, and demand your papers as if you were a criminal!"

"These days anyone may be a criminal," I said. "I don't mind, though; it happens to me all the time."

The woman with the glasses spoke for the first time: "The Pappouli is old and remembers different customs."

"In any case," I said, "the gendarmerie has a duty to see my papers."

"In this village there is no gendarmerie," replied Pappastavrós; a look passed between several of the family.

Soon the two farmers were back again. They handed my papers to me with an apology and said, "We wish you good luck," then departed for the second time.

There was a sense of relief in the room. Someone brought a gramophone, and out of its amplifier issued the swirling rhythms of a *syrtós* as the cousins joined hands, and the floorboards heaved beneath them and several chairs fell over. One of them shouted, "We have a party now, let us go down below."

Then we went out, leaving the women behind us in the house, and with the gramophone and records carried our conviviality through the darkness to the wineshop on the square. There was more room here; the other villagers joined the circle of whirling figures, but I sat next to Pappastavrós in one corner.

"Eh, Pappouli, get up and dance," the villagers called.

"Leave me in peace," he answered.

One of them leaned forward as he went by and put his mouth to Pappastavrós' ear, shouting at the top of his voice, "Get up!"

Someone else reached out and with a sudden jerk on the old man's sleeve pulled him to his feet, then let him go. As he fell back on to his chair the others laughed, "You don't seem to be yourself tonight, Pappouli."

He answered, "I've beaten down more olives today than all of you together."

"Do you think you're a better man than we, Pappouli?"

"Eh, how many olives will you gather when you are seventy-eight!" he called to them above the music.

The rough, hard voice of one young man called, "Don't complain too much, Pappouli. You're still alive, eh?"

"Enjoy your youth," said Pappastavrós softly. He turned to me: "You see how the time is passed in a small village."

No one stayed up late now in the season of the olive harvest, and soon he led me back across the square.

"I want you to be well cared for tonight," he said. "My cousins' house is better than mine. You will stay with them."

They had prepared a bed in a room by myself, where from my stiff straw pillow I watched the tiny light burning before the icons on the wall, and as I fell asleep thought how other small lamps like these once joined in the flames of the burning timbers of six houses.

It was cool and bright next morning. People had gone down early to the olive trees and the village was empty when the woman with the spectacles led me to the priest's house. I asked her when her son had gone to prison.

"In 1945," she said.

"After the December uprising?" I asked, skirting a simpler question.

"He was in the Communist Party," she replied, so that I had no need to ask it. "They took him first to Kastraki where we saw him sometimes—that is, my daughters were allowed into the prison, not I. They closed it down and took all the men to Makronisos and Youra. I think it's five years since I last saw him."

"About Pappastavrós," I said (I heard my own voice loud in the clear, silent air), "did his house burn down with all the others?"

"He has suffered more than we," she said, then drew her head-cloth tighter round her glasses, exclaiming, "Never was there such a Christian in this place, not a stranger passes, not a beggar to whom he doesn't give! The people do not appreciate what he is. They pretend to despise him because he's poor, but they are afraid of him too, because he tells them always the truth and they are not able to destroy him. There are things he has suffered. . . . I wonder how he has not gone mad!"

"What do you mean?" I said, but several yards off stood Pappastavrós in his doorway. So many narratives I heard in Greece broke off in the middle, my last question always just too late. He invited me in to coffee and then we parted, he to his work among the olive trees and I to mine, high on some windy ruins where I saw nobody all day.

Back in the village that night he asked me to stay in his house. "I see I don't have to be formal with you; so if you can pretend you're only a beggar . . ."

He lit the wick protruding from a little iron vessel of oil that hung above the table and we ate the bread and olives from his basket. He had contrived a bed for me out of some more boards and crates and spread a rug beside it on the earth floor. The dull, round flame burned on for hours while we talked from our beds through the penumbra of the oven room.

"Alas," he said, "you have not found great hospitality in this place."

I said, "I'm grateful for yours."

"If only I could have had you in my house when it was standing and my wife was alive to treat you properly as a guest! Before the war everyone would have fought to have you stay. Now, as you saw, they wouldn't speak to you except to ask for your papers."

"Which I was willing to show to the gendarmerie or whoever it is. Can you tell me why they're so afraid of me?"

"It's not you," he said; "they're afraid of each other. . . . This is a hard generation and it's difficult for a priest in the place where he was born and has always lived." Then he sat up in his bed and said, "You know, they come to the church to make their Communion—if they don't, they get frightened—but first they have to make their confession, and certain of them find that hard. For that I try to make allowances, but when I tell them to forgive and that there exists no other way, they sometimes laugh in my face. And what do I do then? Eh, I lose my temper! I ask them, 'Why is it harder for you to forgive than it is for me?' Then they go away. Of course, those who are most to blame are the priests themselves, the holy *keratádhes*! In Corinth the Archimandrite said to me, 'Human beings are stupid; we must make devices to persuade them and feed their stupidity.' So here in this village the people come to me and say they must have miracles in order to believe. *Amán*, when the world is full of miracles already . . . ! 'In the next village,' I tell them, 'is a woman who possesses five fields and twenty olive trees that produce the best oil in the district, and not one of you has married her yet—there, isn't that a miracle!'

"Time and again I wonder what makes the Hellenes such an impossible race. . . . You know that in 1941 the British were escaping from Greece; the Germans were chasing them to the sea, hunting them out and capturing them everywhere. Whole companies of English soldiers came through here and I hid them all—in my cellar, in my barn, in other people's houses, there in the depth of that oven. We kept them for weeks and months until their submarines came and we could get them to the shore at night time. Later that winter we had the famine. Families were dying of starvation because the crops had failed, and it was I then who went to the Kommandantur and persuaded the Germans to let us have enough flour to last till the spring harvest. At that time my sons were away in the Resistance; they were in ELAS.

My two eldest were captured and I never saw them again; my fellow-villagers had told the Germans where to find them. Half the men here were in the Security Battalions under German protection; they said I was their enemy. At last the Germans left and we were liberated. My wife had died in the famine and I was living here alone with one of my married daughters and her baby son; she was to have her second baby in a few weeks. One day I was celebrating Mass in the next village and as I walked back here through the olive trees I saw so many flames I thought the whole land was burning. I arrived as they were setting fire to my house. I was in time to see them drag my daughter out and kill her; they shot all their bullets into her stomach. Then they killed the little boy in front of me."

I left early in the morning and returned to the district town to catch a train that same day for Athens; there was always some train or bus or simply my own two feet to carry me away from lives I could not share or experiences too hard to face. Having, however, several hours to wait before the train left, I went into a restaurant for lunch and the proprietor emerging from his kitchen surprised me by saying, "You have been staying with Pappastavrós, have you not? My father-in-law; I am married to his eldest daughter. His son is here, just back from the army. Do you want to meet him? Come out and meet your father's guest," he called back into the kitchen.

"What a coincidence!" I exclaimed as a very thin young man, pale, with light grey eyes, walked towards me between the empty restaurant tables. "You are expected home."

"Today or tomorrow my father will come here to meet me," he said.

"But aren't you going there?"

"No."

The restaurant-keeper brought lunch for the two of us, and during the meal I said, "Your father accepted me without asking who I was, though some of the people in the village may have thought . . ." I hesitated.

"Thought you were a spy."

"Last night," I said, "he told me what happened to your family."

"Perhaps you can understand, then, why I haven't been back to that place for six years and why I can't go back now?"

I said, "Tell me one thing, though. The people who burned the houses, the men who killed your sister and nephew, what has happened to them, where are they now?"

The young man looked at me with Pappastavrós' same child-like, steady, unsearching gaze. "Where are they now, you say? Why, there where they always have been."

"Do you mean there in the same village!"

"Naturally. Where else would they go?"

"But does he know who did it?"

"In a village," he replied, "everything is known. Of course he knows; he sees them every day, he passes them in the fields, he sits beside them in the wineshop. They say 'Good morning' to him, and he must joke with them."

"It's not possible! How does he endure it?"

"Oh, as for endurance," he answered quietly, "man, you know, is a wild animal."

THERE WERE NATIONAL ELECTIONS that winter for the first time since 1946 when the curtain of enemy occupation had been recently lifted on a country in the midst of revolution, anarchy and civil war. Now the Government communiqués, the public speeches and the Press all extolled the freedom with which the Hellenic race could at last express its will. The results indeed showed a trend away from the Rightist powers that had governed Greece since the plebiscite four years earlier and seemed to prove that the Hellenic race had had enough of both extremes. Three parties of the Centre agreed to coalesce, but after weeks of slippery manoeuvres and carefully arranged delays it looked as if the Right were on the point of resuming power after all; this in the long run would have been to the interest of the Communists, and finally an open letter from the American Ambassador informed the nation that the financial aid to which all Greek governments owed their existence would only be forthcoming to one based on broad popular support. So the coalition of so-called Moderates succeeded in installing itself under the premiership of General Plastiras, the once fiery, now mellow and optimistic but not very intelligent old hero of the Asia Minor wars; and liberal folk believed, as is usual in such cases, that the country's wounds had now a chance of healing. Yet after a civil war it makes little difference to a country what government rules it from the capital.

In Athens one day during the elections I received a telephone call from Pappastavrós' son. We met that evening in Omonia Square, and he told me he had gone back to his village after all.

"And now?" I asked.

He replied, "They said if I stayed there during the voting it might provoke an episode. They told me to get out."

"But that means you can't vote!"

"Does that seem strange to you?" he said. "Have you any idea what it's like in a small village, when you go into a wineshop and see the people watching one another, everyone knowing exactly what side everyone else belongs to, everyone with a weapon in his house and only waiting for the chance to use it? As soon as another war breaks out . . . Till then, however, they know I'm a Leftist, and I know well enough what they would do to me. It's all very well to talk about the secret ballot, but in the provinces of Greece whom does it benefit? In '46, during the plebiscite, I spent four months in Athens and never slept in one place two nights running. I had friends here, but late or early a knock on the door and you knew it was the police coming to search."

I asked what work he was going to do now, and he said, "I used to be a schoolmaster, but after the Revolution they dismissed all civil servants who had any connection with EAM. Last summer I was called into the army, but they discharged me because of a weak heart. I can't do heavy work, you see. Kyr Andrea—"

"And your father," I said, "how is he?"

"He is free because he forgives," the young man answered. "Kyr Andrea, could you help me find a job here in Athens?"

"I can try," I said. "Will you call me at the end of the week?"

I asked two or three people, but without success. Which made little difference since he never telephoned, and I told myself with a certain relief that my lot was not cast among the suffering.

Forest Shepherds
of the Isthmus—Spring

ON A SATURDAY MORNING in spring I packed my rucksack
with provisions for the weekend and took a bus to Megara,
hitchhiked another eighteen kilometres down the coast and then
walked inland from the white shore across rolling stubble fields
with olive trees growing at irregular intervals towards a pine forest that covered the foothills and deeply eroded valleys of the
Yerania Mountains, which rise abruptly to a long, naked ridge
four thousand feet above the Isthmus of Corinth.

I had come once before, late in September of the previous
year, in a great hurry to catch up with a party of Athenian Sunday walkers, whose chartered truck had left Athens without
me. Then too I had hitchhiked down the coast road and walked
across these yellow fields, and a man who lived in the forest collecting resin from the pine trees had given me water to drink and
shown me the way up. I had found the excursionists on the summit—the first Athenians to come here after the Andartes had
abandoned the mountain—with their portable gramophones and
picnic lunches, their blankets for the shady siesta to spread out
over the stony, spiny, rough Greek earth which nowhere fits itself to the comfort of the human form, and their knapsacks to

bring home at the end of the day full of grape hyacinth, autumn-flowering crocus and branches off the dark, thick firs that grow in the cooler altitudes above three thousand feet. On the way back they had talked so loud it was impossible to hear the birds singing in the trees, but all winter I had kept a memory of limestone downs and tufted forests of spruce, fir and balsam where the air was sweet and cold and families of shepherds who lived in huts made of their branches stood here and there among their slowly moving herds, unhurried, patient, high over the Corinthian Gulf.

Now I was coming back, alone. Walking along a dirt track through the lower pine forests, I heard the sound of an axe and saw a man hanging by one arm from a branch and with the other hand scraping at the trunk with an instrument like a short hoe. He dropped down out of the tree and called my name; it was the resin-gatherer I had met eight months before. Rubbing his wrists on his stained and blackened trousers, he called, "Are you thirsty, Andrea? Did you miss your truck again this time? Come and drink some water." He reached up to a branch overhead and brought down a moist leather bag with a pine cone for a stopper. "Drink as much as you like," he said; "our water is good, we get it from a spring down in the ravine. Up on the mountain, though, it's even better—there you take one drink and immediately you can eat a whole loaf of bread. It opens the appetite so."

We sat down on the needle-covered ground and he recounted some of his worries and misfortunes. "What can you do? Life always has such things in store. And I am unlettered," he said, laughing with good-humour. "My father is a *tsélingas*, a wealthy shepherd; he had me and my brothers tending his sheep as soon as we were of an age to be trusted; we never went to school. When I got married, he gave me a hundred goats, my father-in-law another hundred for my wife's dowry. After that came the Occupation, and people who know things because they can read and write all said the English would soon come back to Greece:

with English help we thought we would go to war again and drive the Germans out. So I sold my whole herd thinking I would be taken into the army again at any moment, but the English didn't come till three years later, and I was left with some worthless Occupation money. I had to begin again from nothing. My father, who owns all these trees as well, let me come out and gather the resin to sell to the merchants in Megara. I had never done it before, and I had to teach myself what seasons the sap runs best and how to make the gashes in the trunk just deep enough to keep the resin flowing into the tins, yet not so deep as to kill the tree either. Then, while I was learning all this, the Superintendent of Forests came out and saw me ruining a few trees and told me to stop. He said I was destroying the national wealth. I told him to go and lose himself. He called me a blockhead and I fell upon him with my fists and chopped him up. Ever since, the *keratá* has been threatening to take me to court."

"What will happen then?"

"Who knows?" he said; under these trees his voice, lively and quiet, sounded as natural as the noise of twigs or insects. "I haven't the money to pay him to leave me alone, nor have I any chickens or goats now to give the judge so that he'll let me off . . . And you, Andrea, what do you do?"

I told him about my studies and he looked grave and uncomprehending until I mentioned archaeology. "*Bá?* You dig things up? I ask because when I was young we dug some pots out of a cave once—cups and flat dishes with handles on the sides and figures and writing all over them. I didn't know what the writing said and we broke them up, but afterwards someone told me they might have been valuable. Is that true?"

"They sound like ancient pieces," I said. "Where did you find them?"

"Oh, it's of no great importance," he answered evasively. "Sometimes I've thought of looking for more, but to dig in the ground you need the protection of someone in authority. Greeks are always spying; if they see you digging they report you to the police. My only desire is to be left in peace, yet with what I get for the resin I can barely feed my family."

"Where do they live?"

"In Megara. I live there too during the winter when there's no work on the trees. I've been out here since March, and as soon as school is over my wife will come with the little ones for the summer. We all live in some huts over there on the next ridge."

"How does your work go this year?"

"We eat dry bread," he replied simply.

"You're probably better off here than if your children had to grow up in the streets of Athens," said I.

"Yes. Out here, if we haven't enough food, at least we can feed off the good air that keeps us all alive," he said. "Tell me, how is it you come here all alone?"

"You'd understand if you had to live in a city," I said.

"But alone like this?"

"So I prefer."

"Oh well, the people here are quiet enough. Then again," he added with a quizzical expression, "some are more than others. You shouldn't go alone; people have strange thoughts when they see a foreigner by himself. Why don't you stay with us? Another resin-gatherer has his family in the hut next to mine; his wife will cook for you."

"When I come next time," I said, "but now I go up the mountain."

He walked with me to a clearing where we could see the whole steep flank with one of Greece's half-finished motor roads mounting diagonally across it to a treeless col at the east end of the ridge.

"If you go straight up there to Aéra, you will find my father-in-law and all his family at their goat-pens, and if you go all the way to the spring of Koura at the opposite end you'll find other cousins of mine, for we're all related to each other here on the mountain. Tell them you come from Andoni, tell them I sent you. And yet I wish you'd stay here. I'd feel responsible if anything happened to you. Things seem quiet, but even these days one never knows . . . so, good-bye."

I heard the sound of his axe again as I set off through the trees, then from far away his voice sounded faintly up the hillside, "May your hour be good."

It was a long climb up the open mountainside, where stunted shrubs clung like coils of wire to the rocks and sun glared off the naked stone, to the goat-pens of Aéra. Eight months before, I had found the truck of the Greek Alpine Club parked here, and the driver eating his lunch with a family of shepherds, an old man with curly, silver hair and an old woman with spectacles and a long apron—I had not known then they were Andoni's parents-in-law—and several sturdy young men and their wives and bare-footed children. I had eaten my picnic beside their pine-branch hut, listening to the few words they addressed to one another, contemplating an existence measured by the needs of animals, by patriarchal laws and the simplicities of weather and the seasons; they had not talked to me. Now ahead of me I recognized the huts, and suddenly three huge dogs charged towards me and circled round and round my legs, snarling like wild beasts, their jaws vibrating and slavering, until the same old woman emerged from her hut and with a well-aimed stone sent all three stampeding into the woods. Then she withdrew. For the next two hours I walked along a path that kept its altitude along the mountain's northern flank a few hundred feet below the ridge, breathing again the crystalline air that poured out of the fir forests over the high fields of limestone. These rolled away from the ridge like the backs of whales, rising to smaller peaks that pointed up out of the forests clinging to their flanks, as if hanging in mid-air over the soft blue of the Corinthian Gulf. Far below, the brown fields of the Isthmus—a giant tendon holding the Peloponnese to the continent—and across the water the hazy, warm recesses of Kithairon and Helikon faded into dusk. Even with night falling fast, I felt the marvellous intimacy of the Greek landscape with the sea running in and out of land and the mountain-tops so close to one another. Soon I could no longer see the water of the Gulf; then before me rose the silhouette of a rocky spur above the spring of Koura. Below the path on one of the broad, open saddles were the fires of a shepherds' settlement, and the voices of women carried across the still air. This was not the hour to make my appearance, though they were Andoni's relatives, and I walked quietly so as not to arouse the dogs I could see circling round the firelight. Then at my feet I heard the deep gurgle of water flowing out of the rock into a wooden trough. I drank so much at once it ran down my neck, and it was so cold my teeth hurt. Above the spur, on a little plateau covered with the remains of ancient goat-pens, I was laying out my sleeping-bag when from the forest above came a rushing sound of bells and the dry clatter of innumerable hoofs grating over the stony slope. Suddenly the night echoed to a piercing whistle, yells and imprecations as the shepherd swept the goats before him, flinging stones to right and left.

"Ho ho ho hoo-oo, hey-ey, your father and mother and all their horns and whoooo, your Antichrist, hey-ey!"

A stone rebounded off the rock beside me; I crept off to the top of the spur, while the herd flowed like a dark patch towards the goat-pens on the saddle. For some time I could hear the herdsmen milking and the barking of the dogs and the voices of the women. Then I played the reed flute with which I had beguiled solitary hours on many mountainsides, sometimes pausing to listen to the stillness after a soft or shrill echo had died away. Down the hill someone put out the fire, then all was quiet. I lay back on the ground and received the imprint of stars on my eyes as I fell asleep.

When I opened them again, a sickle moon hung in the sapphire sky of four o'clock in the morning. Gradually it went white. Birds began to sing in the depth of the forest and the goats came up the mountainside again in the shadowless light. Across the Gulf the summits of Helikon and Parnassos showed red through the morning haze, then stood out yellow against the bright blue day. The sun rose like a blazing eye, bringing immediate warmth;

long, dewy shadows of stunted firs stretched over the open slopes where a woman was laying out coloured blankets in the sun. Five bay ponies grazed on the col, their long tails waving. Everywhere the mountain glistened as if the night had washed it.

A second herd came up through the plateau. Two men driving them caught sight of me heating water over a fire of twigs, and came over to bid me "Good morning." I told them of my acquaintance with Andoni.

One of them said, "Was it you who played the *phloyéra* last night? When I heard you I thought it was some bandit and I took my gun and came half-way—why, I was ready to shoot whomever it might be! An unknown person playing the *phloyéra* on the mountain! But . . . after a while I thought better of it."

"So you came back to the pen where it was safe," said the other, who was old and wiry.

"Yet I could have killed you on the spot, an unknown person playing the—"

"But the fact is you didn't," said the older man. "Come, Stelio, the things are already out of sight."

They continued on their way, then from the middle of the slope they called back, "You can sleep in the pen tonight if you wish."

Moisture and coolness, the lingering relics of night, vanished off the mountain by the time I too climbed up to the edge of the forest and looked back at the shepherd women carrying wooden barrels on their shoulders to the spring. I spent the day exploring abrupt little peaks and grey cliffs that dropped almost all the way down to Andoni's pine forests and the coastal plain; in warm dells the sun beat down on to the forest floor, and on the bare ridge it grew so hot I finally sought a circle of shade under a twisted fir. My lids grew heavy over my bread and cheese and water no longer cold, while the great mountains hung like hazy curtains across the water and close by among the rocks the cicadas kept up their dry, shrill antiphon and big flies buzzed under the branches. It was impossible to move away until the fire had died out of the sky.

Down at Koura late that afternoon I found the shepherd women at the spring, with some girls with round, dark eyes and several rumpled children, all progeny of the old man I had met that morning. The wife of the other shepherd, Stelio, had a mischievous face and smiled all the time, showing a gold plate across her mouth in place of teeth. It was still light enough to take a photograph of them, and the young woman smiled obligingly with her mouth closed.

"Imagine an American here!" she exclaimed to the other girls. "Shall we too go to America and laugh at our husbands?"

Stelio and the old man returned to the fold earlier that evening. A girl herded the goats, all rubbing against each other with their shaggy, black flanks and a ripple of clanking horns, into an enclosure of stones with branches piled on top of them in the shape of a horseshoe, with a small opening at one end where the old shepherd and two of the women seized each goat as it came through and milked it. After the whole herd had passed through the opening, the old man, Barba Thymio, drove it off to another part of the col, while the women took the pans of milk and poured it all through a cloth into various buckets and cauldrons and then again into stout little barrels for the night. Our meal was a cauldron of milk over the fire, with pieces of bread thrown into it. The dogs sat close by, watching the flames, and the red sparks spiralled up into the night air. We all lay down then, side by side on a great blanket spread over a platform of flat stones with a rude wall round it covered with rough shepherds' capes to keep out the wind. We were up again and more barrels filled by half past five next morning. One boy left for Loutraki with the milk and the shepherds dispersed with their goats to various quarters of the mountain. For me today was Monday and I must be in Athens by the end of the morning. When I said goodbye to the women, the smiling one said, "Would that we too could go instead of passing our lives here in the wilderness!"

Half-way to Aéra I met some boys from another sheepfold who had heard about me already; for the mountains of Greece are a whispering gallery where everything is quickly known. We talked together in the warm morning sun, and they said, "We wanted you to stay with us, but you must come again often."

By eight-thirty I was down in the hot, sandy gullies where the air was suffocating under the tall, gashed pines. I walked towards the coast road and the gleam of the distant sea, then from deep among the woods a voice called to me and I saw Andoni standing in his loose rags with the axe in his hand.

"I'm about to eat," he said. "Come and join me."

We sat with our backs to the trees and I told him about Stelio at Koura, who came out with a gun to shoot me and then thought better of it.

"Oh, him!" Andoni waggled one wrist contemptuously and muttered in a lower voice, "As for his wife . . ."

Then he told me about his own father in Megara, who at sixty was content to work no more, having married off his daughters with handsome dowries and established his other sons behind the town, tending his flocks. "But I have sold my goats and fallen outside . . . Do you know, Andrea, I have one child still unbaptized. We made three daughters in a row, then our fourth was a son. After that I made a vow in the chapel of Saint Nicholas off there on the mountainside that if our fifth were a boy too I would call him by the Saint's own name. Would you like to baptize him and be his godfather?"

I answered "Yes" without thinking.

Andoni broke into a grin. "Do you really want to?"

"Yes."

"Ah, then you'll be my koumbáros!"

"I'd be very glad."

"Actually," he said, "there's a man who was with me in the army—we walked back from Albania together in '41 after the surrender—who said he'd baptize one of my children some day. Just last week I wrote to him in Loutraki and told him we wished to have the christening soon and would he come. He wrote back he was too busy this summer to come all the way here; so I thought, eh, let him go to the Mercy, we'll find someone else! And here you are, Koumbáre," he said, contemplating the new fact before him. "Surely the Saint desired it. There's a superior force that works in the lives of men—I've heard people talk of it who know such things—and here in a coincidence one sees it working," he ran on. "It would be good to have the *mystírion* take place next week. I'll let you know as soon as I know myself what day."

One morning a fortnight later one of the maids at the Academy woke me up, saying, "Down in the garden there are two men who wish to see you. One calls himself Andoni."

I dressed and hurried downstairs to find him in the driveway, dressed in a suit, his black hair poking out from under his cap, with another man, who said promptly, "You will forgive us for disturbing you."

Andoni began, "What can I say, Koumbáre? I'm not acquainted with the city, I'm a shepherd. I brought with me this one who knows letters and was able to help me find you. He can also explain things; he's my neighbour in Megara."

"And we are friends besides," added the other, a portly man with handsome features and an air of knowing very well what he was about. "Dhimitrios Kharvayiás, electrician. Enchanted with the acquaintance. I've heard many good things about Kyr Andrea, but nothing is so good as the pleasure of meeting him in person."

"I've had no breakfast," said I, not yet fully awake. "Shall we go to the *kapheneíon* in the next street?"

As we walked out of the garden Andoni looked round him at the tall buildings, while his companion repeated some of the compliments he had heard about me. "My friend Andoni—for we are real friends, I'm not joking—is lucky indeed to have Kyr Andrea for his koumbáros. It was a piece of good fortune the other man in Loutraki wasn't free to come."

Andoni said, "The *mystírion* will take place tomorrow."

"You must tell me what to do," I said.

Andoni looked at his friend, who merely said, "Kyr Andrea need not disturb himself on that subject. We'll talk about it later in Megara."

At the coffee-house Andoni sat silent. Once I looked at him questioningly, and he replied, "Nothing, Koumbáre . . . What's the matter? You look disturbed. Myself, I'm lost here in the city; I'm only a shepherd."

Then his friend asked if they might see the place where I lived. I took them up to my room on the top floor, where I had an arm-chair and a fireplace, a desk and crowded bookcase and a view over the umbrella pines in the garden to Hymettos and the eastern slums of Athens. Andoni stood in the middle of the room with his cap in his hand; he was in a world of pine forests, white cliffs and thyme-covered hillsides.

"Mitso," he said to his friend without ceremony, "let us go."

Dhimitrios Kharvayiás looked round my room and a smile lit up his face. "Why, this is magnificent!"

I said, "It's very expensive." In the same moment I felt the false expression of concern come over my own, and was unable to stop the words before they came out, "Actually I'm not sure if I'll be able to stay on here or if I can even finish my studies." Basely I wanted them to think I was poor, so that I would not have to give them money; also I longed for them to take me on their own level.

Then Mitso said in a slightly lower voice, "If this Academy happens to need the services of an electrician—" He stopped; Andoni was glaring at him.

I saw them to the gate and we parted with the understanding that I would take the eight o'clock bus to Megara next morning.

They were there at half past nine in the bleak square that opens off the narrow main street. They had a taxi, loaded with potato sacks and crates of vegetables, to take me over the top of the town to a plain on the other side, where there were only a few scattered houses on the edge of the olive groves. Andoni was diffident in the taxi; days before he must have decided it would be fitting to have his friend Mitso, who had been to high school and was now a prosperous electrician, as an intermediary between himself, an illiterate man of the hills, and the kind of person he imagined me to be. At one moment Mitso would repeat in stilted *Katharévousa* something Andoni had just said to me, at another elaborate on some sentence of mine to Andoni, each time adding a small sting of praise.

The taxi drove up beside a square, concrete house with a cement balcony projecting out into the surrounding bedrock. Andoni's father came out to meet us, white-haired with black eyebrows, followed by the mother who had humped shoulders and a bell-shaped midriff and carried her old head forward on her neck; a white kerchief set far back showed the central parting and the hair drawn tight round her temples, framing a face with deep lines and no expression. Eight or ten children crowded on to the balcony to gaze at me—babies round and wobbly on their legs and elder children with graceful limbs and cropped heads— and then emerged the great-grandmother of them all, who looked hardly older than Andoni's mother and gave me a strong handshake, saying, "Welcome, little Koumbáre."

"She's ninety-five, she can still thread a needle," said the others.

They led me into the house and I ate lunch under the gaze of Andoni's parents and brothers and sisters with their wives or husbands.

"Is it true," they asked, "that in America all factory workers go to work in their own motor-cars?"

"True," I said.

The men turned to Andoni and said, "*Po-pó!* Imagine having a car of your own to drive you to Yerania every day—a golden life, eh Andoni?"

"What do I know about such things?" he said. He looked cross and preoccupied. Then he smiled at me and said, "I'm only a shepherd, Koumbáre." Again I seemed to hear the sound of insects in the hot air under the pine trees.

While I was eating, one of the women came up behind my chair and put a tape measure round my neck, then withdrew rapidly, saying to somebody outside the door, "For the shirt of the Koumbáros."

The meal finished, I was led across a rocky field to Andoni's house a hundred yards away: three small rooms in a row with a scrawny grape-vine stretched across two slanting poles. Andoni's wife came out towards us.

"Here is your Koumbára," he said. "Her name is Katerina."

She said, "Greetings to our godfather," and gave me her hand. She was massive and handsome in her early forties, with the peasant woman's sunbaked skin and a look of serenity and competence, her long mouth and level eyes ready for a half-smile. She wore on her head the yellow printed kerchief of the women of Megara straight across her wide brow, drawn close round her face to cover both shoulders, and down in a long V across her bosom with the two ends stuck into her apron. "You went up the mountain and slept at Koura, Koumbáre? That was where I grew up; my father had his sheepfolds there, but they are ruined now."

I said, "Koura is the most beautiful place I've seen in Greece. I'd like to have grown up there myself."

"What can one do?" she said in a warm, slow, quiet voice that seemed to indicate that any form of wish was on the whole a waste of time.

Andoni said quickly, "Do you wish to sleep, Koumbáre?"

"Why should he not sleep?" said Katerina. "The day is long. Come into this room, Godfather. We shall leave you in peace; nothing happens till late in the afternoon." She led me into the end room, in every Greek house the one set apart for formal occasions and the unbidden guest.

Andoni hovered while I took off my shoes and climbed on to the bed. "Is everything *endáxi*, Koumbáre? It's a poor house, I wish you all comfort."

I lay there two hours and listened to the coming and going of the whole family in the courtyard, Andoni giving breathless orders to the women or hissing at some child not to make a noise and whispered conversations through which recurred again and again the word Koumbáros, referring to me as by some hieratical rank, never by name.

When finally I went out into the courtyard, Andoni jumped up from a chair. "Did you sleep?" he said.

"No, I'm too interested," I replied.

"I haven't slept for a week, Koumbáre."

A woman came into the courtyard with a package and said to Andoni, "The shirt of the Koumbáros."

"Put this on," he said. "It's the custom to honour the godfather," and then: "Koumbáre, we shall go to Mitso's house; he knows how to explain things to strangers."

A few minutes later I was listening to Mitso and his wife explaining to me, over a tray of ouzo and sugared fruit, my duties as godfather and the list of things I was to buy for the ceremony that evening: the baby's baptismal clothes, an ecclesiastical cloth to wipe off the holy oil after the anointing, and a gold cross to hang round its neck. "This may seem to you a great expense," said Mitso's wife, smiling politely; "in any case—how shall I say?—you owe it."

"Of course," I answered airily, "and it's also the godfather's duty, I believe, to pay the priest and in general show generosity—"

"As if the Kyrios koumbáros would fail to understand such things!" said Mitso. "Indeed Andoni is lucky to have for a koumbáros a man who . . ."

While he ran on I shifted in my chair and catching Andoni's eye: "Since the afternoon is going by, perhaps we should—"

"Ah, yes," said Mitso, ready to interpret my wish. "Of course we should see to our purchases, eh, Andoni?"

The three of us went to a haberdasher's and looked at baptismal dresses. Mitso suggested I buy one that was slightly less expensive, made of blue silk instead of white.

"Blue is better for a boy," said I; for I wanted to keep back as much money as possible for the largesse customarily distributed by the godfather on such occasions. Then we went to a gold-smith's, who showed us crosses round and flat, some with more decoration than others; Mitso again tactfully suggested I buy the plainer one, and I did, unaware of how alien it must seem to a Greek to be even temporarily parsimonious for the practical end of being generous later.

As we passed a house from which came the barbaric blare and whine of an instrument such as I had never heard before, Andoni said, "That's old Stamáti, your Koumbára's cousin; he's getting ready for tonight."

All Andoni's relatives and neighbours had collected at his house when we got back. Katerina stood with her daughters round her, all busy combing the hair of my godson-to-be, a heavy, round-faced one-year-old. A wispy-bearded old priest sat limply beneath the grape-vine with the sacristan at his side, holding a packet of candles.

Mitso whispered in my ear, "That priest is going to get everything he can out of you," and he twisted one wrist in the air in a gesture of grasping. "But I'll come to your aid if he really robs you."

Then a truck drove up outside the courtyard wall. Priest and sacristan climbed in the front with their paraphernalia of crosses and candles, cauldron, holy oil and vestments, while the rest of us got in the back, hauling after us the carcasses of three lambs slaughtered for the occasion, the crates of food we had carried up with us in the taxi that morning, a stack of chairs and piles of sheets and tablecloths and blankets for the night. Waving and cheering, we drove down through Megara and out on to the coastal road.

As it mounted up into the cliffs of Kakí Skála where the rusty locomotives derailed during the Occupation still lay about on the scarp of the railroad tracks, the women cried out each time the truck wheeled round the curves high above the sunlit water, and Andoni said, "What name are you going to give my son?"

"But what name would you like?"

The women said, "The Koumbáros must choose; one doesn't pick a name out of the air."

Andoni said, "I told my Koumbáros I vowed the child to Ayios Nikólaos if it should be born a son. It would be fitting to give him that name."

"Think of the little evil-fated soul without a name!" said one of the women, and another, crossing herself three times, added fervently, "The Panagia be thanked the road is straight from here!"

Colour vanished from the sea and the olive groves as we drove in the twilight up a dusty track towards the forest. The body of the truck rolled and sprang from one side to the other, the women seated heavily on the benches leaning this way and that, and the men all standing like sailors on the deck of a ship as we plunged down into a gully and climbed up the other side. The smell of thyme was strong on the air between puffs of exhaust smoke.

Then we came to a halt, and everybody got down and the women unloaded the strange trappings of the expedition while seated on the warm, dry pine-needles their menfolk told me how each was related to Andoni. Somebody's grandfather, they said, had built the chapel here because he was a fisherman and once saw Saint Nicholas in a dream; Poseidon has become Ayios Nikólaos. We were joined by a weatherbeaten man who looked like a Hun or a Mongol, with pointed eyes and skin drawn tight across his cheek-bones. "Health to you, Barba Stamáti," said the others. "Will you be able to play till morning?"

"Eh, it's lucky I have that one, he nearly didn't come," said he, pointing to a young boy who was hanging a big goatskin drum in one of the branches of the pine trees; he had the same features as his father, but being no older than fifteen, the cruelty in his face was fresh and tranquil. The old man went on, "He had a fight with one of his friends at noonday and stuck a knife into his leg. I had to find four hundred thousand this afternoon for the judge to let him off."

Through the gathering darkness someone called to us, "They're ready."

The men got to their feet: "Come, Koumbáre, now it's up to you."

More people joined us under the low branches, and I recognized the old man with silver hair I had seen up at Aéra and his wife in her long skirts and eyeglasses, and among others the shepherds from Koura, Stelio and Barba Thymio. Andoni appeared at my side and next to me walked Katerina with the baby in her arms.

"All my brothers have come down from their sheepfolds tonight," she said. Around me was the whisper of many voices.

We came to the chapel, its eaves level with our heads, and the baby was placed carefully in my arms. We were standing in front of a small rectangle of candlelight and the others were moving back now. Andoni and Katerina said, "Go in."

I ducked my head and stepped through the door. The chapel was so tiny there was barely room for the miniature icon-screen with a door in it and a painted panel on either side; a curtain closed off the sanctuary. The sacristan was pouring steaming water into an enormous copper cauldron, while the priest in his golden robes held the service book and the chains of a smoking censer. The sacristan motioned me to change the baby from my left to my right arm and placed a lighted candle in my free hand. The priest started to intone and swing the censer, then came to a stop and looked round at me. The sacristan whispered in my ear that I must give the response; so I uttered again and again at every pause the ancient word *apetyxámen*, renouncing for this child the Devil and all his works. The baby's clothes were pulled off while clouds of incense rose up on every side, stinging our eyes until he cried and I could hardly see in the little space. The priest's golden arm moved up and down and crosswise, then he turned to me, and I waited with the baby squirming in my arms.

"The name," the priest said.

"What is the name?" the sacristan whispered angrily.

"What, what, the name?" I stammered, then shouted out, "Nikólaos!"

Turning to the open door, the priest called into the black night, "Nikólaos."

Outside in the dark the shopkeepers of Megara and the shepherds, resin-gatherers and charcoal-burners of Yerania with their wives and children cried with one voice, "Nikólaos!" raising a great shout as the priest seized the baby and plunged it down, up, down, up, and down a third time into the steaming water; and amid the immersions and the rolling fumes of incense and the acrid heat of all our candles the screaming infant soul was at last invested with identity.

A towel was laid across my arms; the priest placed Nikólaos in it; again the sacristan motioned me to change him to my other arm and rubbed him vigorously with the towel, while the priest sealed with a finger dipped in holy oil the nine openings of his strong, howling body. Lastly we put on him his baptismal clothes. A lock of his wet hair was snipped off with a scissors and dropped into the font, oil was poured in, the censer was swung over it, and then the three of us, holding on to each other's clothes or vestments, moved slowly round and round the cauldron, stopping at every three steps while the priest chanted and the other man responded and the thick candle began bending in my hand.

We came to the end. The sacristan went out ahead of us, and all the others who had been standing outside shouted and cheered, "Live Nikolaki! Live Andoni and Katerina! Live the Koumbáros!"

Andoni stumbled into the chapel and threw his arms round me. Katerina followed him in, a smile across her face. We grasped each other's hand and transferred Nikolaki into her embrace. They went out again as the priest came up to me and told me to write in his notebook my name, nationality and religion.

"What do I owe you, Pappouli?" I asked.

He answered shortly, "Five hundred thousand."

Then Mitso appeared in the door, exclaiming loud enough for everyone outside to hear him, "Little God and Panagia! How is he not ashamed to ask five hundred thousand from a stranger who has had the kindness—"

"Let the stranger give whatever he wants, then," said the priest. "How much do you want to give, Kyrie . . . Kyrie, whatever you said your name was?"

I was anxious to make an end of the transaction. So was he. He lifted the wad of money from my hand with the same twist of the wrist Mitso had imitated in the courtyard of Andoni's house, then stepped through the door, and I followed him out into the darkness.

Unseen, unknown people caught at my hands and clapped me on the shoulder, and I heard the warm voices all round me murmuring, "Now you belong to us, Koumbáre."

A great bonfire had been built in the clearing. Outside the circle of firelight Mitso was still expostulating over the priest's rapaciousness, until Andoni's father told him to be quiet.

Old Thymio from Koura took me by the arm and said, "Come and look at your godson, Koumbáre."

Nikolaki in his blue silk dress, with two large tears rolling from closed eyelids down his round, little oil-covered cheeks, lay in a low cradle being rocked violently to sleep by the strong arms of several women. One of them said to me, "In a whole year no one has given him the Eye; surely he is a well-fated child. His mother did right when he was born to set out the plate of milk and honey for the Fates to drink from, three nights in a row, the way it has always been."

Voices called from the fire, "Where is the Koumbáros?"

"Why didn't he stay in our sheepfold when he climbed the mountain?"

"Where are you, Barba Stamáti, with your *karamoúza*. And Vangeli with your *daoúli*, where are you?"

"Where is the lamb? Are you still turning it?"

"And the wine? Are we going to begin? Religon makes the throat dry, is that not so, Pappathemistoklí?"

"Plates, plates, glasses!"

"Let the Koumbáros see the lamb before it's sliced to pieces."

I was lifted up by the elbows and brought back to the fire. On rough shepherds' blankets the older women sat with their legs drawn up under their long skirts. To one side a man squatted on his heels, turning slowly in the notches of two short, Y-shaped branches stuck into the ground, a six-foot pole running from end to end through the carcass of a lamb that glistened and spat and crackled over the logs. Someone else was swabbing its flanks with a sponge full of grease on the end of a stick. Finally long knives were taken to it; everyone sat down, plates were passed from hand to hand and big, straw-cradled flagons dragged on to the blanket. Glasses held up to the spouts and passed back, were drunk off one after the other and passed back again to be refilled. We sat in a wide circle—there must have been fifty of us now with the other relatives who had come down off the mountain—balancing plates of meat, potatoes, cheese and bread on our knees, stuffing our mouths and swallowing wine, cheering and calling to one another, while the fire leaped and hissed and the sparks rose up snake-like into the blackness. Beyond the trees the wide land slanted down to the Saronic Gulf, silvered in the rising moon. Even with wine and hot meat under one's nose the smell of thyme was overpowering in the warm night air.

Someone called and pointed up at the black shape of the mountain with its outline unchanging against the sky now growing brighter in the moonlight; a tiny spark showed on the ridge.

Andoni sitting beside me said, "From our bonfire the shepherds up there know the *mystírion* has taken place. They've made a fire of their own to signal to us."

Others began to shout for Barba Stamáti. The old man with the Asiatic face came forward and sat near the fire with a short pipe with a flaring end and a double reed in the mouthpiece like the chanter of a Highland bagpipe. Then, elbows on his knees, he clamped the reed between his teeth and blew so hard the veins in his neck and temples soon stood out like knotted ropes while he raised the pipe into the air and swayed from side to side. The first sound was like an explosion in that silent forest, and after that there was only the hot, weird, shrieking melody with the syncopated thudding of the drum which the boy who had stuck his knife into somebody that afternoon was beating with a stick of polished hardwood. Beyond the fire I had a glimpse of horsemen with high cheek-bones and long bows swarming across plains. But in the dome of orange light under the trees Andoni, tugging at a handkerchief in someone's hand, was frantically shouting, "Why do you sit? Get up!" And a line of men and women moved forward round the fire, rising sometimes on the skip, sometimes swaying like a wave with the occasional backward step, Andoni leaping and slapping both heels in mid-air. He never stopped; others sat down and more would take their place. Those who danced most were the older women in tightsleeved velvet bodices with the fiddle-shaped opening across the bosom, and yellow- and blue-striped aprons over their full skirts slit at the bottom with a piece folded back on either side to show the red lining and their stately, white-stockinged ankles turning in unison. Whenever someone sat Andoni would bend down and drag him to his feet again, vividly swearing at his Antichrist or Panagia. Once I was dancing next to him and he stopped in the middle of a figure and clasped me to him in his winy, bristly embrace, crying out, "I love you, Koumbáre, you have baptized my son! The Saint desired it, and now I am dancing to the fate, dancing to the fate, the fate of my child." He repeated the words over and over as if they were some sort of propitiation and continued dancing until the others gradually stopped throwing logs on the fire and day began to whiten in the sky. Before sunrise we crept off to various parts of the forest and lay down where we fell, covering ourselves in our blankets.

We slept for a few hours into the daylight, but the morning was still early when Andoni, Katerina, a few relatives and I went back to the chapel, where the priest celebrated Mass and the baby Nikólaos received his first communion in the arms of his godfather, according to the custom of the Eastern Church. Throughout the morning lambs were roasted on the spits, blankets were laid out again in a long line and covered with tablecloths, while plates, glasses, wine-jugs and chunks of bread were placed at intervals along them, where we sat or lay propped on our elbows. The meal lasted till early in the afternoon and all the time Barba Stamáti and his son played to us on the *karamoúza* and *daoúli*, and the cicadas were loud in the branches overhead. I began to nod. Andoni called out to his womenfolk, "A blanket, a pillow for the Koumbáros!" and I went off a little distance and lay down in the hot wind blowing up from the sea, and listened to the insects and the murmur of voices and the untiring pipe and drum.

I awoke among long shadows. Too soon the level space under the trees was cleared, the truck was driven in, and, bouncing and swaying on the benches, we returned to Megara and after a few words of salutation everything was over. Andoni, Katerina and I slept beside their five children on the dry earth of their courtyard.

Next day Andoni took me to visit the houses of his married sisters. He told me how one of the husbands had received the truck from the old father, another had been given a butcher's shop in the main street. "The old man thinks his sons can fend for themselves," Andoni said. "True, one must care for one's daughters. And yet all my brothers have fared better than I who fell outside when I sold my goats. Some day you'll take me to America, eh, Koumbáre?"

Every few hours of the day we ate in small rooms where the air sizzled with flies, and in the evening several neighbours, including Mitso, joined us for a stroll along the motor road west of the town. All the young men and women of Megara were out in their Sunday clothes, crowding the road for nearly two miles. I asked if there was some festival going on, and Andoni's brother-in-law winked and said, "It's the weekly wife-bazaar." Mitso asked me my impressions of the christening. "What pleased you most, Kyrie Koumbáre? Were you interested more from the aspects of sociology or of folk-lore? Your opinion is valuable." The others asked me about politics and the likelihood of war. Meanwhile Andoni was far away among his pine trees and his lost goats, asking no questions; it was for the others to be clever.

His family and I were up at five next morning to the sounds of crowing cocks and braying donkeys, and the light of the waning half-moon lay over the courtyard and the sleeping faces of the children. A few hours later, while we were drinking our mint tea together, Andoni's father and mother came to say goodbye and brought a huge christening loaf stamped with ecclesiastical symbols, baked in their own oven, and an old ouzo bottle full of sheep's butter from their flocks to take back with me to Athens. When the time came to leave and make my last formal gesture, I was suddenly ashamed of giving my koumbáros and koumbára the money I had saved from certain expenditures during the last few days. What should have been careless, resembled, in my hands, a sort of barter, as if I could only pay in money for what these people gave of their spirit—the loaf of bread, the bottle of butter and a brilliantly striped woollen bag of the sort hung on donkey saddles, which Katerina had spun and dyed, woven and embroidered herself; in it was a bunch of dried mint from the slopes of Yerania.

"You will make yourself tea with this in Athens, Koumbáre, and think of us," they said.

I said, "But what have I done for you? You barely know me."

A puzzled look passed between them that seemed to ask how I could place so little trust in love.

Andoni walked down with me to the ten o'clock bus. We had time for coffee with the brother-in-law who drove the truck and Mitso, who came to see me off. Both were effusive and cheerful as I got on, but Andoni gave me his hand in silence.

CHAPTER 8

Taygetos—
Summer Lightning

"THE GENTLEMEN PASSENGERS are begged to mount the vehicle departing within five minutes for Corinth, Xylókastro, Aigion and Patras"—from the megaphone outside the ticket office a furry, dehumanized croak boomed over the little square. In the shadow of the bleak, high, brown façade of Saint Constantine's Church travellers bound for various quarters of the Peloponnese waited over their morning coffee while ragged boys with shoeshine boxes sidled in and out and old men with trays of sweetmeats strapped to their shoulders limped between the crowded tables. The sun had just come up and the trams of Athens were already starting on their noisy circuit in the neighbouring avenue. A bus drove up in front of the ticket office, and as soon as it was full the door was closed, the motor roared and it drove off. Another took its place and again the loudly filtered, granulated syllables burst from the megaphone: "The gentlemen passengers are begged to mount the vehicle now leaving for Corinth, Argos, Tripolis and Sparta."

I was going back to Mistra for the first time in two years. Throwing a rucksack packed for the whole long summer ahead on to the bundles in the street, I joined the crowd pressing noisily into the bus. The familiar hush fell as a gendarme, sleek in his battleship grey, climbed in after us and turned the narrow eyes in his pouchy icon-face upon each passenger's identity card and travel permit. He stepped back into the street without a word, then the driver climbed in and a sturdy, prosperous-looking young man with a camel's-hair cap and a burnished mask of sunglasses sat down next to him; the ticket-taker, coming in through the door at the back, called "All set, Niko!" and the motors roared beneath the driver's foot. The women with the headcloths and the sun-dried faces crossed themselves three times as the bus lurched forward among the trucks, carts and tramcars where twenty-five centuries ago a road called the Sacred Way led out to the holy places of Eleusis.

Two years before it had taken a week to get to Sparta; today it took eight hours over the smooth macadam road built by the American engineers. The Corinth Canal was cleared and we rattled over the Bailey bridge without stopping to have our permits checked, though among the mountain passes in Arkadia I noticed newly built barracks and concrete gun-emplacements where in 1948 there had been only dug-outs. The passengers talked together as if they were in a *kapheneíon*, and I struck up an acquaintance with the man in the front seat, who inquired at length about my studies and said expansively to the others sitting behind him, "Here is a foreigner who is drawn by the unknown!" He hung his jacket on the knob of the windshield, and throughout the journey kept shaking and re-folding it to hang free of the door. We had lunch together in Tripolis. Then in the middle of the afternoon the bus drove down the short, broad, dusty street of Sparta and halted outside a coffee-house; the other shops were still closed.

The man with the camel's-hair cap invited me to join him in a glass of ouzo. "And now," he said, "where do you go from here?"

"I'll find a place in Mistra. The last time I was there they tried to make me stay in a hotel in Sparta, but I slept out in the woods."

The man laughed. "Come to my village tonight," he said airily.

"But it doesn't do to disturb you," I demurred.

"On the contrary we Lakonians have a great feeling for strangers, and without flattering you I like the way you travel so carelessly."

I decided that anyone who could appreciate me was a kindred spirit; this was my third summer in Greece and I had still not learned to be careful.

"A bus will be leaving in an hour or so," said he. "Meanwhile my name is Tasso. And here—let me introduce you to my uncle, Kyrios Panayioti Pappadhópoulos. Eh, Barba Pano," he called to an old man sitting by himself in working clothes white with saw-dust. "Come and meet my guest. You will excuse me," he added. "I must attend to some business."

The old man sat down beside me and blew his nose between two fingers. "Archaeology, history, I know all about such things. I used to be a quartermaster in the cavalry; we went abroad to get our horses. . . ." The air was hot in the dark coffee-shop while Barba Pano talked on. "In 1920," he was saying, "the French and English wanted Greece to be a republic, with Venizelos for pres-ident, but the Greek people"—this phrase invariably indicated the speaker's own political views, and the Peloponnese was of course traditionally Royalist—"wanted the King; for Constantine was adored by his people and by his soldiers. There was fighting in the streets and Greeks killing one another," he went on, "but it was nothing to what we have gone through these last years. On one side the Communists massacred people and burned down villages for no reason, and on the other side those who are thriceworse."

I began to pay attention.

"Thrice-worse," he said again. "One man alone with his own hands has slaughtered thousands. He used to go into a village with a band of armed ruffians every Sunday, take hold of the nearest twenty or thirty boys and line them up against a wall and shoot them."

"But why?"

"Merely to show who was the law in this province! From '46 to '48 when he rode out from Sparta on Sunday mornings no one knew what place he would choose next. That one man drove whole villages into the Communists' arms, and now the same villages are safely gutted and empty; the army, the gendarmerie, the *Khi* and the other bands did a clean job—people wiped out who had done nothing but try to defend themselves against a homicidal maniac paid by one of our Members of Parliament to keep order in the district. The amnesty three years ago absolved Pavlakos from his sins, and now he's back in his village where nobody's going to take the trouble to go after him. Eh, the time will come when the Government will need him again; he's the kind of agent they find most useful. That's why the Greek people have always fought against their rulers." He glared at me out of his big, flushed face. "They took my two sons, twenty-two and twenty-six, and killed them one night outside my window. And all my life," he exclaimed, "I have been Royalist! Fifteen years I fought for my country—against the Bulgars in 1912, the Germans in 1914, the Turks in 1920. And so the people who lately collaborated with our enemies come and kill my children! Thanks to the British and to you Americans!"

"Why to us?"

"You like to think you are here to do good. You want us to be grateful for your canal-dredging and your road-building, at the same time that you support those who paid Pavlakos, and finance the camps like Makronisos and Youra."

I then made the mistake of telling him I had seen people that winter who came out of Makronisos, just as Tasso came in again.

"Well?" said he with a smile.

"Tasso, the Kyrios knows what has been happening in Greece!" exclaimed Barba Pano. "He knows about Makronisos, and I've just told him about—"

"Oh, these are deep matters," said Tasso, glancing at me. "You've finished your coffee? I see there's still time before the bus goes. Why don't you take us to look at your workshop, Barba Pano?"

The old man, disregarding him, leaned forward across the table and whispered in my ear, "That man there, the proprietor— three years in exile. Those two at that table—two years on Mak- ronisos; they got out last month. They could tell you things you'd never hear from—"

"Come," said Tasso, who had already got up. We followed him out to a carpentry shop where Tasso showed me briskly around, pointing out pieces of half-made furniture until Barba Pano over- rode him and insisted we come to his house.

Tasso looked at his watch. "Very well, but quickly, eh?"

Next door Tasso drank his ouzo down impatiently; then Barba Pano said in a sombre voice, "Perhaps the Kyrios will allow me to show him a picture of the slaughtered ones." He took out of a drawer a mounted photograph of two boys dressed in coats and neckties for the occasion, with earnest eyes and proud lit- tle new moustaches; both had the smooth, unreal look of faces made over by the provincial photographer's pencil or the under- taker's hand.

"This is all I have left," said Barba Pano and turned away from us to put the picture back in its drawer.

Tasso shook his head weightily. "What can you do? Things in Greece are so complicated you can never find an end to them. Well, it's time to go."

Barba Pano followed us back to the main street and stood on the sidewalk looking old and foolish as we got into the bus. In a minute we were rolling through the olive orchards of Lacedae- mon, and after a few kilometres stopped in a village where two- storeyed porches on wooden pillars were partially hidden behind a profusion of dense, glossy orange leaves, cypresses, plane trees and long vines hanging from the dark verandas. Tasso took me to a large upper room filled with furniture and photographs and picture-frames, all decorated with sea-shells. Female relatives crowded in the doorway and for ten minutes his hospitality was vociferous in their presence; after that I found myself alone with only the photographs to look at, when he and the women all went out together. Dusk soon fell. It was dark when he returned, say-ing, "I'm afraid I'm a little busy. I have a large property," he added with a winning smile. "I have many responsibilities . . . Now, before going to bed, do you want to come downstairs and eat? I also own the wineshop on the ground floor."

So much the better, thought I; perhaps there would be com-pany. I was installed, however, alone within while Tasso sat and talked with the villagers outside. Sometimes he would dash back to fill the beakers of his clientele from the barrels along one wall, with an occasional polite glance in my direction, then out again fast. The apron round his waist made him look different from the prosperous traveller I had met on the bus that morning. Once he came in and gathered up the plates from my finished meal and took them back into the kitchen, then returned and to my sur-prise sat down opposite me.

"You have had enough?"

"Thank you," I replied.

"A cigarette?"

"Thank you."

My eyes wandered round the room and rested for a moment on a lithograph on the wall; a cluster of medallions framing goatlike heads and a scroll along the bottom: PANTHEON OF THE KINGS OF THE HELLENES. I turned my gaze from it too quickly, and Tasso prevented the casual expression I was on the point of assuming. "You know," he said, "these political matters are more than any-one can understand. On one hand you have people like Barba Pano—in few words, the Leftists. Because some of them are in prison the rest are inclined to consider themselves saints."

"They have that tendency," I said. "But on the other hand there are those who shot his sons. Indeed, what can one do?"

"Of course," he sighed. Then he turned to greet a man who walked into the wineshop: "Kyrie Dhimitraki. Won't you join us and keep company with my guest, an American?"

We talked about the retreat of the United Nations forces in Korea, and after exhausting the subject lapsed into silence.

Tasso was the first to break it. "The Kyrios was just saying how sad it was, the death of Barba Pano's two sons. When you think of the old fellow bringing them up, sending them to school, teaching them a craft, working for them, and then to lose them—sad, of course . . ."

He was called away by his patrons drinking outside in the warm summer night. He must have regretted his invitation from the moment Barba Pano had blurted out that I had actually heard about two sides in a civil war. I was not a convenient guest; so he was now keeping me hidden from both his family and his fellow-villagers, till at last they finished their wine and he returned to take over his duties of host and showed me to the bed in the room with the photographs and sea-shells.

Next morning as he and I stepped out of the bus from his village into the main street of Sparta he asked, "And where do you go from here?" since now he could afford to seem cordial and interested. "Ah, to Mistra? Good. I have some business to attend to at the moment, you'll excuse me. Responsibilities," he murmured, "one of my aunts ill today. . . ."

I said, to help him save his face, "Perhaps we'll meet again." And he laughed, as if delighted with the thought. "There's no doubt of it! We are friends."

We shook hands and he clapped me on the back and vanished.

ALL THE WAY to Mistra I wondered fervently when I would learn not to open my mouth on political subjects. Walking between the olive groves, row after row of shade-drenched treetrunks dwindled away on either side into the miles of glistening stubble, while far and near the cicadas shrilled out their long, diminishing festoons of sound, endlessly repeated among the black branches and stiff, grey, pointed leaves, and the menacing little hillside with the infinitesimal, white walls of the crusaders' castle, etched with black shadows in the early light, rose high and pointed overhead. I walked through the village and up the road towards the ruins and the fountain at Kryovrýssi, where Kleoméni would probably be all smiles and welcome whether he remembered me or not. I hoped I would find somewhere the good-hearted Kostandí who had killed his chicken for me the evening I had not stayed to eat it. Ahead of me on the terrace sat some farmers with a carafe of wine. As I approached, one of them leaned over the balustrade and called, "Come and make company with us. Afterwards, you, me, Ay Yanni."

"Tell me, does Kostandí still live there?" I asked.

The man replied, "I am Kostandí."

For a moment I stared—trying to recall some feature of the dashing, hearty young peasant I had known—at this man's lantern jaw, thin neck and narrow, fleshless temples, and the pinched, grizzled look about the eye-sockets. I climbed up to the terrace and pulled a chair over, saying, "Is it really you? I must have gone blind." Then I recognized the chestnut-coloured eyes and the warmth and friendliness that seemed to flicker inter-mittently like a snake's tongue round the edge of something else deep inside him that was not gentle.

He said, "I recognized you down the road. This time you'll stay with me in Ay Yanni. Drink." He shoved a glass across the table. "You find us sitting—Andrea, I believe your name is—but what else can one do in the heat? Eh. Let us go now."

As we walked together I reflected that two years is a long time in a Greek's life; Kostandí moved with short steps as if the joints of his legs were stiff, and his voice had grown husky and in-distinct.

"Do you remember, you came here once," he said. "You met my wife, I believe." He had the courtesy to say nothing more. We passed through several archways into the court of Ay Yanni, where smooth marble columns on the flagstones carried their graceful vaults round three sides, the fourth open over the far-spreading olive groves. "You were here," he said, "when all the families of the district lived inside the church. Last year they moved back into their own houses; but we ourselves are still here. We have rebuilt the staircase that was ruined then."

I followed him up a flight of wooden steps inside a framework of poles under the colonnade where two years before I had seen a mound of fallen masonry and a hole in the floor above it; they shook slightly as we mounted to the second storey of the loggia; here a wooden balustrade and plain upright timbers supported the ruinous tiled roof slanting downward from the church and the buildings on either side that once formed the monastery and palace of the bishops of Mistra—a whole building had fallen in at one end. Kostandí's voice rang out, "Panayiota! Eh Panayiota!" and his wife opened a door in front of us.

Dumpy in her plain shift and head cloth, she looked at Kostandí, then at me; she had a small, round, honest face. "Who's this?" she whispered.

"Don't you remember the *Amerikános* from before last year? The one who was coming to supper? He's staying here."

"*Bá?*" she said, smiling.

"Come in, Kyr Andrea," and Kostandí ducked his head; I followed him—the Byzantine Greeks built miniature doorways—into a dark room with half the plaster fallen off its walls and the rest blackened by smoke. Under its high roof-beams lost in shadow, the room was empty except for a cooking-pan and a kerosene stove several inches high in one corner. There were no windows, though a few chinks of light showed through the roof like distant stars. There were two more rooms beyond: one little bigger than a cubby-hole with a metal bed in it; the other large like the first but lit by one small window, with a pile of blankets, a few stools improvised out of boxes, and a table against the wall. "Kyr Andrea will sleep on the bed," said Kostandí. "Drop your knapsack in there. Now I show you the 'place.'" Another door led out on to a stone-paved balcony, at the end of which a flimsy stone turret with a hole over the open air served for a latrine.

"Now we shall eat," said Kostandí, and we went back into the room with the table. "Sit. Be comfortable."

I sat on one of the boxes. Panayiota came in. A thin little boy of six with cropped hair and a frightened face followed Panayiota, who took a great loaf off a shelf and sliced it with all her strength against her bosom.

Kostandí said, "This is my son. Eh, Kharíli, come and greet the Kyrios."

The little boy looked at me round-eyed and hid behind his mother, who turned and whacked him on the head, and he ran out of the room, howling.

"I don't want you to be shy, Kyr Andrea," said Kostandí. "Eat your bread." He dipped his own—it was stale and covered with dust—into his glass of water. I followed his example and we both chewed in silence. A fat and sturdy two-year-old with long, blond ringlets and the bloom of health on its round cheeks and half-naked body toddled in barefoot. Kostandí said, "Greetings to Vangelaki," and took him up on his knee.

"A boy?" I said. "May he live many years for you."

The corners of Kostandí's mouth moved slightly. "We don't have the heart to cut his curls off."

Panayiota came in and filled our plates with bean soup. Again Kostandí told me to eat and not be ashamed—it was his way of apologizing for his poverty. However he was still addressing me formally in the plural; so I had to do the same with him, and as a result we were both reserved. As my eyes became accustomed to the darkness inside the room I noticed one wall was hung with rifles and machine-guns, covered by khaki greatcoats hanging from their muzzles. Kostandí looked up from his soup.

"You have an arsenal here," I said, casually chewing a mouthful of beans.

Kostandí merely replied, "Some of us have not yet moved back into our houses."

Attention was drawn away by a sudden whimper from the far corner of the room, where for the first time I saw a very small, thin baby moving its arms and legs on the stone floor.

"You have another one?" I asked.

"A girl." I had the impression he would not apologize for her either.

By the end of our meal he had changed to the second person singular and told me he now had rheumatism in the legs. "They have also pulled out six teeth, here and here." Hooking back his lips with one finger, he showed me the gaps in both jaws. That was why his voice sounded muffled, although a tone of command rang through it when, rising, he said, "You will sleep now, Andrea? Panayiota, make up the bed for my friend."

"But it doesn't do that I should sleep in your only bed," I protested tactlessly.

Kostandí gave an impersonal wink. "Behave as if you were in your own house. I see your shirt is torn. My wife will patch it for you."

I went into the room with the big bed and took off my shirt. It was one I still had from the army, with breast pockets that buttoned down conveniently over the wads of money I always carried. I wanted Kostandí to know I trusted him; so I gave him the shirt without saying anything about the money. Several minutes later he reappeared. "It's better if you keep this in here while my wife sews on the patch," he said, handing me both packets.

"Oh, it makes no difference," I said breezily. "Expenses of the journey, you know. . . ."

"Children play about with it. Keep it in here," he replied.

I took the money and shoved it carelessly into my rucksack.

"Sleep as long as you would in your own house, Andrea," he said. "In this heat there's little one can do in the afternoons."

"What are you going to do?" I asked.

"I have work," he answered as he closed the door.

I lay down. On the opposite wall was an election poster of three former ministers of the Metaxas dictatorship who had banded together in the last elections in a new party of the extreme Right: one of them had founded the concentration camps on the Aegean Islands before the war; and another, a director of the Bank of Greece under the Germans, had organized the Security Battalions in 1944—a triptych of grim faces with the slogan: WE ARE RESOLVED NOT TO ALLOW A FOURTH ROUND IN GREECE.

When I woke up at five-thirty the sun had already passed behind Taygetos. On the small balcony Kostandí was stretched out on the paving-stones with two of his children. He looked up—his clipped shrub of a moustache gave him a humorous expression—and said, "I play with my sons."

With one leg over the balustrade I watched the shadow of the mountain spreading over Sparta. In a few minutes it reached the foothills of Parnon on the other side, and soon all the hot earth turned grey, though for several hours the sky would be full of light. "They say from the top of Taygetos one can see the shadow of the summit all the way to Crete," I said. "Is that true?"

But Kostandí did not reply. I was soon to find him reluctant to talk at all about what one saw or did on Mount Taygetos. "Shall we go to Kryovrýssi, Andrea?" he suggested.

Kryovrýssi had now become the most public place in Mistra, he told me as we walked down together. People from the village and farmers from the houses in the ruins of the old city came here every evening; this year Kleoméni was doing a lively business too with parties of Lakonian gentry, Athenian tourists, and foreigners who came to see the antiquities and stayed to dine before returning to their hotels in Sparta. Mistra had no hotel—the Bureau of Antiquities was still holding out successfully against the Ministry of Tourism—but Kleoméni had his radio; to my horror I could hear it already. The towers along the hillside, the great plane tree and the dark sea of orange groves below us all echoed to the husky roar of a voice from Athens floating through the evening air: ". . . reductions in the price of corsets and cotton stockings. Lady-listeners, fail not to visit during the next three weeks the second floor of Lambrópouli Brothers!" And the next moment I caught sight of Kleoméni on his terrace with a napkin over his arm, scanning the road for a possible taxi from Sparta.

Kostandí hailed him unceremoniously: "Still waiting for the aristocracy, eh Méni? In the meantime you can bring some wine for me and the American. You remember Andriko?"

Kleoméni turned to re-arrange some chairs and tables with his half-smile and downcast gaze, and murmured, "Ah ha." A glance at my clothes told him I was not his sort of customer.

Kostandí and I were joined by some other villagers, and later when it was dark and no new arrivals were forthcoming, Kleoméni himself sat down at our table and said, "Well, Kyrie, you are back in Mistra again? Let me stand you another carafe of wine. You are welcome here."

"I have found you well. And you have a new radio," I said, glancing with detestation at the loud-speaker in its coloured box attached to one of the branches overhead, vibrating and shattering the silence of the summer night. Then I looked at the relaxed, indifferent figures of Kostandí and the others in their ragged shirts. "Does it improve business?"

"Ah, yes," said Kleoméni.

"I suppose your tourists stay in Sparta now the way they should, what? You had a hard time with me two years ago, do you remember?" I tried teasing Kleoméni, but without success; the Greek's shrewd wit and passionate pride leave little room for sense of humour.

He replied, "We didn't know what to do with you. While you insisted on sleeping out of doors, all night we had to stand watch round our houses."

One of the others said, "Wasn't Kyr Andrea here when the two Andartes came into your cellar, Méni?"

"Oh?" I said. "What was that?"

Kleoméni replied casually, "Two came down one night looking for food."

"Into your cellar?"

"Underneath where we're sitting."

"Did you see them?"

"I had a gun."

"Nothing happened to you?"

Kleoméni leaned across the table for the wine-tin, while Kostandí answered instead: "He killed them both!"

During the next few days I saw more of Panayiota and the children than I did of her husband, who went off early to his coffee in the village square and stayed away till nightfall. When he and I met in the evening for our meal of bean soup, we had little to tell each other. He had changed since I last knew him, and not only in appearance. His whole manner had grown brusque and sombre; it seemed to say that as far as he was concerned my activities were my own affair, while something equally prevented me from asking what he did during the day. Anyhow I was busy myself. Because of the heat it was necessary to rise at five in the morning to eat the bread and drink the warm milk Panayiota brought up for me from the goat on the lower floor, then climb the hill to start work on the castle. On that narrow ridge, high above the plain and isolated from the huge mass of the mountain behind it, there was generally a breeze till nine; after that, through the long hours when the sun seemed to stand in the middle of the sky, there was a cistern which had preserved a moist chill underneath its vault during many summers since the thirteenth century, and certain corners of the circuit wall that cast a shadow wide enough for me to sit and scribble my notes.

When I went down again at noon it was as if the entire hillside dropped away beneath me; here and there the big, untidy, tumbling growth of a cactus or a prickly pear attached by a single root hung out haphazardly over the steep rocks, while at every step my boots dislodged small showers of thirsty pebbles down the path between the warm, truncated walls of what had once been houses, until I came to the courtyard of Ay Yanni and the cool of its empty, stone-floored rooms. Sometimes I would meet Panayiota coming with slow steps up the path from a spring in the gully with an earthenware jug balanced on one shoulder, or she was inside, preparing lunch on the stove; for Kostandí had told her she must always cook a hot meal for me at noontime. While I ate she would sit on the floor giving her baby the breast, and talk of Kostandí and of his family who lived outside the walls of Ay Yanni among the ruins; she seemed glad of the opportunity. "Only the Panagia knows what I have suffered from these people!" she would exclaim, and I soon found myself asking her questions as if she were an oracle on the arcana of Greek family life. One of Kostandí's sisters was the half-idiot girl with the short, black hair, whom I had seen lying on the floor of the clerestory inside the church two years before, paralysed by epilepsy. Now she lay on the balcony of a house across the lane and some days regained the power of speech sufficiently to sing songs in a loud, broken gurgle, while she leaned her face on the parapet; little girls from the surrounding houses going to fetch water from the spring looked up from under the stone pots they carried and greeted her, and idle boys accustomed from an early age to no such tasks would call up, "Things go well today, eh Dhimitroula?" Another sister had grey hair and lived with her parents. "The old man never married her off," said Panayiota, and from the woman's own brisk, kindly, victimized expression the reason was obvious: it was her life's work to take care of a girl who had to be fed by hand and carried from room to room. "Anyway it's too late," said Panayiota. "He should have married her when she could still have children. Who wants her now?"

I said, "This system of dowries and arranged marriages can be a cruel business sometimes. He must be a harsh father."

At which Panayiota pulled a long face and expressively waggled her wrist. "*Pó-po-po-pó*, what things has he not done to all of us! Kostandí is too good to him. Whenever he earns any money the old man comes and says, 'This is mine. Give it to me.' Or else he plays on Kotso's good nature and says he's old and feeble and his sons should lend him money to buy food. All the time he has money stored away and olive orchards in the plain, but never once has he let us have any oil, not even when my children had nothing to eat. He says to his sons, 'Now I am old. Let me enjoy myself, Charon take whom he will.' The worst of it is that when there is a fight between Kostandí and his brothers, the old man always takes their side. For instance, there's the family lime kiln down the road; the other brothers are working it and earning money. Kostandí can't work there because he doesn't speak to them— they have been fighting since they were small boys. But if Barba Kharíli were a good father, he would say to the other two, 'Come, agree to work together. The kiln belongs to us all.' But he is an egoist," she concluded.

After lunch I would carry off a rag rug into the church and spread it out on the clerestory floor. Here in the half-light under the little domes I would sleep in the cool till well into the afternoon. Then it was an easier climb to the fortress where I worked till sundown, when Kostandí would have returned, with one or two of the children already bedded down on the balcony over the courtyard. Panayiota, reserved but good-humoured, set our food before us and nothing would be repeated of what she had talked about during the day.

One night he said, "Andrea, I want you to write to America for me. I am heavy in the brain and don't know letters. I have a cousin who lives in Ouasigton Di Si and has a big restaurant. He is rich, the *keratá*; last summer when he came back I went to Athens and met him; in his hotel room he had a cupboard full of suits hanging up and he never even said to me, 'Here, take a suit.'" Afterwards he came to Mistra and promised to help me in my work."

At this point I finally asked, "What work do you do?"

"*Magazí*," he replied, which is the word for restaurant, wine-shop, or coffee-house. "I used to have the other place down at Kryovrýssi. I did better than Kleoméni does now."

"What other place at Kryovrýssi?"

"It isn't any longer," replied Kostandí. "Anyway, this cousin of mine said he would help me, and he hasn't done anything about it for a whole year now. I want you to write him."

Panayiota took away our plates, murmuring, "A pity for the trouble!"

"What do you know about it?" said Kostandi sternly. "He said he would help me, didn't he?"

I got some paper and sat down to paraphrase Kostandí's blunt statements into long, discursive sentences describing, I thought admirably, the plight of a poor European too proud to ask for help.

Kostandí then said, "Now read me what you have written," and after I had translated my Americanisms back into Greek: "That's not what I said, however. Do it over again. Say this: 'Dear cousin, You told me you had enough money in America to give some to me for a *magazí*, to feed my children. Since you were here I spent three million drachmae on a mule to earn money with. The mule died. Seven years I have been fighting Communists and now poverty and hunger have reduced me to half a man. God grant you health.' So, Andrea, have you finished? Tomorrow I take it to the post office in Sparta."

ONE DAY WHILE I was working on the broiling hillside a woman with two boys climbed up the path. "Does one go this way to the castle?" she asked with a smile, and I saw inside the black shroud of her head cloth the face of a young widow waiting for old age. "Since one travels, it is a good thing for children to see these places."

"You're not from here?"

"No. We have come from Messenia," she replied. All three of them were barefoot. "We are from Meligalá, but there is nothing left of it. My husband was killed in the massacre in '44. When the ELAS troops came in, they shot all the men and threw their bodies into a great pit, though some were still alive, and they buried them all at once. Then they set fire to the village. My son here was inside when the house fell down on him. Argýri, show the Kyrios your foot."

One of the boys stuck out his leg; shin and ankle looked as if they had been shrunk by some chemical, and the foot, twisted and blackened, only had two toes. "I was stuck under a timber for eight hours," he said proudly.

"You have no possessions in Meligalá," I asked; "no land or olive trees?"

"My husband was a Frankish tailor," she explained, using a country word meaning a maker of European clothes. "He had only what he earned, which was little since he was twenty-three when he was killed. He left us nothing. Now we travel from place to place—I and my son and this boy whose family was killed also—asking here and there for bread and olive oil."

I offered her a ten-thousand-drachmae note, enough for a meal. She took it and said, "The Panagia grant your heart's desire."

On my way down to Ay Yanni one of the neighbours greeted me from her top step, "So Andrea, you saw the woman from Messenia?"

"Why yes. Did you?"

"Oh, she told us you gave her ten thousand."

"Where do such people sleep?"

"No one in Mistra would let an evil-fated soul sleep out at night!" exclaimed Kyrá Photiní with a laugh. "Our village itself is full of widows and orphans. Greeks learned to be kind to each other while the Turks were here, and it is natural to give hospitality."

Panayiota had seen the woman too. She told me how the Communist bands had besieged the Security Battalions in the village of Meligalá in November, 1944, while the Germans were withdrawing. The village surrendered on terms, and the Communists entered and massacred the inhabitants. "As for what happened in Mistra at that same time—!" she exclaimed. And that day and many days after I took long over my lunch while she sat on the dark floor with her arms clasped round her knees, rocking back and forth, talking in her quick, high, urgent voice, and like a pedlar with his wares around him, spread out for me the story of her life in the southern Peloponnese during the last ten years.

"*Ach*, Andrea, if you knew what I have suffered from this family!" she said again, but without a trace of rancour, then screamed at her eldest son, "Get out of here, you *vláka!*" and slapped him on the ear as he dashed past. His yells resounded in the courtyard. "Eh, he's a coward like his uncle Leonídha, Kotso's eldest brother," she went on. "He's forty-five and still lives at home with his mother and father, and they call him the Monk because he has never married. At least he does no harm, unlike the others who were born to trouble. There's Spyro who had to go off and join ELAS—the beginning of it all. It's true, when the Occupation started, EAM and ELAS were organization anyone could join to keep on fighting the Germans and Italians after they defeated us. Kostandí would have joined it too when he came back from Albania in '41, except that his brother Spyro was in it already. Oh, those two. . . . Last winter Kotso bought a mule, Spyro borrowed it, the mule died; each said it was the other's fault, and so it started all over again, *pó-popo-po*! Anyway, Spyro soon learned the Communist Party was getting control of EAM and ELAS; so he left them, but they never forgave him for deserting and swore vengeance against all his family. One day an ELAS man from the next village lay in wait for his brother, Pandelí, as he went out to sow his fields, and shot him. That was in '43. Pandelí was the only brother Kotso really loved. So Kotso joined the Battalions and has been getting his revenge on the Communists ever since."

"Was Kostandí with Pavlakos?" I hazarded.

"So you know about Pavlakos?" Panayiota's eyes narrowed slightly. "No, Kostandí was never with him."

"Oh? I thought Pavlakos was against the Communists."

"He was against anyone who wasn't Pavlakos," replied Panayiota. "To him it made no difference whether you were Communist or Nationalist if you happened to have goats or a barrel of olives"—and she drew her fingers swiftly across her throat. "Pavlakos tried to make Lakonia a country of his own. Two years ago Kostandí went out one day to kill him, but he had already gone. There wasn't room here for the two of them."

From the other side of the wall came the sound of her son's voice whining, "Manoula, I want some bread."

"Come and get it, then."

The little boy appeared, glancing at her and at me from under his eyebrows, snatched a piece of bread from the table and went out faster than he came in.

"*Vláka!*" she called after him. "So there Kotso was—as I say—from that time on his life was made. Over and over again the Security Battalions have been dissolved and reorganized under different names, but my husband is still *kapetánios* of Mistra. Since he was a baby he has never been peaceful. The old man used to break his head every day; that's how he grew up."

"What did he do in the Battalions?" I asked.

"He lived at night," said Panayiota. "ELAS set ambushes for him all over the country, but he always escaped them. Once he came into my village—Levétsova, near the sea—to find out who belonged there to EAM and ELAS. He saw me then the first time. When he next came back to raid the houses of the ELAS families, he kidnapped me. The Germans had just killed my father, and I had no brothers. . . . Eh, why make excuses? I longed for him! He took me away and we lived together in a cave on Parnon, so, without crowns," she said, referring to the double crown held over the heads of a man and woman in the Eastern marriage service. "They crowned us properly long afterwards, but it was living like that in the beginning which has been the cause of all my troubles. He brought me back here, but his family didn't want me. From then on he was away all the time; the most important thing for him was to avenge his brother Pandelí's death. I had to live with the consequences, what else can a woman do? Once he led the Germans to a big ELAS hide-out up in the mountains, but he didn't know how strong they were. There was a battle. The Germans were driven off, but Kostandí stayed fighting to the last, and was captured. As soon as the news reached here I set off with blankets and food on my back. For a week I walked through those mountains over there until I found the ELAS camp. I told them I was the wife of Kostandí, and if he was still alive I wanted him to have these things. They laughed at me but let me pass.

They took me to the place where they kept their prisoners. 'There he is,' they said. 'You can give him anything you want, since he's going to die.' At first I didn't recognize him; he had a wound in the head, and the blood had dried all over his hair and face. As soon as he saw me with the bundle on my back, he burst out laughing and I knew him. 'It's lucky I married you!' he shouted. They drove me right out again, though, and I had to find my way back across the mountains, thinking all the time that by now he was probably dead. When I got back here, Barba Kharíli said, 'Why do you weep so much, since he's dead, the *keratá!*'

"We didn't know it for a long while, but the Germans came back a second time, hundreds of them; during the battle the Communists began to shoot their prisoners, but Kotso had stronger hands than the man who tried to kill him. A German gave him a gun, and between them he and the Germans killed every last Communist in the camp. All the time I was sitting in this house, wondering what would become of me, a widow. One day the rest of the family all went out, and in walked the other brother, Akhilléas—the little shrivelled-up one—and he put his arm round me and said, 'My doll, why are you so unhappy? Resign yourself. He's dead.' That moment I saw Kostandí standing in the doorway with a stick in his hand. He broke it against his brother's shoulders as he was getting out. Kotso shouted after him, 'I'll be waiting when you come again.' Nobody saw Akhilléas in Mistra for the next ten months! However, Kostandí was hardly home before he was off once more. The others would come for him in the middle of the night to get their guns"—I glanced at the row of fire-arms and greatcoats hanging on the wall—"and days would pass, sometimes weeks. Finally my time drew close, and Kotso brought my younger sister from Levétsova to be with me, since he had to be away when the baby came. No sooner was he gone than little Akhilléas tried to get my sister to sleep with him. He used to follow her out into the fields, and the news of it got around; so Kostandí heard before he even got back; and then they met, the two of them, in the main street of Sparta. People still say they have never seen such a fight; the little one is wicked. Kotso almost killed him, though. Akhilléas got away and ran back to Mistra. He got his gun and lay in wait at Kryovrýssi, behind the big tower, where he would be able to see Kostandí coming up the road. Little God of mine, I shall never forget that day! I sat in here with the new-born baby in my arms, listening to the shots. I could tell where they came from, then I knew they were both coming closer; that meant Kotso was driving his brother back. The noise grew so loud I thought I would die. The rest of the family were all hiding, and even the neighbours came into the church here.

"My husband is dangerous when he gets angry; he will not harm a soul, but if someone harms him, not the Panagia herself can help that person. . . . Then I heard them shooting in the alley under this building. I thought Kostandí would defend himself in here, but no, he drove his brother into the ruins, up on to the open slope where there are no more walls, just under the castle. And then from this window I saw their father climbing on to the tower you can just see from here, and there he stood with that white beard of his, roaring at the top of his voice, 'Kill him! Kill him!' God only knows which of his sons he wanted to kill the other. . . . At last there was no more sound. After a few minutes Kostandí arrived in the courtyard. I heard his step and ran out with the baby to show him his own son. I said, 'Eh, Kotso, did you kill him?' because I saw his clothes, his hands, his whole body covered with blood, but he only laughed. 'Him? No. He got away through the upper gate. He'll be half-way across Taygetos by now. Why do you look at me like that? This morning I killed sixteen men near Pend' Alónia. Now give me my baby and take my clothes and wash them.'"

"And Akhilléas? What happened to him?" I said. "I see him quite often around here, although we haven't yet spoken."

"Oh, he knew what was best for him. He stayed away in Patras or Aigion or somewhere for a couple of years. What he needs is a woman all day and all night, but Kotso doesn't take him seriously any longer."

"After that, did Kostandí stay here?" I asked.

"He stayed here," replied Panayiota, "because ELAS captured Sparta and drove the Security Battalions back to Mistra. By then the Germans had left, and there were only six hundred of the Battalions against six thousand ELAS. Everyone from the village took refuge here in Ay Yanni or else up in the castle. ELAS was encamped in the plain all round the bottom of the hill. The battle lasted thirty-six hours. We had seven machine-guns: two in the castle, three on the ramparts round the big palace half-way up the hill and two more down here. Kostandí went up and down, up and down the hill, all the time, from one post to the next. He never stopped. His friends were shot one after the other at the guns; Kotso had to take the place of each one of them as they died, till he could get someone else. Then he would go up again to see what was happening in the castle. Wherever he went he was in full view of the ELAS positions as they advanced. Once he came to see how I was. I said to him, 'Are you mad? Don't you know it's you they're after? Take cover, for the Christ!' But he ran out into the gunfire and climbed on to that tower and waved his arms and shouted to the ELAS, 'Try if you can destroy me, you never will!' Our men knew it was no good surrendering; we had already heard that the ELAS had captured Meligalá. Finally after three days there was no more ammunition, but when the ELAS began to come in through the gates, Kotso went out with his bayonet. I don't know how many he killed. But they got him. They shot any number of people, but him they kept for the last. They took him away to the prison in Sparta, then a week later the British came and disarmed ELAS and took over the prisons themselves. Kostandí was kept for a month in a camp near Yítheion. They were going to try him as a traitor because the Security Battalions collaborated with the Germans. But in December when they found themselves attacked by ELAS in Athens, they needed their prisoners; they were fools not to see it from the first; but the way they acted all through the Occupation and after—supplying arms to ELAS and up in the north to EDES also, and finally

fighting ELAS with the help of the people they had been keeping imprisoned—all they did was to make enemies of everyone.
The British like to keep people fighting each other so that no
one else can grow strong. Now they have left Greece, but I tell
you frankly, Kyr Andrea, it's difficult for us Greeks to understand
what the Americans are up to either."

"Then Kostandí came home?"

"He came home, but he never stays home," said Panayiota. "He
has been much busier since 1944—till last year, that is, when the
ninth division of the national army came into the Morea."

"It was they who finally put down the guerrillas?"

"Is that what you read in the papers?" asked Panayiota, and she
told me no more. I could see, however, that since the end of the
guerrilla war a year ago, Kostandí was finding inactivity a burden.

One night he showed me photographs, pictures of Marshal
Papagos on a recent visit to Sparta shaking the hand of Barba
Kharíli, and of himself looking much younger as a soldier in
uniform.

"When did you serve?" I asked.

"Several times. Two years ago was the last."

"But you were a civilian when I was here two years ago."

"Oh, I put away the uniform," he said. "They called me up and
I went to the camp at Nauplia, but I soon had enough of it. Why
should anyone give orders to me?"

"So what did you do?"

"I deserted."

"But what did the army do about it?"

"What would the army do about it?"

"But if you were a deserter!" I exclaimed.

He laughed. "Do you think anyone would come after me? The
gendarmes in Sparta, do you think? *Bá.* Nobody is enthusiastic
about coming after me as long as I have this"—and with his most
humorous expression he clapped one palm over the revolver he
always carried on his hip.

"So when I was here in 1948—"

"I was busy," he said coolly. "Much busier than sitting in Nauplia, polishing buttons and obeying orders from young lieutenants. My job is in Mistra and others do well to leave me alone."

"But now there are no more Andartes in the Morea, how do you occupy your time?" I made bold to ask.

"With different things," he replied. "Two months ago I earned two million driving a truck. I work sometimes at the lime-kiln, though at the moment I till the ground."

After that he sometimes took me with him to a tiny terrace outside the old city walls near the communal spring, where there were several plots measuring six feet square; while he planted his vegetables I would hand him the hoe or the trowel, and he showed me how to divert the water into the irrigation channel; or we would climb the poplar trees to pull off leaves for his goat. At that hour he had the Greek's urge to do something in company, and he would make an outing of it even if we only gathered figs to eat ourselves, or went down to Kryovrýssi for a glass of wine. He was at his best after three or four glasses, knowing just how to make Kleoméni uncomfortable as he bustled out to greet a party of foreigners with his napkin over his arm. We would support each other home up the dark, cobbled pathway through the ruins, singing. Once he began to shoot burning glances at Panayiota while she was preparing our supper. "*Ach, ach, ach,*" he muttered; "only the saints know what I feel like at this moment. May the Panagia save me, I can stand it no longer, I'll go into Sparta! There in a certain street . . ." He rolled his eyes and ran his tongue over his lips. Then his face straightened. He put one arm round Panayiota and looking at me, said, "I don't go to other women, because I have a good wife, you understand."

As THE WEEKS went by he and I spent more and more time together. Saturday was market day in Sparta, and once the arthritis in his legs was so bad that, riding in to buy food for the household, he asked me to come with him to a doctor. "An old army doctor," he said. "I knew him in the Battalions. . . . You've heard tell of the Battalions? Well, he's a good man."

We walked up to a door on which the doctor's name was inscribed on a brass plaque. There were no letters or titles after his name, only the words: STUDIED IN PARIS. We climbed to an upper floor and Kostandí knocked on a door that rattled unsteadily.

"Forward march!" wheezed a voice from within.

The two of us entered a dirty little office with piles of periodicals on the floor and ink-stained newspapers all over the desk, behind which a heavy old man rose to his feet, gasping huskily, "Good fortune to Kotso and his companion!"

"This is an American," said Kostandí.

"American? Ah ha! Well, well, please be seated. I beg you first of all to tell me what is going to happen in Korea. And what is your opinion of Communist China? We shall drop the bomb on Peking, eh? Ha ha ha ha."

Kostandí said, "Andrea doesn't know about such things; he's an archaeologist.

"Archaeologist!" the doctor exclaimed. "Why, my heart opens to welcome an archaeologist. I in my youth—"

"Andrea has come with me today because my rheumatism is worse, Kyrie Doctor."

"Ah ha-a-a, so? It's worse, you say? Well! Patience is what I counsel; God will put His little hand into the affair. However"— he sat forward and made a great stir among the litter of newspapers in front of him—"we shall do a series of injections."

"Will it do some good?" asked Kostandí quietly.

"I have absolute confidence," the old man replied. "In fact we shall begin now, today. This very moment I am writing out the prescription. . . . There we are!" he concluded, as if the series were already accomplished. "The medicine is to be found at the pharmacy. If you will come back—"

Kostandí interrupted him, "Andriko, go and get it. Here's some money. I stay with the doctor."

The medicine was French, I discovered at the pharmacy, and in the box were instructions as to dosage; each injection (costing the price of a week's food for Kostandí's family) guaranteed *soulagement* for at least four hours.

When I returned to the office, the doctor lumbered out of his chair, swept a mound of Athenian pulp magazines off the desk with his elbow and began to prepare the syringe.

"Amán!" said Kostandí. "I've never had an injection. Christ and Panagia, are you going to stick that into me, Kyrie Doctor?"

The old man sneezed, blew his nose and wiped the syringe carefully with his handkerchief. Then he took hold of Kostandí's forearm and plunged the needle into his biceps. I jumped up in time to catch him before he fell off the chair, nearly fainting.

"I'm dying," he murmured as the doctor drew the needle out.

"There we are. You can come back whenever you like for the next one. I assure you, this time you'll notice an improvement."

"What do I owe you?" asked Kostandí, breathing heavily.

"O-oh, you can give me twenty thousand—the price of a melon!" the old man exclaimed, beaming at the comparison. "Today is market; so I shall think of Kotso and his companion when I eat my lunch."

I went with Kostandí on other days when he tried in vain to sell his pig in Sparta or to get money back from people to whom at one time or another he had lent with his usual carelessness. He behaved shyly with his debtors, as if asking for money, even one's own, were something indecent. When I suggested he make his intention plainer, he would only say, "So-and-so and I served together once," and if I reminded him of his children's need he would reply, "How do I know if So-and-so is not poorer than I am? What is given should be given willingly. What would people think of me if I wanted something back from them?" I thought of the blood he wanted back and said to him outright, "Does it matter to you how many widows and orphans you make?" But he made no reply and his face was expressionless.

I was with him too when he sat with cronies (to whom I was never introduced) in the coffee-houses of Sparta; they had served with him also and for all I knew had nowadays as little occupation. I took no part in their conversation, carried on in an undertone, so that I would have to listen carefully while looking casually in another direction. They talked of the past and of people whose names I had never heard. One of these had died recently in his village, and Kostandí said, "He was really hard. Do you remember the way he used to take out a prisoner and tie him by the legs to the back of his jeep and then drive full speed round town? One day when he heard I had been killed, he hung eighty." Sometimes they made veiled references to preparations of some sort, and I learned that once a week they forgathered for rifle practice. The Athenian papers kept them in touch with the outside world, particularly with the news in Asia, to which Kostandí voiced their general reaction with the brief words, "Things are tightening. We shall have war by the end of the month." He said the same thing day after day with a confidence that amounted to desire. And when they talked of politics in other countries it was always in terms of a Greek civil war, as when, hearing of the proposed abdication of the King of Belgium, "In Vélgio too things are tightening; this time the Communists have won against the Nationalists."

One night over supper he told me how far the American forces had been driven back that week by the North Koreans and Chinese. I thought I had heard the end of it when Panayiota went to spread our blankets on the loggia, but after we lay down—they and the children slept on a rug in one corner while my bedding was a few yards distant next to the wall of the church—he went on to say that Americans did not know how to fight in a country like Korea. "What do they know about guerrilla warfare? We Greeks could finish off the Chinese in half the time. Look how the Americans are running away now, just like the British ran out of Greece in '41."

I was thankful to be able to lie there in the dark without answering.

"Are you asleep, Andrea?"

He called again, "Hey, ragamuffin, I know you're pretending to be asleep."

I continued to pretend, and later heard him say to Panayiota, "Andriko has taken offence because I said the Americans don't know how to fight."

Next morning we breakfasted together in the sun. Kostandí gave me a cigarette and said quietly, "You went to sleep early last night?"

"Oh, yes," I said. "Why?" It amused me to see him look so boyish with his brows meeting in a slight frown of anxiety.

"Today, you know, is the Feast of Ayios Pandeleímon; they're celebrating in Paliánitsa, do we go?"

Panayiota came out on to the balcony and said, smiling, "Do I go too?"

"No," said he, "you stay in the house."

We could already hear voices and footsteps coming through the ruins; Paliánitsa was a hamlet just across the gully.

I followed Kostandí into the courtyard, then ran back to get my hat. Panayiota was weeping in a corner of the dark room.

Catching up with Kostandí in the lane, I said, "Panayiota's crying."

"Eh, so," he grunted.

"She's sad not to come."

He retorted with a laugh, "God forbid that we should take orders from women!"

We joined a line of men walking up the path on the farther hillside, dotted here and there with houses among the olive trees. I went on ahead with the middle-aged brother, Leonídha, the quiet one of the family, while Kostandí fell back, talking in the low growl he reserved for one particular subject. I heard him say, "He came back from Makronisos three days ago. We've told him never to stir outside his own garden. We don't want an episode."

Numbers of people from Mistra, Paliánitsa and other villages stood about outside the white-plastered church where the liturgy for Saint Pandeleímon's Day had already begun. I went with Kostandí, Leonídha, and two languid, vain young farmers with thin, black moustaches into the church to light candles and kiss the icons. A few people remained through the whole service which a priest chanted inside the gimcrack sanctuary; the five of us, who formed an inseparable group for the day, crossed ourselves three times and went out again into the open. Almost everyone who had gathered in Paliánitsa that day did the same and no more; the Greek word for worship also means a bow or a paying of respects.

Down the hill I could hear the rich note of a clarinet, and said excitedly to Kostandí, "Are they beginning to dance now?"

"They are practising. It is not done to play instruments or dance during the Liturgy."

At nine o'clock a wild burst of music from fiddle, clarinet, and drum announced the Mass was over. We followed the musicians to a little wineshop, where they seated themselves in the half-shade of a canopy of calamus reeds plaited with fir branches, and the man with the drum began a song in a ponderous, mournful rhythm about a girl who did what no Greek woman should ever do in public, so that her family might kill her and not marry her to the man she did not love. Kostandí and the others took up a verse of it here and there:

Have you heard what has happened, you villages of Sparta?
They have killed Pephronía, the wicked woman with the
    European dress.

There in the square of Sparta, near to the coffee-house
They saw her, evil Pephronía, smoking a nargilé.

O sing for all the poppies with laughing and with joy
And for guileful Pephronía with the two wounds in her side.

Mistra, the castle and the northwest walls of the upper town

When they brought her through the market place,
Young and old wept for her long, fair hair:

Poor burning Pephronía, a pity for your body;
You have brought shame on Sparta, shame on all your race.

—But I never dared to hope you'd kill me, Vangeli my brother
And so not give me to be Petropoulaki's wife.

The sun mounted across the sky; there was one song after
another, and we kept the musicians going with glasses of ouzo
and ten-thousand notes clapped on to their steaming foreheads.
When it was our turn to dance the others sent us trays of wineglasses from their tables. We drank them quickly not to miss the
beat while we moved on, hands joined in an open circle; three

Acrocorinth, Venetian artillery platform

steps forward while on the fourth whoever was in front leaped into the air or whirled on one foot and struck the ground with the palm of his hand, four more steps forward and two steps back, then forward again, round and round that little space of beaten earth while the low canopy slowly reeled above our heads and the shadows of near-by ilex trees revolved around their trunks and slanted farther and farther down the hillside. At the front of the line I pulled and hung on to the end of the handkerchief which Kostandí held in his steely grip, singing huskily and gazing at me out of his half-closed, chestnut-coloured eyes with a look of exhaustion and sublimity. At some time during the day the five of us went into the wineshop and leant our hot backs against the chilly wall; mules arrived laden with barrels of beer from Sparta and we called for another meal, our heads swimming from the music booming and rippling outside the door. Across the room a large company of people dressed in town clothes were eating and talking noisily together, and in their midst I recognized Spyro with his young wife.

I looked at Kostandí sitting beside me. There was a strong resemblance between them—the same features, the same colouring—yet everything that was straight and strong in Kostandí produced in Spyro's face an effect of softness, with one side of his mouth, one eyebrow, one shoulder ever so slightly higher than the other.

"Eh, Kotso, that's your brother, isn't it?" said I. "One can tell it's the same family." Kostandí did not answer, and so I said again, "He certainly resembles you."

Kostandí growled, "And what if he does resemble me?"

Outside, the musicians stopped playing. Kostandí stood up and at the same moment Spyro rose from his table. There was a sudden hush in the room as both brothers walked towards the door. Then all at once some people from outside burst into the shop with two of the musicians, waving their instuments over their heads, shouting for food and drink; no one noticed which of the brothers got out of the room first. Everyone began talking loudly once more.

Not many days after, I offered to fill Panayiota's water-pots at the spring. Kostandí was home too that day; so he came with me to the gully where people were sitting around the fountain in the shade of the big plane trees that grow to a great height in watery places. I filled our pot and lifted it on to my shoulder. Kostandí walked beside me while I staggered up the hill. This labour was beneath him, and back at the spring they probably thought me a fool, but I was flattered that Kostandí made no offer to carry it himself; this, I thought, is what it is to be accepted in a place. Then we went back a second time. Spyro was there, sitting on the edge of the stone basin, not two inches away from my elbow while I leaned over and set the jug under the curving jet of water; it filled silently while the minutes went by. Kostandí sat a little distance off and I listened to the others talking now to him, now to Spyro, and with equal friendliness, taking great care not to address them both together. In the hamlet of Ay Dimitri a civil war turned on the mutual hatred of two brothers reclining in the still, green light under the plane trees.

CHAPTER 9

Taygetos—
The Thirsting Noon

I READ IN THE PAPERS that summer of plans for opening up the country to foreign travel; new hotels were to be built and new roads to remote places like the Monastery of Hosios Loukás and the Temple of Apollo at Bassae in Arkadia, which one could only reach after long hours of tortuous mountain paths. There were new postage stamps with the motto "Reconstruction," showing cogs of machinery and the map of Greece with electric light bulbs to mark the provincial towns. Posters appeared on the public buildings of Sparta, showing mules, grain sacks, trucks, tools and farm implements from America greeted by the smiling faces of Greek peasants and factory workers.

I climbed Taygetos at last, finding the high villages re-inhabited, and spent a week in a sheepfold half-way up the mountain, climbing fifteen or eighteen hours a day alone. Here and there along the highest ridges I came on rude fortifications, low walls of stone wrenched out of the mountain-top, relics of the guerrillas' defense against expeditions led by men like Kostandí the previous year, and at the bottom of one ravine I saw a skeleton on a bank of snow. These were days of solitude and mountain silence broken only by the cawing of small, grey rooks under the limestone

176

precipices, days of wind, sun, cloudbursts and glimpses of the
Peloponnese with all its capes and islands spread out seven thousand feet below me. Once I stayed on the summit to watch the
sun set across Messenia, while the chock-a-block mountains of
the Mani merged rapidly into the darkness, and it took five hours
to get down to the sheepfolds where the shepherds lay wrapped
in their goat's-hair capes, but the fire was still burning and they
had left me a cauldron of milk and some bread. We ate the same
thing each morning, watching the shadow of the earth's eastern
rim descending the ridge like a curtain as the sun rose.

The first evening back at Mistra I left Kostandí at his hoeing,
and going up the path towards the old gateway passed under the
lime-pit belonging to his brothers. Spyro stood above it, feet wide
apart, with his naked back to the warm, russet walls, his oddly
slanting mouth bared over his teeth and his hot, red shoulders
and long muscles shaking in his arms as he raised both hands
grasping the crowbar high over his head and drove it crashing into
the stone. He did not glance in my direction; though Kostandí
was nowhere near, it was out of the question that he and I should
address a word to the other. Akhilléas too knew better than to
arouse Kostandí's wrath by speaking to me. He was living now
with a girl whom I saw one day singing in the ravine, and someone said, "That's Akhilléas' girl. Always she goes about like that,
singing; nothing matters to her." She had no family except for
an old aunt, who would urge Kostandí in a low, worried voice to
force Akhilléas to marry her. But he and his brother were not on
speaking terms; clearly, since the girl had no menfolk, the situa-
tion would remain the same.

In Mistra nothing ever seemed to happen to upset the pre-
carious and perilous balance of these people's relationship to
one another. Among our neighbours was a family whose father,
a quiet man whom I only saw once, worked in Tripolis and came
home for a few days every two months. The mother was well built
and had a laughing eye. One Sunday Kostandí and I and several
others stood in the clerestory of Ay Yanni, looking down on the

service. The woman was leaning with her elbows on the marble balustrade, while behind her three young farmers lounged against the wall; she turned her head slightly round and swiftly lifted the back of her skirt. Later Kostandí told me, "There are women who give themselves to any man who wants them. Take Merópi; her husband is stupid, he suspects nothing, so no one is going to tell him, unless it's some other woman with a grudge against her. . . . A woman who puts horns on her husband wants butchering on the spot, don't you agree?" Since this was the general opinion, no one would blame her husband if he killed her, though they themselves might take advantage of his absence.

Then there were the women who had lost their husbands during the battle of Mistra or before it, whose lot would never change, old or young. Kostandí's sister-in-law was very pretty and had a seven-year-old son called Pandelí. "We called him after his father," she said to me one day, "but it was an evil-fated name, for he was killed a week after the christening." Next to her lived a pleasant-tempered, older woman whose eldest son came back from the army on a week's leave. The neighbours came to greet him the night he returned. "With good fortune receive him," they said to her, and she offered them wine and food, and soon everyone was dancing. Once I called to her as we passed, "Won't you lead us?" and she answered with a laugh, "It's not done for a widow."

One morning I came on Kyrá Photiní sitting by one of the parapets on the hillside, with a distaff under one elbow, spinning thread out of a mass of wool. She wiped her eyes and looked out over the plain, saying, "My husband manned a machine-gun here. With Kostandí he led the defense when ELAS besieged us. He was the bravest man in all the Battalions. He was like Kotso. Nobody had more honour. He always had compassion on travellers and poor people like that beggar-woman from Meligalá. He used to come to me and say, 'I've just seen some poor wretch from England or France or Germany who has come all this way to see our antiquities and is far from his home and his own people. We must take him in.' Things that he and Kotso did together here during the battle! They had so many people to defend they had no time to be afraid. ELAS knew him well; he had been leading expeditions against them for two years. It was him they wanted, but he was killed the second day of the battle. For seven days after the ELAS troops came in I hid in the cellars and cisterns of the ruined buildings where I could hear them tramping about overhead, saying, 'Where is she, the *poutána*! Her man is dead, let us at least get her.' At the end of the week when the British arrived in Sparta I found my husband's blood here soaked into the earth. I piled these stones on the place where he died, so people should not walk on it."

That evening in the ravine I mentioned to Kostandí that I had met old Photiní among the ruins.

"Crying?"

"I think so."

"She sits up there day after day," he said. "Give me the hoe, Andriko. Now go to the spring and send the water down to me, I'm ready."

One morning—it was the Feast of the Assumption—I was waiting in the village square for an early bus to Sparta among the usual crowd of villagers sitting in the open windows of the wineshops and round the close-packed tables; today they were listening to a radio address by General Plastiras from the island of Tenos. Still Premier after four months, he was taking part in the annual pilgrimage to the miracle-working icon of the Panagia. In the square I could hear water gurgling out of the lead pipe between the roots of the plane trees while the grave, sonorous voice of the old politician carried to us clearly through the warm morning air. He was taking the occasion of the feast day to call for national unity and an end to civil strife, telling how many Greeks, men and women, had been let out of the political prisons during his term of office, and appealed to the rest of the population to accept them in their midst once more as brothers. "My Government," he was saying, "has endeavoured to follow Christ's injunction to love our neighbour—" During the moment's quiet after the radio was switched off I heard again the drip of water from the pipe and glanced round me at the dark and hungry faces of the farmers seated on the wooden chairs, smoke floating upward from the cigarettes they held between lips drawn rigid with contempt.

Then the bus drove into the square and I spent all day in the plain north of Sparta, where the main street ends in a broad, gravelly space and a dirt-track winds up to a rise of ground just a few feet above the level of the surrounding treetops. Under a few olives and thin-needled pines growing over the hill were the foundations of a wall that once enclosed a temple; while Sparta was at the height of her power Thucydides wrote, "If some day Lacedaemon were devastated and there remained only its sanctuaries and the foundations of its public buildings, a distant posterity would have difficulty believing its might could ever have equalled its renown." Farther out were traces of a vast perimeter of walls built against the rebellious cities of Greece in the third and second centuries before Christ. But when the Romans destroyed all fortresses within the empire, these walls were abandoned and it was not till centuries later when the barbarians came that, far and wide, cities which had long since shrunk to villages had to defend themselves alone. From that period dates the remnant of a rude retaining wall along the south side of the hill, of column drums and massive marble blocks of stylobate and architrave all plundered from ancient buildings and thrown together with every mark of haste, bricks and tiles and boulders filling up the interstices, in which may be read the history of a whole world going to its ruin. Late that afternoon I was standing on top of the wall, looking out across the cloud of grey leaves stretching over the plain like floodwater to the foot of Taygetos and distant, minute Mistra, and I saw through the light foliage four men walking close together very slowly between the trees. It was easy to imagine a lonely farmhouse somewhere in the silence of the plain, and perhaps these men were heading for it; they would draw close, disperse and then converge upon it; a shot might echo in the distance. . . . The late afternoon held a moment's terror. Then they were gone. Walking home, not by the road from Sparta but straight across the chessboard level of the plain, I kept looking to the right and left down the long, barred shadows of the olive trees.

It was dusk when I got back, Kostandí was irrigating his vegetables in the ravine. I asked if I could help. Crouching close to the earth, with his back to me, he replied, "There's nothing you need do here, Kyr Andrea." He was using again the plural forms and I connected his distant manner with the band of men I had seen moving with that slow, resolute tread like scouts setting off on a night patrol, but perhaps it was only because I was leaving next day and in Greece friends often become strangers before a departure.

"So you think you can cross Parnon?" said Panayiota in the morning while I was closing my rucksack. "What can I say, Andriko? It's not so steep as Taygetos, but once in you never find your way out."

I had chosen my route, however. The *Guide bleu* recommends to those interested in Byzantine and Frankish remains an excursion on muleback through the hills east of Sparta to Monemvasia, which can be reached by the end of the second day. After Taygetos I was confident I could find my way and trusted to my feet to carry me faster.

"You may need this," said Panayiota with a doubtful expression as she handed me the end of a bread loaf. "But come back here for the fair at the end of the month, eh?"

By eight-thirty I was already hungry and looking forward to the moment when I could take out my canteen—behind my back I could hear the water inside it gurgling reassuringly with every step. In the first village across the plain something prompted me to walk straight past the groups of people standing about in the rutted roadway, and I took long strides to show them I knew where I was going. But the road forked and I had to call to some women, "Which way to Khrýsapha?" hoping a confident tone would prevent them asking questions; it was so easy to waste time chatting in mountain villages. They waved me to the right, and I was just leaving the last houses when a voice called behind me, "Eh, you!" I paused to scratch my shin and continued with leisurely steps. My rucksack had excited suspicion and now they were coming after me. The voice called a second time, "Eh, you who are walking!"

There was nothing to do but turn and greet three men as they caught up with me and, before they had time to ask, state my nationality, occupation and purpose of travelling in this district, the well-worn words rolling smoothly off my tongue. Two of the men were soldiers, the third was a short man with a bulbous growth over one eyelid.

"Papers?" said he.

I brought them out. After perusing them carefully, the third man tilted back his head and looked at me from under his growth. "What if you're a Russian?"

"What if I am?" said I with a helpless smile. I brought out more papers, among which an elaborately worded letter stated that all civil and military assistance to a certain student of medieval fortifications would be appreciated by the American Academy in Athens.

"Excuse us," said the man with the growth, "but it happens we have been burned too close. You may go on."

Soon I looked back for my last sight of Taygetos—shadowy and majestic—and I wished myself back in a place I knew rather than in this hideous landscape of brown hills rolling like waves and terraces curving on every side with not a tree to be seen nor any trace of water in one shallow valley after another; these were the very hills I had watched being scorched the summer before last from the other side of Sparta. Some women on donkeys came riding through the black stalks.

I asked, "How far to Khrýsapha?"

"Ach óu," they called in strident voices, "you have a long road before you!" Their swaying, jolting figures vanished round a turn in the path.

Then I sat on a hot rock and drank a little water from my canteen, but the pack felt heavier as I shoved my elbows through the straps. I walked on, imagining guerrillas retreating over these low horizons where all covering foliage had been burned away. After three hours on a track meandering through the leafless hills, the existence of a big white village with church domes, open windows and seated figures in the cobbled street, seemed as unreal and inconsequential as an island in mid-ocean. Then I saw the familiar nationalist slogans in blue paint splashed across the walls and on every door the letter X with a crown above it. The inhabitants must have returned here only last year after the guerrillas were driven out of Parnon. In a few minutes I would be assailed with questions, and I must appear natural and careless, good-humoured in my answers, patient and not too clever; I must project, like an actor upon a too attentive audience, a type of innocent and respectful person anxious to go quietly about his business. Above all, I thought during the last moment before I stepped into a wineshop, if I wanted to make a rapid exit, I must not let them know I was hungry.

They were all inside, the village strong men, as if waiting for me to cross the threshold. There was the hush as always when I came in, then the grim surprise of fifteen strangers turning slowly in their chairs. Being a little weak from hunger, it was more of an exertion than usual to explain why I particularly wanted to see the Byzantine churches here or the Frankish castles farther on. Then having made my business a subject for whispered conversations, I waited until someone was summoned to take the American to every church in Khrýsapha. During the next two hours the glare of the alleyways alternated with the desolate chill inside narrow, malodorous churches with mud-coloured frescoes, where the guardian jangled his keys and, more patiently, stood behind the trays of candles of varying price inside each door. Under his furtive gaze I could not bring myself to buy a single one. The last church seen, the obligation still remained and I invited him to have some wine with me at the shop. More people had gathered there, waiting for me to come back. The guardian sat sullenly to one side, while I heard myself repeating for the third time that day words that seemed to belong in a dream from which one never awakes. I remembered not to ask for food or water, but waited to get out again into the wilderness where I could eat Panayiota's bread crust without people asking where I had got it or why, being a tourist, I was not better provisioned. Once their attention wandered inexplicably and I seized the chance to announce that I must be on my way. There was no objection.

Late that afternoon I passed below a solitary shepherd with a rifle under his arm. Then I was in a pine forest, where as my shadow lengthened before me along the tree-trunks in the cool air, I could at last allow myself to think of water and my mouthful of bread. Across the valley rose the high tower of a castle on a rock, pink in the soft evening light like a church tower in an English landscape; through the branches I saw the village of Zaraphóna, a little bunch of walls against the far mountainside. Walking fast, I could perhaps reach it before dark and then I could drink water until my throat became unglued, and in some house or shop get a meal and sleep through the night soundly. And then I realized that to come into a village in the heart of Parnon, on foot, at nightfall, unable to prove where I had come from, barely able to speak for hunger—I said something out loud there in the middle of the forest, to hear my own voice—I might have to talk all evening. I could not make the effort. I turned off the path and descended to a round plain where in the shadow of a dense ilex under the rising moon I devoured the last of my crust and took two gulps of water, leaving a little for the morning. Several times while the moon travelled through the silvery sky I sat up, thinking to hear the scratch of a boot against a stone, then lay back and tried to produce saliva in my mouth. Sometimes I slept, only to wake with a sensation of something twisting about inside me, wondering whether, if some shepherd came upon me, I ought to lie quite still or stand up immediately and greet him. Three times during the night I had to sip from the canteen, putting it down carefully lest it make a sound.

It was empty by morning; there was nobody in sight, so I let it fall with a clatter. Only half an hour away was the village on the hill with its wells or cisterns, with perhaps a shop where I could buy something to eat, or kitchens with small fires heating the morning coffee—and with its police. Where, they would ask, since I arrived so early in the morning, could I have spent the night? Then why did I choose to sleep out where any armed shepherd would have the right to shoot me? So the interrogation would begin; without food I could not face it. I started off through the rocks and bushes towards the castle directly south.

Less than a mile distant, it rose up over the plain with its scattered olive trees and the naked mountains all round it: an inhuman landscape in the fresh, clear light of six o'clock. I was slow to understand why I took a whole hour to reach it, climbing at last hand over hand up the jagged rocks that bristled with sharp bushes to the foot of the tower, eighty feet high on the clifftop.

I began to pace each sector of the curtain wall, and noted down the measurements. I made sketches of arches, parapets and niches, my mind working quite clearly; it was good to have something definite like this on which to concentrate, yet one thing was very simple: I must finish quickly; it was nine already and the sun was well up in the sky.

The map in my guide-book showed a distance of five miles from the castle to the next village. The road had a well-beaten surface that even sloped slightly downhill; I counted on two hours to carry me this next stage of my journey. Below the road I passed a group of shepherds around a well. Fortune always changes at the right moment, I thought as I scampered down the slope into their midst, holding out the light aluminium flask.

A woman filled it from a bucket. I drank it down, tasting nothing, hearing only the heavy bubbles rolling through the nozzle.
She filled it for me again; I drank it all, and again a third and a
fourth time. I could easily have drunk more, but remembered it
would be unwise. Filling it one last time, I climbed back to the
road. In a few minutes my legs were weak under the sun burning
on the wide and lifeless earth; I had to keep my head bowed and
my lids half-closed, seeing only my feet moving very slowly one
in front of the other in the dust. The way wound again and again
over the glimmering hillsides and I had been walking four hours
when I came to another well, looked down over the edge and to
my inexpressible relief saw my own head reflected in the round
little disk of sky. Then I tied the canteen to my belt and tied that
to one sleeve of my shirt, knotting the other to a towel. Leaning as far as possible over the well-head, I could still see my own
face, small and far away, moving on the untroubled surface. The
ground was warm underneath my body where I lay for the next
hour with the towel over my head. Finally I was hardly aware of
my actions as I got to my feet again, and when I reached the village in the middle of the afternoon it had taken me eight hours to
walk the five miles.

There was a wide square with shade along one side, tall houses
and a sweep of hills above. As I walked into a cool and airy *kapheneíon* where large windows framed the shimmering light, I
told the man behind the counter I had walked from Mistra and
would like now as many glasses of water as a tray could hold. Out
in the square I sank into a chair, put my feet up on another and
said carelessly to all the men who drew round me in a grinning
circle that I had walked from Sparta without eating or drinking
because I had been afraid of the police; they could think what
they liked of an American student who chose of his own free
will to live in such a manner. Then I asked where I could order
a meal.

"No need for you to do that," said a boy. "You can stay in my
house and we shall eat together." He had an easy smile.

"Perhaps I can wait till evening," said I, thinking that with thirst quenched by eight or ten glasses I could still go without food. Then I remembered I had come here to see the Frankish castle and set off alone to a towered hill an hour's walk away. After climbing through rocks and ruins to the top, I only had strength left to place my feet carefully so as not to fall. Late in the afternoon I met the young man back in the square and he took me round the village, telling how he had just returned from Epiros with a discharge from the army and pieces of a grenade in his right leg; he was waiting to go to America for an operation that would heal it. In the dusk he took me to see the earthworks recently dug in a prehistoric acropolis in the middle of the town; we talked with men who were on guard there still, and the well-roofed trenches were stacked with guns and ammunition.

"Do you see how the Hellenes fight?" he said, with a note of gay accusation.

"Evidently," I replied, "the *Khi* is vigilant throughout the district."

We went by such a circuitous route I thought I would lose consciousness, stopping at houses of friends and relatives, where he introduced me with a certain proprietary and scornful air, every time saying, "He's an American, I've been showing him how the Hellenes fight." I paid little attention to anything until someone said the Government had fallen that day.

"You heard old Plastiras on Tenos the day before yesterday, telling us to love our enemies? Those words have done for him," said the young man with a look of delight.

"And who is Premier now?" asked the women. "Is it good news? We don't know, being women."

"One government feeds off the people, the next one does the same," he replied. "But on the whole for Greece it is good news. It means now the Communists will remain in prison till they're dead, all of them."

One woman said, "But not all, surely. Some are less bad than others."

"All," repeated the boy almost in a whisper, with a delicate smile on his lips. "All. Let not a soul remain."

At his house I was not surprised to see the election poster I had first noticed at Kostandí's, of the Rightist triumvirate with their slogan about a fourth round in Greece.

The boy's mother brought us a dish of green weeds for our supper. In the morning I walked with weaving steps to the gendarmerie, took advantage of my nationality and requested a lift with the police chief in his jeep all the way down to a town on the Lakonian Gulf. Here at noon I caught the bus which goes every week day from Sparta to Monemvasia in four-and-a-half hours.

AT THE END of August the olive groves below Mistra were transformed into a vast barnyard of goats, sheep, lean cows, horses, mules and donkeys all braying, snorting or pawing up the dusty earth as far as the eye could see, with here and there odd little enclaves of bedding and pots and pans shaded by blankets tied into the branches overhead, where people slept on the ground with their families during the nights of the great summer fair. Across the road there sprang up that week a city without walls but with olive trunks for columns and leaves for ceiling: little booths and shops, restaurants and gaming tables, while up and down the stubble-carpeted corridors between them villagers from all the region of Sparta sauntered and haggled, drank and quarrelled and threw away their money. From morning till late into the night they thronged round the booths. Each installed under an olive tree were the merchants with their rugs and blankets, kitchenware and household icons, gipsies with ironmongery fresh off their anvils like new bread out of an oven, monks from Mount Athos selling wooden charms and lockets against the Evil Eye, taverners with their paraphernalia of heavy iron trays and spits, singers and musicians who played during the winter in the slums of Piraeus and Salonika, and gamesters amid their litter of prizes calling the light-hearted and the openhanded to forget daily fears and trust to fortune—a migrant flock wandering all summer with their mules, trucks and wagons through the district towns from Thrace to the southern capes of the Morea.

Intending to stop off in Mistra on my way to the castles of the Messenian coast, as I walked along the road towards the village, Kostandí hailed me over the heads of the crowd. He looked more gaunt than ten days before; he was limping with rheumatism and his eyes were bloodshot. While he led me up and down I told him about my trip through Parnon, but he paid little heed and looked round him all the time at the various gaming tables. Finally he said, "Go up to Ay Yanni, they'll be glad to see you. I have a job of work."

At six next day he took me with him to the fair ground. Through the long, hot morning we strolled about, looking at the wares and sometimes pausing at the gaming tables where there was always a tight knot of people watching eagerly. Whenever I made to go on he would stay me with a powerful grip on my forearm and I would remain, watching the back of his neck with his big jaws sticking out as he gazed with all the others at the green cloth covered with chips and numbers or at the whirling wheel with the little balls dancing up and down. I knew he had no money to spend, yet nothing could drag him away.

Toward noon the crowds began to thin and people lay down beside their booths eating on one elbow among the stubble stalks. Under a sheet of canvas stretched between four trees where we took refuge from the overpowering light, Kostandí whispered in my ear, "Those games, they're a crafty business, I'm in it too. At those wheels the man has a pedal underneath the table; he presses it with his foot and the thing stops where he wants it to, never at the number where somebody might win." He grinned with a sweet, misty expression in his tired eyes. "Most people don't know about such things. So I hang around, to watch how much they earn. I could expose them if I wanted to, couldn't I? At the end of the day they pay me."

That afternoon he and I were standing by one of the roulette tables when someone dashed up, waving a thick wad of money and crying out, "The evil-fated mule, I sold it for a million!"

Others patted him on the back and said, "Now you'll get rich, eh?"

"Shall I not!"—and he thwacked the table exultantly. He was a young man with most of his teeth gone, which gave him a soft and guiltless expression. His delight lasted for the first five minutes. He was the centre of attraction; everybody urged him on, and when they groaned over the sums that vanished one by one he turned round and grinned at them all with his pink, ravaged mouth, laughing, "*Bá*, I still have more." In ten minutes it was all over. His hands hanging limply, he walked off, staring straight in front of him like someone who has been hit on the head. The owner of the wheel was calling vigorously, "Who will come forth? One loses but the next man wins!" Kostandí gazed at him and their eyes met briefly. Late at night under a few kerosene lamps hung from the trees, someone took Kostandí off into the darkness. He said to me when he came back, "Not bad tonight. Seven hundred thousand. The stupidity of people who sell an animal; the money goes to their heads and so they run to the games, thinking they can make some more. *Ach*, the stupid country people!" he exclaimed softly, without scorn or compassion. "Tomorrow I'll buy a scarf for Panayiota, poor burning soul."

Early in the morning we slaughtered his pig in the courtyard, then carried the carcass down to sell at one of the restaurants. He asked four hundred thousand for it, but the restaurant-keeper told him the animal had been half-starved and only gave him two hundred thousand. Kostandi, cursing under his breath, said with a shamefaced look, "Andriko, don't tell Panayiota I only got two hundred thousand. We'll tell her I got three hundred, eh? She won't speak to me if she finds out. It's true the pig would have died of hunger anyway, I had nothing to feed it."

Again that night he waited at his accustomed place; the operator of the roulette wheel walked away with him to a distant tree where I saw their hands meet quickly. Kostandí shoved something into his pocket and stood with clenched fists while the other man waved his hands in the air. He was angry when he came back and for a long time would not speak. "They're losing," he finally said. "The colonel of police has been here all day long and everyone's on his guard, even the gendarmes."

"Why they?"

"They're in it too, what do you think! Why should a gendarme resist temptation! But now the chief has come down from Tripolis, so they must pretend to do their job. The lotteries have made nothing all day. All the man gave me was a hundred thousand, the *keratá!*"

Next day he was even more put out because his father had at last succeeded in selling an aged cow and walked away from Kostandí without paying a debt he had been owing him for the past three years.

I said, "But why didn't you ask him for it?"

"One doesn't ask one's father to pay back money."

He was vexed because last year he had won a cooking-pot and a tin icon, and this year he had nothing.

The last day of the fair the booths were demolished one by one, their counters and side-walls stacked together like stage props and thrown into the waiting trucks on top of everything else; these drove off, and heavily laden mules moved on to the main road. Here and there patches of flattened stubble round the trees showed it had been a fair ground, and during the day one heard again the cicadas singing in their branches. The last to go were the gaming tables and the lotteries, and even after sunset people were still standing round one little booth where one could pull strings with numbers whose total might correspond with any of the numbered articles within. Kostandí and I waited for an hour, but here too chance was elusive; the man behind the counter would add up the numbers before the customer had time to think, offer him a quick, regretful smile and shout out, "Who comes next, please? Step up."

Kostandí whispered, "He counts so fast no one can keep up with him. Naturally the total's not going to be any one of the numbers marked. But now and then the man will pick on some- one who—"

His words were interrupted. "Kyrie, Kyrie, why do you lag behind," the man was calling to him. "All this time you've been standing here. Do you still not dare to come forward and try your luck. For shame! Surely the Yerákovítes are bolder than that! Who will step up and prove the saying that of all the Lakonians the people of Mistra are the luckiest in games?"

"Let me try, then," said Kostandí gruffly. He threaded his fin- gers through the rings and gave a tug; up went five numbers.

"Ten, fifty-seven, sixty-two, nineteen, twenty-one—that makes one hundred and sixty-nine," the man called. "What have we with that number? Let me see . . . Unfortunately—but no, the Kyrios has won a glass pitcher, bravo! There you are, Kyrie, may good fortune always be with you. Who is next now?"

"About time!" Kostandí said when we got out of the crowd and found ourselves under the deserted trees. "I was almost think- ing I'd have to threaten him if he didn't let me win something. He and I, you see, have the understanding that sometimes he will show people his game is *endáxi*; so he chooses me when I happen to be near. For me he counts correctly, and now I have a pitcher to bring home to—" He paused, hearing a voice in the crowd behind us. Several people ran past us saying, "*Po-po-pó*, what happens now?" In three springy steps Kostandí was back at the booth. There, surrounded by four gendarmes, a man was arguing violently with the operator of the game.

"Tell me that number again!"

"Seventy-nine," said the man behind the counter very quietly.

"Lies!" shouted the other. "I know what my numbers were. Do you think I can't add? Eighty-two is the number of that fry- ing-pan. You counted wrong and thought I wouldn't notice. I can count as fast as you, and any one of these gentlemen here" (he indicated the gendarmes) "can tell you nineteen and twenty-three and seven and twenty-eight and five make eighty-two. Do you take me for a *vláka*? My father sent me to school to learn letters and numbers so that deceivers like you shouldn't laugh at me." He turned to the gendarmes and said, "You saw the numbers I pulled. Is not the sum eighty-two?"

The gendarmes shuffled around him without answering. "Why do you make such a commotion?" they said.

"Because I have proof this man has cheated me. You saw it with your own eyes."

"Such a commotion!" the gendarmes repeated. "Be quiet. The fair is over. Next summer you can take up your quarrel. Now leave it alone."

"Bravo!" cried the other. "When wrong is done we turn to the police to help us in our difficulty."

One of them hissed, "People will hear you."

"Aha," cried the man, "you admit I am in the right! Am I permitted to ask for what reason you try to defend this cheat here?"

"How do you know he's a cheat?" said one of the gendarmes lamely.

"And if so," persisted the man, "why is it that robbers and the police have this agreement between them? I have shown you all up for what you are. This is what has happened to heroic Mistra, the pride of the Morea! Bravo. And this is what I get for fighting thirty-six hours on the hill-side against our enemies. Now we're defended by people like you who—"

"Silence!" a gendarme shouted.

There was a bustle around the booth as a tall man in uniform with decorations covering his chest appeared, the crowd stepping back to make way for him. The gendarmes stood all round the man so that he had to face the newcomer.

"Here," they said, "is the Colonel himself."

The district police chief gazed down at the hothead in front of him. "What is the matter?"

"I have been cheated at this game," he answered bluntly.

"How so?" inquired the chief of police in a regal, benevolent voice.

The man, subdued, replied simply, "I counted the numbers right and he counted them wrong on purpose so as not to let me have the frying-pan numbered eighty-two, Kyrie Director."

"Ah," murmured the police chief in the inimitable tone of an Athenian Member of Parliament presented with a petition: a voice that contrives to say all at once, "I completely understand your plight; I am here to serve your interests. Come back tomorrow."

"And why," one of the gendarmes pleaded, "why do you make yourself so nervous?"

"You might have counted wrong," the Colonel kindly suggested. "I myself won at this same booth yesterday a set of glasses with a decanter on a tray. Nobody was cheated in my case."

"It's quite true," parroted the gendarme. "Only yesterday at this same booth, this same person you say cheated you—"

"But, Kyrie Director, I *counted* the numbers, everybody here saw—"

Kostandí stepped forward and said to the man in a lowered voice, so that only the policemen round him could have heard, "Mitso, are you by any chance turning Red?"

The man turned without a word and slipped away.

For several more days I stayed on in Mistra, going once more over the fortifications and taking my last photographs; that winter in a distant library I would sit writing about it. After the fair Kostandí got drunk one night at Kryovrýssi, sitting with an exalted look on his lean and cavernous face. A taxi from Sparta drove up and halted in the road, and a party of American tourists got out and were climbing up the steps when Kleoméni dashed out from his kitchen to meet them. Kostandí hooked one foot round his leg and sent him sprawling. Kleoméni on all fours, with a napkin in his fist, raised his face to greet the foreigners. "Good evening, ahaha, good evening," he said, struggling to his feet, and swept his guests to the opposite end of the terrace.

Kostandí murmured mournfully, "Why is it that Kleoméni never likes his tourists to sit anywhere near me?" He emptied his glass so vigorously that a red stain spread over his shirt across his narrow chest. Without changing his expression, he said, "I have the inclination to kill somebody."

At the end of the week a village beyond Paliánitsa was celebrating the feast day of its patron saint. Kostandí and I got up at four o'clock to water his garden. Lightning flickered across the night sky and when it got light, early risers from Mistra began to pass by.

We finished watering and I said, "Do we go now?"

"We're not going," he replied.

"In Greece," I said, "one changes one's mind quickly."

"Mind your own business, Kyr Andrea," he said, picking up his tools, and I decided then to leave the following day.

That afternoon as the two of us were going down through the ruins towards Kryovrýssi he said to me in the rather shy voice he had sometimes, "You know, Andriko, there was a reason why we didn't go to the festival. Everything's quiet these days; so be it. I don't want to start murdering people again."

"What has that to do with the festival?"

"Because the men live there who killed my brother. At festivals one drinks. When I'm drunk—" He stopped.

"You kill people, you mean? But you'd be with me; I wouldn't let you."

"You don't know me yet, Andrea," he said. "Can you guess how many I've killed?"

"Eh, how many?"

"Over five hundred."

I had the sensation of sinking to a great depth. Nevertheless I brought myself to say with easy mistrust, "That's impossible!"

"What do you think I've been doing for the past eight years? When I set fire to their hideouts in the forest, when I surrounded their caves and after a week they crawled out half-dead of starvation, do you think I brought them down with me, just to hand them over to someone else to put in prison? *Bá*, I killed them where they stood—fifteen one time, six another, thirty the next week. The number mounts up, like in these games you saw at the fair."

I looked at the dead city on the hillside.

"Of my own accord I will not disturb or harm a soul," he said.

"But people who have never even touched you?"

"They killed my brother," he replied.

I left at six next morning. Panayiota packed in a napkin some chunks of stale bread which was all she had in the house.

"Somewhere at a spring you'll be able to wet these and eat them, and then you'll think of us, eh Andriko?" she said, following me out through the tiny doorway. Her two-year-old son trotted after her and began to cry as I went down the rickety wooden stairs. When Kostandí and she reached the edge of the ravine I told them to come no farther.

He said, "If anyone harmed you, I'd kill him. Don't think ill of me, Andriko."

He embraced me, while Panayiota laughed shrilly, "Look at them saying farewell like sweethearts! Kiss me, Andrea. You're better than any brother. Good hour to you, may your road be good, go with good fortune." Her voice echoed above me like an incantation as I made my way down with quick, stumbling steps into the ravine, shifting my rucksack from side to side to balance it properly.

MY ROAD LAY WEST to Kalamata, fifty kilometres away on the other side of Taygetos; but first I had to pass through the village where I had missed the festival. It lay an hour to the north and when I came in sight of it, being used to the ruins of Mistra, I was not surprised at first to look down into roofless squares of walls spread out below me. But as soon as I came into the street I could see the walls stood intact up to their normal height, with here and there a fountain playing at a crossroads. Old women and little girls bustled about on their verandas among flowers and pots and pans, although in every house the doors were empty and the windows showed the sky. Verandas and balconies were made into little rooms with the side-walls built up under roofs of loose planks and sheets of tin.

Somebody coming towards me called, "Eh, Andrea, how is it you come here now? The festival was yesterday." I did not recognize him, but he went on, "Over at Paliánitsa you danced all day." Then he turned to some others behind him and said, "This is Andrea who was at Paliánitsa with Kostandí." But they answered nothing and looked at me with a strange expression.

At a half-ruined coffee-house I asked a few idlers tossing strings of beads around their hands, how long it would take to reach the top of the pass.

A man with his back to me replied without turning round, "Four hours."

I asked promptly, "Was it the Security Battalions who burned this village?" There was no answer. I said, "How many houses were destroyed?"

The same man replied, "Out of two hundred houses, one hundred and twenty."

No one seemed disposed to continue the conversation, and I continued out on to a wide road leading up into the mountain. A little way ahead a man on a donkey mounting from a path called to me, "You're heavily laden. Put your pack on this saddle."

He slid down off the donkey and reached out for my rucksack as I approached. "There's no reason for you to carry it," he said in a thin, cultivated voice, "since I have the donkey and we can walk together. I'm going up to my potato patch; just above it is the chapel of Prophit Ilías at the top of the pass. You're bound for Kalamata, I suppose. Are you American or English?"

I walked beside him, relieved of my load, for five hours. He had been a merchant in Smyrna and had come to Greece in 1922. Since then he had been growing potatoes. Nowhere near here, he added, as if there might be some significance in the fact, but on the other side of Taygetos, in Messenia. He asked why I had shaved my head and I told him it was to save trouble in the summer heat.

"But your clothes are in tatters," he said.

"That way I don't stand out so much as a foreigner," I replied.

"You don't want to appear foreign?"

"To foreigners Greeks don't tell the truth," I said, "or rather they tell them what they think foreigners would like to hear. This way I get closer to people; there's less flattery on one hand, on the other less mistrust."

"It's not wise," he said, "to travel about looking like a beggar."

"Oh, I've had to answer many questions, but I've always got out of difficulties. People have only to feel one respects them, which I do, and then all goes well."

"Things happen suddenly in a Greek's mind."

"But since I'm American, I prefer to expect good instincts in people. It sometimes even draws them out," said I.

The man shook his head.

"Can you tell me," I asked, "since you're not from here, what happened in that village? I suppose it was the Security Battalions?"

"They were justified in part"; he sounded cagey. "But one must look at such things from a long way off. If one is too involved nothing is comprehensible. Our troubles started, as you know, during the Occupation. Over in Magóula certain families were friends with the Germans. One night in 1942 a band from here burned down nine houses in Magóula. A few weeks later a band from Mistra came here and burned down a hundred and twenty houses. Why so many, you will ask? Because an act of violence produces not another act of violence, but ten or twenty more. There are other feuds between the two villages, but that is what Greek history has always been. In Greece people take up arms against each other not because of politics or ideologies, but simply because the individual can't stand another individual as strong as he or in authority over him. As with persons, so with villages and towns and bands and nations and alliances of nations."

Then I asked the question for which I had long been seeking the answer. "Which side, then, has committed more crimes, the Right or the Left?"

He said, "I can only tell you that the side which happens to be in power has more opportunity to commit them. Once, north of the Corinthian Gulf, I saw a group of ELAS Communists pull a man's teeth out one by one and then, while he was still conscious, dig out both his eyes and shove them into his mouth. Another time, here in Lakonia, I saw some Rightists of the Security Battalions form a circle round a prisoner and kick him from side to side till he was dead. People take sides depending on what happens to them personally or else for what they see happening to their friends and families. No one takes sides for abstract reasons. In Greece it's considered dishonourable not to take revenge—terrible. And yet those who find reasons to avoid taking sides are often the least interesting persons; haven't you found it so?"

We talked on without clash or discomfort while the pines gave place to firs and the firs grew smaller among the white cliffs, until at noon we came to a hut just below the road where I expected to be invited in to a lunch of hot potatoes. However, my companion merely said, "Here I stop. In half an hour you will reach the pass."

Since the motor road mounted in long zigzags and descended into Messenia by a roundabout way, I followed a mule track leading directly up the col, where inside a white chapel was an icon of the prophet Elias on a mountain-top. I wetted my lumps of bread in a spring and thought of my friends and their children.

The descent was easy at first down a long path covered in pine needles, winding in and out of some folds in the mountain, then reappearing a long way below on an open slope. Thinking to avoid the unnecessary detour, I cut straight through the forest and soon found myself waist-high in a dense growth of scrub ilex with prickly leaves that tore my trousers. In the middle of the afternoon I reached the first village in the province of Messenia, where I asked my way of some women on the path. They smiled at my torn trousers and gave me some walnuts. Half an hour beyond, I came upon three young shepherds sitting by the path, who told me I would have to hurry if I wanted to reach Kalamata before nightfall.

Pleased with the distance I had already travelled, I told them I had come from Mistra that morning.

"What village are you from?" they asked.

"Oh, I'm not from here, I come from America."

The sky had begun to cloud over and I said good-bye to them in haste.

The path curved down into a deep gully. Twenty minutes later I had crossed it, when from high above me on the hillside I heard faint voices shouting; the silhouette of the three boys stood out on the skyline waving their arms.

"Come back," they called. I put my hands to my mouth and shouted across the valley, "What's the matter?"

"They want you up at the village. The police are calling for you."

"I have nothing to do with police," I shouted back, walking on with somewhat longer strides. I neither wanted the gendarmes to catch up with me nor the boys to notice I was walking faster. After a hundred yards the path mercifully turned into a narrow gorge where they could no longer see me.

A few minutes later I heard voices behind me. The three boys ran pell-mell round the corner, one waving a big stick over his head. I stood where I was until they caught up with me and two of them seized me by the arms, the third dancing up and down in front of me, shaking his cudgel.

"Not a step farther," he panted.

I said, "I'm going to Kalamata. You told me yourself I'd have to hurry. It's already half past four."

"You can go there tomorrow. My father will lend you his mule."

"But I want to get there tonight."

"Why?"

"Because I have to catch a bus early tomorrow morning. I have to spend a month in Methoni, working every day, to get back to

Athens by the end of September, where I have more work during the winter."

They stared at me uncomprehendingly. "But the police were calling for you to come back. They shouted to us to catch you."

"Tell them you didn't," I suggested. "Say I disappeared. Or else you can look at my papers, search me up and down and then, having found me *endáxi*, you can tell the police you didn't want to hinder a foreigner who had to be in Kalamata by nightfall and was too tired to come all the way up again to your village. To begin with, here are my papers."

The boys took the papers and looked at them upside-down. "None of this means anything to us. We don't know much about the alphabet," said one.

I spread the papers out. "See, here it says: Nationality American, Occupation student, Permission to travel throughout Hellas, permanent address—"

"Look at his photograph!" the boy with the cudgel suddenly exclaimed. The other two crowded round to look first at the picture, then at me.

"*Bá*, it's not the same," whispered one.

The other said, "Look at him now. He has let his moustache grow for disguise until his hair grows long again. Eh, they had you locked up in Tripolis or Sparta, and you escaped before they took you off to Makronisos. You think you can laugh at us with your forged papers."

"If you think I'm an escaped convict," I said, "look at my belongings."

"Let's see," they said eagerly, pressing round my rucksack as I pulled out, one by one, sleeping-bag, clothes, camera, binoculars, compass, notebooks, maps of Lakonia and Messenia, and plans of fortresses. Every object aroused their interest and curiosity, then their suspicion. One moment they were saying, quite off their guard, "What's this, Uncle?" and the next turning on me with "You go around measuring and taking photographs, eh!"

I looked dubiously at the opaque, grey light all round us in the ravine.

"If you're American," said the boy with the cudgel, "why have you walked all the way from Mistra on foot? Why didn't you go by bus, straight to Kalamata, or take a taxi?"

"I happen to like walking in the mountains."

The boy with the stick kicked one of the outer pockets of my rucksack. "What's in here?"

"You can open it," I said.

"Open it yourself," he commanded.

I kneeled down and unstrapped the pocket. "These are not dangerous weapons," said I, bringing out two of my calamus flutes.

"*Po-pó*, look at these!" exclaimed one of the shepherds. "Do you play it?"

Laughing, they examined the flutes carefully. One of them tried unsuccessfully to blow a note, but the eldest, sticking the cudgel under his arm, snatched the flute out of the other's hands. "Will you make me a present of this one?"

"With pleasure," I said. "And now it's late and—"

"You think I'll take this?" He flung the flute down on the rocks, stamped on it and with a kick sent the broken pieces flying into the ravine. "You're coming back with us. Get ready to walk."

The other two, searching through my rucksack, had just come upon the pieces of bread still tied up in Panayiota's napkin. "Dry bread!" they cried.

"Is that the last of your provisions?" said the boy with the cudgel. His eyes were cold and angry. "So you're the last of the band that burned my father's house."

"Let us go then to your village. I'll leave this pack here, it's too heavy to carry up the mountain again." I turned on my heel and started up the path. I had gone twenty paces when, looking round, I saw them still standing near the abandoned rucksack. "Don't you want to take me to the police?" I called.

"If you leave this here and something happens to it while we're gone, then it'll be our fault," they said, climbing on to a rock above the path. "Come back here."

I walked back, saying, "I thought you wanted to take me to your village."

"Are you American?"

"I told you I am."

"You have the pronunciation of an Albanian or a Serb."

"That may be."

"Why do you walk over the mountain when you could take a car?"

Once more I described my mode of life.

"If you're American," said the eldest shepherd slowly, "you'll give us all the money you're carrying and we'll go back and tell the police we couldn't catch up with you."

"Then we shall all go to your village this instant and tell the police you were ready to lie to them," I said.

They climbed down on to the pathway and one of them muttered, "Let's go then." Close behind me I could hear them talking in excited whispers. I walked on, paying no attention. In a few minutes they were by my side.

"Hey," said the eldest shepherd. "You can go where you want. You walk well."

The compliment was unexpected; it was now six. Two hours later I came in sight of Kalamata, indistinguishable from the surrounding countryside but for the harbour works standing out like pencil-strokes across the silvery sheet of the Messenian Gulf. I walked for hours more, observing nothing in the rapidly falling dusk and thinking only of the night's rest ahead of me, glad for once to be coming back to civilization. I was close to my goal now; all I had to do was to keep on walking down this same road between the pointed tents and bright fires gleaming in the dark; too late I realized I had come into an army camp. Voices were shouting all around me, "Hey hey, where is he going!" and a squad of soldiers hurried up and told me to get out fast. I had to go back the way I had come, grudging every extra pace, but came at last to the other side of the encampment, and a restaurant surrounded by plane trees with electric lights strung along the lower branches. The restaurant-keeper eyed me curiously when I asked him for whatever he had in the way of food, but chiefly for some water, at once. He told me to go through the house into the garden and draw water from the well myself if I was in such haste. The garden was swarming with soldiers washing and drinking. I jostled my way through to the well, drew up a bucketful, drank, washed my face, and after taking off boots and socks splashed the rest of the water all over my feet.

And now for food, I thought as I went out to the front of the house and collapsed into a chair.

"Oh, how marvellous this is!" I exclaimed when the restaurant-keeper came out and deposited a plate of macaroni on the table. I fell upon it with a sense that my troubles were over; too relieved to object to the concentrated gaze of three or four young officers on a bench a few paces away from me. Let them suspect anything they want, my thoughts ran gaily on; I have walked to Kalamata in a day. Then, to put them at their ease, I struck up a conversation with the keeper of the restaurant.

"I've walked all the way across Taygetos by the Langádha Pass," said I, with a glance at the three officers as they moved closer to my table. "Do you know how far it is from here to Mistra? Fifty kilometres, I believe. Ah, well," I said, wiping my mouth clean, "I've never appreciated food so much. All day I've eaten only a few pieces of stale bread. Some shepherds on the mountain even tried to rob me, but I said I'd report them to the police, and they finally let me go after two-and-a-half hours. *Po-pó*! I see it's almost ten o'clock. How much farther is it to the centre of the city?"

The restaurant-keeper glanced at the three officers before he replied, "Oh, half an hour, an hour."

I paid for the meal and lifted the rucksack on to my shoulders with extreme difficulty. "Good night to you all," I said to him and the three young officers; these had disappointed me by not seeming to take the least interest in my story, but that too was unimportant now. In the darkness I could feel my boots plough-ing through the soft dust of the roadway. And then I heard foot-steps padding behind me, and the clank of leather and metal. Someone grasped my elbow, saying "Come with us. The captain wants to talk to you."

I suffered myself to be led back to the restaurant where the officers were sitting in a row, a jaunty-looking tribunal.

There is a certain stage of exhaustion when it is easier to act a role in front of other people than to be oneself. "Bring a chair," I said briskly to the keeper of the restaurant. "And what do you want?" I said to the officers, and after that I lost track of time as I tried to make them forget my shaven head and piteous state of clothing. At first it seemed that all was going well. They had been to high school and were glad to see if I knew as much as they. We chatted about the Fourth Crusade, they asked me the date of the Battle of Lepanto, then told me all about Don John of Austria while I obliged with an excursus on the War of the Holy League; but none of it was getting me nearer to my long-awaited rest. I suggested they might now be satisfied.

Once more I was rising from my chair, my arms assisted through the straps of the burden on my back. Once again I was walking down the dark, dusty road, two soldiers beside me, their rifle butts beating rhythmically against their cartridge-belts. The night air was heavy with the smell of mimosa, and then the soft dust changed to a concrete pavement; street lamps passed over-head, familiar boulevards in the centre of the city, more dark streets, and more powdery sweet-smelling alleys on the other side of Kalamata, till we halted at a gate with a sentry-box on either side. The soldiers were talking to two brown-clad figures in white leggings, their faces quite obscure under the white helmets that gleamed like big eggshells under the arc light over the gate. Fig-ures retreated into the dark as I was guided across a gravel space into a square, white room. For a long time I listened to a monologue on American politics by a glib, courteous sergeant. "We knew in your last elections that the Truman was too peaceloving. Had the Dewey become President we should certainly have had war"—and I heard my own voice interjecting a feeble "Yes? Really?" as I tried to keep my eyes open. The man proceeded, "And I may say that the Greek people wanted the Dewey." Then others came into the room and again I found myself walking through the darkness. A staircase rose up in front of me; I was mounting a passage with lights all the way down it and sounds of snoring issuing from open doors. I was propelled into an office where a man was sitting at a desk and someone said, "Here he is Colonel"; the door closed behind me.

I came rapidly to my senses. Right hand extended, I strode across the room, announced my name and said I was *enchanté*. The officer behind the desk half-rose, shook my hand uncertainly, and announced his own.

I grabbed the nearest chair and sat down. At the end of an hour he was convinced of my identity, though a little incredulous. "You have walked from Sparta, but when did you leave!"

"At six o'clock this morning."

"*Amán!*" he exclaimed. "Not in one day?"

I produced a modest shrug. "To each his own madness."

A heavy rain that night continued into the early morning when I woke up in a little hotel to which I had been driven in the colonel's jeep the previous midnight. I barely remembered how I had come here, and yesterday's events had slipped obscurely out of my mind. I was missing Kostandí, who had given me his hospitality for months on end and had killed more than five hundred people.

I walked up the boulevard to a certain coffee-house where at eight o'clock a bus would be leaving for the western coast. Kalamata was empty in the grey morning light, with the rain spitting upwards off the pavements and splashing in the wide puddles of the street. Perhaps the rains were starting early this year; certainly Methoni would be dull after this crowded summer. I was thinking sorrowfully how I would have to finish all my work during the winter and after that return to America at twenty-seven, still uncertain of a career. Independence, excitement, vagabondage seemed to lead only towards rain and loneliness.

Behind me a quiet voice chuckled, "Ah, ha, in my young years I too travelled the way you do." A man with a flat fish-basket on his head leaped barefoot across a puddle and walked beside me up the street. "Yes, all over the world—Africa, Australia, South America—with all I needed on my back, just like you. Man needs very little for happiness. Indeed the inner life is the most important, as you have probably discovered on your travels."

He put down his fish-basket outside the coffee-house and we went in off the streaming sidewalk. Sitting over our coffee, I said: "On my travels I've discovered that very few have anything in the way of an inner life. I have a friend who, as I know him, is altogether good, the best husband and the kindest father, a person who hates to cause the least embarrassment or unhappiness to those he loves. Yet he has slaughtered so many people he has lost count of the number. I hesitate to say how many, because the number doesn't matter. I am disturbed for his sake."

"Perhaps now he has no inner life," the man said, "and all that matters to him are the outer forms of revenge and honour. But some day there will come to him a moment of crisis, of judgment, when he will have to face himself—it comes to everyone sooner or later. You need not worry about him." He smiled and looking out through the window, shrugged his shoulders at the persistent rain.

CHAPTER **10**

The Shepherds—Winter

IT HAD BEEN A long summer's journey, half a year, since the christening on Yerania. Soon after returning to Athens in November I went back again and at the edge of the forest played my *phloyéra* to the echoing hillside. From high up on the slope I heard a voice roaring and a few minutes later Andoni was running with long strides towards me, his crude shoes of rubber tyre sewn with string nearly flying off his feet. He collided into me and we clapped each other on the back while he cursed loudly, "How shall I give you hospitality such as you deserve! I do this to my poverty," making an obscene gesture. "And are you still alive, Koumbáre? How is it possible! I thought you dead all summer. Never a word from you all this time, four months—"

"Six," I corrected.

"Seven, eight, nine, a year—how long? All I know is that sometimes I was disgusted with you, Koumbáre. Yet it was all my fault. I said to your Koumbára, I said to Mitso, 'He was not pleased with us at the christening. We didn't make him comfortable enough, he left dissatisfied, and all because of my poverty.' *Ach*, Koumbáre, I'm so glad you are alive," he panted. "Do you know, I went to hospital; they took my appendix out, and when I came back to consciousness I heard them saying, 'Here are your wife and children beside you.' I said, 'I know that, but where is my

Koumbáros? He's dead and we displeased him.' I swear to you
I said those very words, by the Panagia!" he exclaimed with his
hand on his chest.

As usual he was out of work for the winter; all he could do till
spring was serve among his father's hired men tending a herd of
goats. A few hours later they came down the hill, driven by the
others. In a cave where they were kept during winter nights the
beasts were milked, and I helped them carry the pans back to
the hut.

There was a hole in one corner of the low roof and a tiny
hearth beneath it, where we cooked our supper of boiled potatoes
under the saddle-bags hanging from the smoke-blackened rafters,
and after the meal the men sang an old song about a brigand captured by the Turks:

> The mother of Kitso sat by the edge of the river;
> She scolded the river and threw stones into it.
> "River, flow less strongly, river turn back your water
> That I may pass over to the other side
> To the place where the brigands have their lair,
> Where the warriors are waiting, and all the captains.
> Kitso has been taken. River, let me across."

We drew the huge, heavy blanket over us where we lay, and
one of the men stamped out the fire.

In the morning Andoni went off to saddle a mule and a donkey, announcing, "Today we shall go to a monastery up on the
mountain, where I used to go often when I had the goats."

We set off with provisions, climbing to where the trees thinned
out over wide, level spaces—brilliantly green among their own
blue shadows on the limestone, filling the cool, moist air with
their honey-sweet and spicy smell—and a white chapel stood by
a cypress. Mounds of fallen stones surrounded it in a quadrangle
of what had once been the cells of a small monastery. Inside was
a plaque in the floor of the aisle with the date 1463; the monks

must have taken refuge here a few years after the Turks overran the whole of Greece.

Andoni said: "Some day when I am old and my children are all grown, I shall come here and live alone as a monk . . . I don't know how I am to feed my children. Sometimes I want to die. Tell me, is there going to be a war, Koumbáre? I wish there would."

Riding back in the late afternoon, he tried to interest me once more in the ancient cups he had discovered years before, but when I asked him where he and his friends had found them he was again evasive. Then he made obscure suggestions about certain machines he had heard tell of, with which one could divine metals underground. I had so often referred to the work I was actually doing that I brushed aside these present suggestions lightly, and an hour or two passed before he again broached the subject on his mind. "I don't know what you do, Koumbáre, I don't know who you really are," he said, "but if a war breaks out and you need a place to hide in, you can always come to me, for I know these mountains better than anyone; there are places where I can keep you hidden for as long as you like."

"Thanks, Koumbáre, I'll know whom to come to," said I. In Mistra Kostandí had said once, "Andriko, you can fool us no longer; you are in the Secret Service. Why else would you bother with us who live in the country, or explore the mountains where foreigners never go?" Nothing I could say ever seemed to drive this idea out of people's minds; so now I passed it off with a laugh.

We rode on in silence through the woods, then behind me Andoni said, "Now I know what you are. I have been observing the way you sit in the saddle. You are an officer."

I laughed all the way back to the hut. He laughed also, delighted with his discovery. "All this time you have tried to keep it hidden from me! For shame, Koumbáraki! But I know your secret now."

All his family were at the hut; the brother-in-law had driven them up with the week's provisions in his truck and they were to spend Saturday and Sunday night here. Together we herded the

goats as they came down the hillside into the cave above the ravine, then ate the hot meal Katerina cooked for us and drank a
great deal of wine which they had brought with them from Megara. Again in the flickering light we sang *Tou Kítsou i mána*, and I
told them all how Andoni had discovered that day I was a smug-
gler of antique objects, a digger after precious metals, and in ad-
dition an officer, a cavalry officer, carrying out secret missions in
these hills. Everyone seemed pleased.

At four o'clock next morning the dogs in the goat-pens were
barking at the moon, and I went outside to look at the eastern
peaks shining in the bright blue night. Andoni came out to tell
one of the shepherd boys sleeping under a tree to take the goats
up the mountain. Then I went back inside and blew up the fire
among the embers. Katerina lit the wick in the tin of oil, while
Andoni's mother and aunt, my godson and his four-year-old
brother rolled and murmured under the blanket that had covered
us all. The old women mumbled, "*Ach*, may the little Lord pro-
tect us!" Katerina handed me a plate of meaty bones and bread
slabs from our last night's dinner; she had already filled my pack
with bread, cheese and fragrant mountain tea. I met Andoni driving the last goats up from the cave, bells clanging, horns knock-
ing and hoofs scraping over the rocks; we wished each other a
good hour.

I reached the coast road after an hour's walking into the sunrise and there stopped a truck driving up from Argos with a load
of vegetables for the city. Back at the Academy the students were
eating their breakfast of porridge and ham and eggs.

THAT WINTER I ASKED Andoni and Katerina to find for me a
certain kind of heavy woollen coat with a hood such as the shepherds wear in winter. Early in the new year I had a letter from
Andoni, dictated to his eldest daughter, telling me he had found
the stuff and that I must come to Megara to have it made to measure. I found him in Megara alone, taking care of the children;
Katerina had been sent away to fetch some hens from the for-

212 THE FLIGHT OF IKAROS

est. He and I took the massive bolt to an old tailor in upper Megara, who said there was not enough to make the sleeves. Andoni
said he would find more from someone else. A fortnight later he
himself brought my finished coat to Athens. I was called over
from the library to the Academy across the street; the servants
had allowed him inside the door, but not so far as the common-
room where guests customarily waited, and I found him standing in a dark alcove with his cap in his hand and an enormous
bundle tied up in a sheet. A week later I took the opportunity of
a trip to Corinth to stop off at Megara on my way back; I knew
Andoni would be there now for the rest of the winter because he
had written me that he had had a disagreement with his father
and refused to herd his goats. The first thing he told me was that
the Superintendent of Forests had been threatening to take him
to court to pay him back for hitting him, years before during the
Occupation. He begged me to write a denunciation of this man
to the Ministry of the Interior, or at least petition for his transfer
to another region where he would cause him less trouble. When I
protested it was not up to a foreign student to transfer the agents
of the Greek Government from one place to another, Andoni
said: "But Mitso and many others have told me all that's necessary in this case is one little word from an American, no matter
who he is. How often have they not said to me, 'Would that we
had Andrea for a koumbáros! We would have him working miracles for us, while you, Andoni, simply sit and entertain him in
your hut and never ask for anything.'"

"I can't be useful to you in that respect," I said.

"All right, Koumbáre," he said, smiling.

During the morning we went back to the tailor, who had only
given me one pocket in my coat. While a second was made, the
tailor said to me: "The Kyrios is American? My youngest son has
made an application to go to America, to study business. I began
life as the poorest shepherd north of the Corinthian Gulf; all
my life I worked; I learned this trade and made enough money
to send my son to high school, and now he himself has written

to a business school in Chicago, who say they have a place for him. All that is needed is a word with the United States Consul in Athens, just a word, to say my son is deserving and intelligent. I know it would not be too much trouble for Andoni's koumbáros."

Once again I explained that anything to do with government regulations was beyond my capacity; I could not arrange for people to be sent to America.

When we left, Andoni said, "You know, of course, why the old man only put one pocket in your coat?"

"I have no idea."

"So that you would come back to his shop and he could ask you that favour for his son."

"Perhaps you see now that I can't do things like that," I said. "In spite of all you think about me, I am not an important person, and don't want to be."

"Naturally, Koumbáre, I understand," he said gently. "By the way, there's the old woman from whom I got that extra length of stuff for your coat. She's a neighbour. It was quite hard to find the material, you know. Well, it happens she has no children and only one adopted son who has just been called into the army. She asked me the other day if there was anything we could do about it."

"Anything who could do about what?"

"I know, there's nothing you can do about such things, but since we're passing by her house we can just step inside and tell her so, eh?"

"Koumbáre Andoni," I said reproachfully, "you haven't been putting me under obligations in advance, have you?"

"All I have done is tell a few lies about you, Koumbáre. With Greeks you have to tell lies."

"You put me in an uncomfortable position before these people," I said with gravity.

He replied without a trace of it, "Eh, just tell a few lies yourself, Koumbáre."

We walked into a grocery shop where an old woman greeted us both affectionately and sat us down to a table and an ouzo.

"I was telling my Koumbáros it was you who gave me the extra material for his coat, Aunt Evridhikóula. Without you the coat would never have been finished. My Koumbáros is under obligation to you," said Andoni treacherously. "In fact if there is anything he could do for you—"

The old woman wailed, "If only your Koumbáros knew my plight!"

"If he only knew it, Aunt Evridhikóula, I am sure there's nothing he wouldn't do for you," he went on.

Our eyes met. He threw his head back and tossed off his ouzo with such rapidity that he choked, and he looked at me again with tears streaming down his cheeks. Finally he had to get up and go outside. I was left with Aunt Evridhikóula.

"You saw how touched your Koumbáros was," she whispered to me with a glance towards the open door where Andoni stood gulping and coughing and making strange, weepy noises. "He feels for me so strongly because I have no sons to help me, poor evil-fated soul, in my old age. Only that one boy who is more than a son to me, and now they have taken him away. It was he who ran the shop for me; he did everything. Now I have to do it all alone. And how many years will he not be gone! I was thinking"—she lowered her voice—"that if he were transferred to some post here in Megara, poor burning child, he could continue helping me in the shop. It is a good idea, is it not?"

I looked desperately for escape towards the open door. Andoni had abandoned me.

"Come," said the old woman, "would you not go to the Chief of Staff in Athens and tell him to let the boy stay here in Megara?"

"I'm obliged to you, Kyrá Evridhikóula, for the material you gave for my coat, and I don't know what my Koumbáros has been telling you about me, but I cannot request the Chief of Staff to transfer the boy to Megara."

"Eh well," she said philosophically, "what can one do? God will put His little hand into the affair, as we say. And yet it might be so easy . . . just a word, if only one knew the right person to go to. Anyway," she said with a broad smile, "I hope your new coat keeps you warm now in the cold weather."

I rejoined Andoni outside in the street and asked him earnestly never to do that to me again. "What do you think I am!" I exclaimed.

"I have told you I don't know who you are or what you really do, Koumbáre," he replied.

A new test of my extraordinary powers came that evening when Mitso paid us a visit. He proceeded to business after the minimum of compliments. "If the Kyrios Koumbáros will listen, perhaps I could tell him about the scheme I have in mind to build a wineshop near here, just a hundred metres away at the start of the road to Alepokhóri. People coming from the country villages in that direction have no place to sit down and rest when they reach Megara. Why, I have often thought, should the poor villagers not have a resting-place of their own? And so it happens that recently I have found myself in a position, Kyrie Koumbáre, to build just such a centre in an extremely good location. But it also happens in that same spot a festival is held every year. Easter Tuesday, when women dress up in their old costumes and people come from all over the world to see the interesting exhibit of folklore. In few words I am not allowed to build because the Church and the Municipality both hold that the place should be reserved for the traditional festival. Of course, we also know they are only interested in the tourist trade, in taking advantage of foreigners, poor souls, who come this long way to see it. Since the time my friend Andoni—and you know, Kyr Andrea, Andoni and I are nothing less than the best of friends, I don't speak of the subject lightly—had the good fortune to make your acquaintance, I have thought that if you were to put the case to, say, the Nomarch himself when you get back to Athens, with your own particular recommendation to the Nomarch to force—yes, why not?—force our Municipality to give me permission to build my wineshop on the Alepokhóri road . . ."

"Better not to force my Koumbáros, however," Andoni intervened with decision. "You know well he can't do that sort of thing."

The expression that passed over Mitso's face seemed to say, "Andoni, why have you betrayed me?"

Yet for all Mitso's eulogies over the friendship that existed between them, Andoni himself never seemed to echo it. It seemed as if only a national penchant for complexity in human relationships could explain why, with more and more open dislike and ill humour, Andoni continued to send for him and to insist that we call at his house whenever I was there.

I went to Megara again in March to see the famous dances of the women in the public square on Clean Monday, the last day of Carnival and first of Lent in the Eastern Church, when people eat a quantity of garlic and onion with the frank intention of blowing the Devil out of their bodies. Andoni and I called on Mitso in the afternoon and suggested that he and his wife give a party in his house that night. Andoni told me afterwards that he was probably going to misbehave; he had not liked the ill grace with which Mitso's wife received our suggestion. Then he had a fight with Katerina, who said she would not come. We both pressed her, but she shook her head. "Nikolaki's ill," she said.

"That's not the reason," Andoni said. "You won't come because I haven't bought you a new pair of shoes."

"Much it bothers you!" she retorted.

"*Ach,* I want to leave here, I want to get away!" he exclaimed. We were sitting in the other room not long after when he said to me: "I trust you absolutely, you are as close to me as anyone, Koumbáre, by the Panagia! I was in love once . . . eh, it was long ago. I was passing the girl's house in the middle of the night and she rushed out and threw her arms around me and said, 'Andoni, I love you, let us run away.' 'Be quiet for God's sake!' I said. 'Do you want somebody to come out and kill us?' Well, she was married off to someone else. Then my own marriage was arranged. I had never seen your Koumbára before our wedding. She is a tough person; honourable, a good wife. I am pleased with her." He spoke with subdued exertion.

Katerina, however, was prevailed upon to come. She wore her one dress and brought Nikolaki in her arms. The party was a failure. Mitso had invited (on his wife's suggestion, he told us later) only one other guest, Barba Stamáti to play on his *karamoúza* and make a great deal of noise, and no one else to enjoy it. Katerina sat in a corner, caressing the sick baby and murmuring to it over and over again, "What's the matter, my little he-goat? Why are you crying?" Wine there was, and we all drank copiously without growing any the more cheerful. Andoni was the only one who made any pretence to high spirits when he burst into a song that had for its refrain:

Ez ez ez
Let me piss in your fez.

Mitso told him to be quiet. Mitso's wife suggested his leaving. We did so without further ceremony.

All the way home Andoni delivered himself of his more intimate opinions of his neighbours. Mitso's father had killed a man, he told me. Mitso himself was a person I should be on my guard against. Mitso's wife had delusions of grandeur, particularly in the way she had her hair cut short and permanently waved, which was a shame in any woman; he called her a "mignonne" and more could not be said. "Except for this," he added: "not long ago Mitso told me he would get his wife pregnant and they would have another child and ask you to be godfather, so that you would be their koumbáros too. They want to have you for themselves . . . *keratádhes*! And at the same time they go about telling everyone in Megara you are a spy, working for the *Intéllitzents Sérvis*. They laugh at you behind your back because you wear that shepherd's coat. What need have I of such people? None. I want to get away from here."

"Back to your forest where you don't have to buy me a new pair of shoes," said Katerina in her clear voice.

"Oh!" was all Andoni could say.

Nor had anyone's mood improved by morning, except perhaps for Mitso and his wife who came to pay us a call. "Would you like to have some visitors," said she coyly as they walked into the courtyard.

"Now they want to be friendly," whispered Katerina.

Andoni nodded. "That's right. They're ashamed of throwing us out last night. Mitso has probably told her they must come and make up with us, to get on the good side of our Koumbáros."

Yet the visit passed off well. Reconciliation was effected by a piece of news of which the interest to everyone far outweighed any personal antagonism of the night before. Up at Koura the shepherd Stelio had stabbed his wife, the girl with the smiling face and the gold plate for teeth, twelve times all over her body for enticing the young shepherds on the mountain into her goat-pens during the day while the men were gone. The wife was still alive, but Stelio was bringing suit against her, and the trial would take place in Athens. Best of all, one of Andoni's brothers, who had had several "uncrowned wives" already, was implicated in the affair. Mitso wound up the story by saying to Andoni, "Could it be that you too have soiled your whiskers?"

Both wives laughed when Andoni protested, "I don't go to other women, I tell you! Not since I was married have I—"

"*Po-pó*, I think I see Andoni's whiskers twitching," said Mitso. "We shall see what comes out at the trial."

There was a festive atmosphere all over Megara that day. Shops closed and all the girls and younger women of the town dressed themselves up in their mothers' costumes. One saw them during the morning in the drab, whitewashed, sun-drenched alleys, wearing head cloths of white silk falling in long folds over their backs and shoulders, plum-coloured velvet jackets tight and stiff

with a profusion of gold embroidery, with lace at the cuffs, strings
upon strings of coins hung across the breast, and silk aprons
heavily embroidered over their long skirts that swirled around
their gold-slippered ankles. There were some however who had
no golden slippers, and one caught sight of cheap shoes with
open toes and sling heels. The young women who no longer let
their hair grow long wore false braids, which they allowed to show
under the bottom of their kerchiefs. Lipstick there was also in
abundance, as if with all these costumes the play of colour were
not brilliant enough already. In the afternoon we went down to
the main square to watch them dancing the much-reputed *Trata*,
but all there was to see was a long line of a hundred and fifty or
two hundred women with false hair and gorgeous clothing holding hands across each other's waist, simply moving with short, un-
rhythmic steps slowly round and round the square, their mouths
tight closed, not daring to sing. There was no music anywhere,
and it was small wonder they were so selfconscious, threading
their half-splendid, half-tawdry line through the teeming multi-
tudes of townspeople all dressed up in city clothes with no city to
go to, and the American Embassy and Mission families watching
from their Cadillacs with the badges of their office, the Leica and
Rolleiflex, around their necks, and the languid Athenians with
their travelling-bags and thermos flasks, uncomfortably seated at
the coffee-house tables. I looked in vain among the crowds for
some of the people from the christening on Yerania.

Jaded and bored, we returned to Andoni's house in the late
afternoon. Nikolaki was much sicker; his face was red and his
brow hot to touch, and he was running about the courtyard in the
chilly evening wind barefoot and half-naked. When night fell his
mother took him into the house, and while he wept and whim-
pered she caressed him, murmuring endlessly, "What is it, my little goat, what is it? What's the matter?" Until I could stand it no
longer and said I would go for the doctor.

"Doctor!" muttered Katerina under her breath as she crouched
over her child on the empty hearthstone.

"Koumbáre, what can the doctor do? We don't go to doctors," Andoni said.

I finally persuaded him it could do no harm, and the two of us walked to the quarter where the doctor lived. But every light was out and all the shutters tight closed. "They might know at the pharmacy," Andoni said, but that too was closed, and we had to ring the bell until a shutter opened above our heads and a man leaned out and directed us to the doctor's house. "But he will surely be in bed at this hour, and you will have to get a taxi to transport him; he's very heavy." When we found the house we had to stand outside the door there too, ringing the bell again and again until the doctor let us in and showed us up to his study while he went off to get dressed. Andoni went to the main square for a taxi. The two of us had to help the doctor into it. Rolling and bouncing in the darkness, the doctor talked expansively of his lifelong love for archaeology. "Ah, when I think of the glorious history of our country!" he said. "Andoni, you are indeed fortunate to have a koumbáros engaged in such pursuits."

"*Phtou!*" Andoni replied unceremoniously.

An hour later everything was quiet in the house, and Nikolaki fell asleep after a dose of purple medicine the doctor gave him. It was very cold next morning at five when Andoni came into my room with a brazier of live coals. Katerina was up in the other room, heating tea while the five children wriggled beneath the blanket on the one bed. When I said good-bye, she kissed my hand in an old-fashioned gesture. I walked out of the courtyard, flooded in moonlight, and once again the earliest bus out of Megara brought me back to Athens in time for breakfast at the American Academy.

ANDONI CAME TO ATHENS for the third time in his life the following month. He told me with composure how he had borne false witness in the suit which Stelio had brought against the wife he had stabbed twelve times and the various men with whom she had been involved. Andoni's brother was the only one of these let

off. We sat with some others from Megara in a coffeehouse opposite the ruins of Hadrian's Library, where the Megara buses left
every hour. They congratulated Andoni on the happy issue of the
trial: "It goes without saying that a member of your family need
not expect to be condemned. Your father has enough sheep and
goats to keep any judge content." Andoni's father-in-law, the old
shepherd with the silvery curls whom I had seen among the pine-
branch huts at Aera the first time I climbed Yerania, was also in
Athens for the day on business of his own. Shifting uncomfortably in his chair, he glanced up the street at a public urinal and
with a shrug said, "I suppose I must go there. For myself, I wish
there were branches round about; I like it when there is a smell
of pine branches."

Andoni and I had time to go up to the Acropolis, where he
had never been before. He fell silent as we climbed the steep
steps into the Propylaea and passed under its coffered ceiling on
to the bare, grey summit. I had been there with many people
who lectured or listened or studied or registered different forms
of amazement, but I had never seen anyone accept what he saw
here with such simplicity and awe, the only person who did not
look out of place. He gazed across the ugly, smoky little city at the
blue outlines of the mountains which he knew, then looked up at
the columns of the Parthenon and said, "Who built these things,
Koumbáre?"

"People who lived here thousands of years ago."

"Things like this are from God," he said.

Many months later in the autumn I was driving back from
Corinth to Athens with some friends in their car. We had crossed
the Isthmus at dusk and were going fast along the straight road,
the yellow funnel of the headlights swallowing up the far-
spreading branches of the pine trees overhead; we were coming to
the place I knew and I asked them to stop. A minute or two later
I was alone by the side of the road, watching the distant lights
of the car dwindle rapidly away. Around me I could see nothing,
but my feet found their own way to the dirt track leading inland.

Darker than the night, the olive trees passed me as I walked. Far off the solitary spark of a shepherd's fire glowed on the highest ridge of the mountain, like the one we had watched from our own bonfire at the christening. The soft track climbed into the forest and I played *Tou Kítsou i mána* on my flute. Someone called from the distance, guiding me in the direction of the hut. Climbing the hillside, I passed through the midst of some people lying out under the trees. A man sat up and said, "Your Koumbáros waits for you."

Andoni was alone. We made a fire and while we waited for the potatoes to boil, one of the other resin-gatherers who was also a koumbáros of Andoni's because Katerina had christened a child of his, poked his head in the door, bade me good evening and withdrew at once.

Andoni said in a whisper in case the other were lurking outside, "That's a strange one, he can read and write; I don't trust him. His village is on the other side of the mountain towards Thebes; one never knows with Thebans. One night not long ago he came to me and said, 'Andoni, you shouldn't be a Royalist. The King is a bad thing for Greece; it's only the Leftists who have the interests of the nation at heart' or some such stupid words. As if anyone remembers the people's interests when he gets on top. So he goes on to say, 'Andoni, they tell me I'll get paid by a secret office. You must join too; all you have to do is cross the mountains once a month into Boeotia.' Suddenly I think to myself it would be nice to give him a good fright. So I stand up and shout, 'How can you say such a thing to me! My father's for the King and so was his father before him, and the same with me and my children. I'll go to the police down at the coast and tell them all you've told me about being paid by a secret office,' and I rush out into the night and saddle the mule, shouting all the time, 'I'm going to the police, this is a national emergency!' Then I gallop off down the path until I'm out of hearing and very quietly ride back again by another way. When I get back to the hut I can still hear him far off down the road, thinking he's following me, trying to catch up and shouting after me, 'Andoni, stop for the sake of the Panagia! I don't recommend the secret office any more. I'll join the Royalists, I promise you.' When he finally got back he could hardly believe his eyes; he had run all the way down to the sea, but he got frightened of meeting up with the gendarmes and so ran all the way back again. I never laughed so hard. As if I would do such a thing to a person whose child my wife had christened! 'Beware of mischief, you who can read and write,' I said to him, 'You're not so crafty as you think when a mere shepherd like me can laugh at you.'"

We ate our potatoes in the light of the fire.

"Did you know your Koumbára gave birth to another son?" he said.

"When!" I exclaimed.

"Two weeks ago."

"But I never even knew she—"

"You haven't come to see us for a long time, Koumbáre. Yes. So now we have six—eh, the herd grows bigger. What can one do? One is married!" he exclaimed simply. "Children are a festival in the house."

I told him I was leaving Greece at the end of the month.

After a long silence he said, "Who knows when we shall sit here again together?"

"Who knows?" I said.

In the morning we heated up some of last night's potatoes for our breakfast, then kneaded some dough and placed it on a flat tile in the middle of the live coals to bake while we went to the ravine to fetch water from the spring. On our way down Andoni told me he had asked a neighbouring shepherd to carve me a crook as a souvenir. The man was known for his woodcarving, but there was a little matter of a kindness I might be able to do him in return. Andoni was not quite sure what it was, but the man himself would explain it all to me when we went to his sheep-fold in the evening. We happened to meet him in the ravine; he had a mule with him and was going to fetch some belongings from another part of the mountain; he had finished the carving, he said, but now must be on his way, for next day he was leaving with his flocks for the Peloponnese. In the late afternoon Andoni and I went down into the plain where the man had his sheepfold. Andoni looked across the fields to a clump of trees a hundred metres away and said, "Let us sit down here, Koumbáre."

"Why here?" I asked as Andoni sat down with his back to an ilex tree.

"It is not done to go to somebody's place when he's not there," he said, then raising his voice called across the field, "Eh! Is anyone there?"

A child's voice called back, "What is it?"

"It's about the crook your father carved for my Koumbáros," Andoni shouted.

"My father will be back presently."

"Why do we have to be so formal?" I asked. "Can't we go and look at the crook at least till he comes back?"

"It's not done," said Andoni. We remained under the ilex while the sun went down behind the mountain.

Finally in the dusk the child called to us again, "My father has come back," and the two of us advanced cautiously across the field.

The man we had met in the ravine was there with the women of his family, busily packing up. They came from a village in the Argolid where pasturage was bad during the summer months; so for several years he and his family had come here every summer with their flock, but now it was time for them to return again. "Your Koumbáros asked me to carve you this," he said, handing me a crook made of the hard, straight branch of a wild olive, with a curved head fantastically carved in the form of a serpent devouring a fish with a dog's head, minute and elaborate like the carving on a Byzantine marble.

"The wood is very hard," I murmured, not knowing what to say.

"I've worked on it all summer," he replied.

"I can well imagine." It was idle to ask this shepherd if he knew where he got his inspiration, and he was not interested in talking about it.

While I was examining the head of the crook in the light of the fire, a dish of fried eggs with several big bread slabs was placed on the ground in front of me. Andoni and the shepherd were served in turn. We ate, saying little, while the women went on about their packing, rolling up the bundles of rough blankets, gathering their pots and pans into one place and setting the donkey saddles in a row, ready for the morrow.

"Your health," said the man, and we drank our wine.

I wondered how I could repay him. To hand him money, here beside his own fire, was unthinkable. To send him a food parcel from America when I got back would be easy and mechanical, costing no effort, expressing none of the dignity of this present which I had not asked him for.

At length he indicated to me the way: "Your Koumbáros asked me to make something you could take with you when you go back, with good fortune, to America. I told him I would if you could do me a certain kindness. As you know, we are strangers here in the country around Megara. People are jealous of me. They say, 'Why does this outsider come and pasture his flocks on land that should belong to us who live here?' Last spring three boys who wanted to drive me away fell on me and beat me up. I am lame in one leg and was unable to get away from them. In self-defense I struck one of them with my knife. Nothing happened to him; he didn't die. But now they have brought suit against me. I am awaiting trial next month. You would be doing me a kindness if you went to the judge in Athens or talked privately with the jury during the—"

"Next month," I said, "I shall have left Greece already!"

He made no further suggestions or demands, for which I was partly grateful, but in his eyes it was plain what he was thinking: if I really wanted to do something for him, why not go to the judge before the trial and arrange that it should not take place? With money was not anything possible? In four years I had had to accept so much generosity and kindness without knowing how to repay it that it had become almost a habit, but now I felt the obligation more keenly.

I asked Andoni what I could do in this case as we walked back to the hut.

"What can you do?" he said.

"You put me under obligation to this man."

"Eh, I just said a few lies about you, if that's what you mean. Otherwise he wouldn't have made the thing, and I wanted you to have it, Koumbáre."

"Where I come from a person like you would probably be an artist," I said.

"What's that, Koumbare?"

I had no answer ready.

Everything we did the next day was coloured, tinged, thrown into relief by the oppressive imminence of departure, and the sense of standing on the outermost boundary of that personal kingdom which Greece had become for me. The future was an unknown country. Very simple, familiar, unhurried actions took on a heightened reality, like a walk we took through rolling forest and meadow to a group of pine-branch huts where Katerina's father and mother, brothers, sisters-in-law, and small nephews and nieces were all settled for the coming winter. These people were like the trees around us, gnarled and thin, rough in texture, graceful in their movements. The brothers took turns on my flute, playing as I could never hope to play. Hearty and cheerful in the shelter of the wind, we ate a hot meal the old Koumbára made for us, and they talked of recent events on the mountain.

"Do you remember, Koumbáre, our cousin, Thymio, the old shepherd? Lately there has been no peace at Koura. Thymio's son had a quarrel with another boy in Megara who insulted his sister. He got angry and waved his stick at the boy and by mistake the pointed iron end flew off and hit him in the eye. The boy did nothing about it. He let the eye fester for several days, then lost it. Barba Thymio went to the boy's father and they agreed not to do each other violence. Barba Thymio gave him one of his fields in payment for what had happened. So the father took the land and then brought suit against Barba Thymio and condemned his son to a year's imprisonment. Now Thymio is waiting to kill him. Who knows what will happen?" They told the story without distress or agitation; they would have it to think about—the insult, the accident, the agreement, the treachery and the murder perhaps impending—during the winter after I was gone.

We said our farewells to each other. Andoni and I went back to his hut and tidied up the grimy little room where I had slept so often. Then we set off for Megara, not by the coast road but over the high country behind the cliffs of Kakí Skála. After five hours' walking we reached his house where Katerina showed me the tiny, dark baby born to her two weeks before. Andoni was up early next morning; I heard him out in the courtyard giving orders to his wife and eldest daughter to go to his father's oven and bake biscuits for me to take away. The two of us went to the barber to be shaved and then went from house to house of his friends and relatives to say good-bye. Mitso was not at home, but Andoni left word with his wife that he must come as soon as he returned. News of my leaving travelled quickly; people were waiting at the house to greet me. One woman took Andoni aside, and I overheard her say, "Could not your Koumbáros take my husband with him to America? You know all he does here is drink. Come now, ask him." For once Andoni was firm in his reply. Mitso arrived at lunch-time and sat with us for two hours, talking steadily. At first I thought this was too much to bear on my last afternoon, and I wished the women and children of the entire family might come in from the other room and overwhelm his discourse, but this was not according to custom. Andoni as usual sat mutely by while his friend held forth about his schemes, his ambitions for his children, politics, folklore, and the example of international friendship which he saw before his eyes, in this very room where he sat. Then, hearing only the half of what he said, I gradually became thankful for his presence which saved me from any sensation whatever.

At last Andoni and I sat alone over the end of our meal. One of the girls came in and put on the table a bag full of biscuits she and her mother had baked that morning, a bottle of some kind of red syrup and a jar of sweets. "For you, Godfather," she murmured softly, looking at me; then she lowered her eyes and went out of the room. I sat gazing at the objects on the table and suddenly turned my face to the wall. Andoni leapt up and clasped my head in his arm. Then I had to put the things into my satchel and go into the other room where Katerina and the five eldest children were waiting for me. The eldest daughter cried. Katerina wiped her face with the end of her yellow headkerchief and kissed my hand stiffly. One by one the children bent down to do the same as I tried to embrace them.

Andoni came with me to the bus, where Mitso and the brother-in-law who drove the truck and some other neighbours were waiting to see me off. We were an hour early and there was time for us all to sit about and drink cold lemonades in the chilly square.

CHAPTER 11

Olympos—Ikaros Rising

I MADE RESERVATIONS and bought my ticket home. I packed my trunks; an agent of the shipping company came and took them away. Day and night I was busy in the library collating manuscripts. Sometimes I was able to get off for a few hours in the evening to say good-bye to friends. Once I went to Pangráti to see Nikiphóros, but nobody was at home; I got no other opportunity. The weather, which had been threatening an early winter, then changed quite suddenly; summer seemed to be beginning over again, but it was only the last fine spell which country people call the Little Summer of Saint Demetrios. It was hard to believe that in a few weeks I would be in New York, and in a last act of irresponsibility before my youth, as it seemed to me, were ended, I hurried down one night to the Greek Alpine Club for information on Mount Olympos. Two parties had climbed it the previous summer, but there were still bandits about; detachments of the army and gendarmerie were all over the lower slopes, and a posse of these accompanied all climbers to the summit.

One of the club members, a retired army general who had often climbed Olympos, drew me a map of the mountain with meticulous directions how to approach it: from the railroad station on the coast I must walk eight kilometres southward to the village of Litókhoro where I could engage the services either of a squad of police or of an old guide who had conducted the first "Europeans" to the summit in 1913; from there I would climb again in a northerly direction, to a headland called Stavrós three thousand feet above the sea and continue for three hours on the same level, southward again, to a place called Priónia in the middle of a gorge that drops from the highest summit to Litókhoro and the sea; from Priónia (where the water was seven degrees centigrade at midsummer) the path would mount steeply westward for another three thousand feet to the Alpine Club Refuge, which I would naturally use as my headquarters since my comrades would have the key; it would be a steeper climb from here to the various summits three thousand feet higher. Times, heights, distances and places where I would find water were all drawn on the map while other members of the Alpine Club looked on and said, "Wherever the general goes, he is continually taking out his watch and noting down the time." I was much obliged to the pedantic old mountaineer, who assured me I would find no shepherds anywhere on Olympos. Next morning in the police department of the Aliens' Bureau I ran from office to office with my credentials while officials with their backs to me pored over my dossier. I had to hurry up and down many flights of stairs for stamps and applications, and emerged into the teeming noonday streets with a permit to travel in Macedonia. Next morning I boarded the Athens-Salonika express.

Riding past Thebes and the Copaic Lake, under Parnassos and Oeta, over the Gorgopótamos Bridge and across the wide, brown plains of Dhomokos and Pharsala where Julius Caesar defeated Pompey in 48 B.C. and Crown Prince Constantine fought the Turks in 1897, I concentrated on ways of avoiding my familiar antagonists, the Military and the Law, and how to get from the coast alone to the summit of Mount Olympos. I would get off the train at a station close to the shore—fortunately only a station, not an inhabited place—late that night. If I could avoid notice there, I would sleep somewhere in a field and early next morning cut straight inland to the monastery of Metókhi, which the old general had drawn on the map, from which there would probably be some way up the headland called Stavrós where I could gain the path; that way I would by-pass the village of Litókhoro with its guides and its police headquarters. I must trust to ingenuity to pass through the military installations I would find, as they had told me at the Alpine Club, all over the lower slopes; Andoni would have given me good counsel here: "Tell them a few lies, Koumbáre." I also thought how he would have deplored this voyage. "Never go to the North," he had told me once; "there are wolves, there are Bulgars . . . Nothing is more foolish than to travel alone in Greece these days. Don't throw yourself away. Think of your future." I reflected sadly that I had been living in the present for the last four years, and now the future was too close.

At seven-thirty we reached Larissa and continued on into the great plain of Thessaly; dotted with flocks of sheep and ancient grave tumuli, it drank up the onrush of night so fast I could not see where the flatland ended and the hills began again. In a few minutes we were in the Vale of Tempe, the lights from the train windows falling upon masses of dense foliage and trunks of willows and plane trees leaning far out over the black swirl of the river; and on the other side the silhouette of cliffs blocked out the night sky. We stopped for a few minutes in what looked like an inn yard beside a cove in the river bank, with one or two lamps hanging from the branches of gigantic sycamores, where people stood under the windows of the train, holding up little baskets of vine leaves full of ripe figs, calling to the passengers, "Figs from the banks of the Peneiós, only two thousand!" Ten minutes later I could feel the train turning sharply; we had reached the shore of the North Aegean. The windows framed only the empty night till we stopped again, and I heard the conductor shouting along the station platform, "Litókhoro . . . Litókhoro."

I climbed on to the platform and watched the windows of the train flash past like a reel of motion-picture film, while the roar of the cars was carried into the night. Around me every-

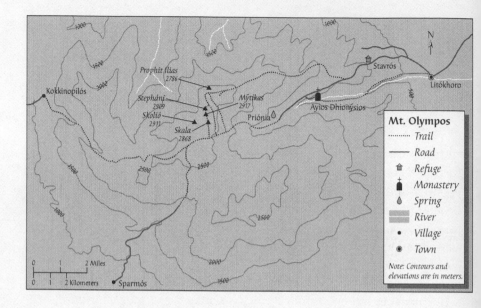

Mt. Olympos
.... Trail
——— Road
🏠 Refuge
✚ Monastery
◊ Spring
▒▒▒ River
• Village
◉ Town

Note: Contours and elevations are in meters.

thing was dark except for the open door of the station-master's office. I walked quietly past a man at a desk with his back to the door, then climbed down into deep sand pricked by esparto grass waist-high, to a stony beach where I took off my clothes. The air was warm and I could see the stones under the water as I walked in, washing off the day's dust and soot in a foaming sparkle of phosphorus. I swam under water through filtered moonbeams under cold, yellow light spilling all over the surface. I fell asleep that night by the little splash and fall of the Aegean a few feet away; on the other side the massif of Olympos reared up into the stars.

Between four and five I watched these paling into the white light. I swam again far out and looked along the level of the water, barely rippled by the dawn wind, straight into the big, red eye of the sun, which only a few minutes before had touched the domes and towers of Constantinople across that same sea. The pink and green water rippled back towards the shoreline, behind it a shelf of land, then a surge of forested heights rising one behind the other to an upper world of plateaux, ravines, ridges and one bright wall of rock nine thousand feet high, crowned with five summits sparkling in the early day. Only when I had passed through the intermediary strip of coastal plain and the first forested headlands could I visualize myself up there. To the south the houses of Litókhoro clustered together at the mouth of an enormous gorge running up into the mountain, cleaving its eastern side in two; directly inland rose the Stavrós, and somewhere at its foot would be the Metókhi monastery where I must be ready with any number of falsehoods on the tip of my tongue. It was six when I started off through the soft sand. A stubble field across the road looked as if it stretched all the way to the foot of the Stavrós. A man on a donkey turned as we passed each other at a distance, but did not stop. Soon I was crossing an uncultivated tract carefully flattened out like an airstrip, with a big shed at one end, through whose open door I could see the blunt snouts of bulldozers. Then the ground began to rise as I entered the mouth of a wide, shallow gully between scrub-covered hills leading back to a higher shelf. High up one side two men were working in the brush, building concrete foundations for what might be a pillbox. They called, "Where do you go so early in the morning?"

"To the Metókhi."

"You won't be able to get there this way. You have to go round by Litókhoro."

I shouted up the hill, "It'll take hours to go all the way back."

"But the soldiers up ahead won't let you through."

"But I have to get to the monastery as quickly as possible," I called back. "Friends are waiting for me who have come all the way from Athens; if we can get guides we may go up the mountain."

"You'll find the soldiers at the top of the gully."

"Thank you," I called.

"May your hour be good."

So I continued. The ground rose steadily and the walls of the gully narrowed together. Then the path came to an end at the confluence of two sandy ravines where a squad of soldiers were mixing lime in a pit, bared to the waist against the heat already beating up from the earth.

"Excuse me, but is this the right way to get to the Metókhi?" I asked. "I meant to go round by Litókhoro, but this gully seems to have led me in the opposite direction."

"Do you want to go to the monastery?" said one of the soldiers, peeling a river of sweat off his brow. "I'll show you the way."

He set off with long, swift strides and I followed him into a wilderness of small tracks leading this way and that through the dense and brittle scrub. He showed me a big rock pointing up out of this jungle of dwarf ilex and said, "You'll find other soldiers there; they'll tell you what path to take, but don't lose it, for you'll never find it again."

"Thank you very much," I said.

"Since I was there to help you!" he exclaimed, and strode off.

At the rock more soldiers were digging trenches. One of them called as I passed, "Eh, *patrióti*, do you have the time?"

"Half past seven," said I, walking on at a steady pace—I could already see the white walls of the Metókhi embedded in a clump of cypresses under the headland.

But I would have done better to ask the way; the level surface of the coastal plain had risen like a dish in an oven and I found myself in a mass of little hills ringed about by gullies of surprising depth where it was hard to follow any direction. It took three hours to reach the monastery, only three miles from the shore. Here an avenue of cobblestones, shiny and smooth with age, led into a courtyard where tight, tufted cypresses with trunks like organ pipes rose up between the wooden galleries and only the splash of water pouring out of a carved stone mouth disturbed the silence. The place seemed uninhabited, and there was a chill of autumn in the shade. I soaked my head in the jet of water, then saw two army officers watching me from the doorway.

"Good morning," I said. "Could you tell me if a group of climbers stopped here on their way up the mountain?"

"When?"

"Either this morning or yesterday," I explained confidently. "We had arranged to meet at the Stavrós, but I don't know if they came by here or went up some more direct way from Litókhoro."

"Some people did pass," said the officer. "I didn't see them myself."

This was a lucky chance. "Do you know how many?" Questions of one's own were useful for dissimulation.

"I don't know," he said, then called, "Yorgi!" and an old man appeared in the doorway, wiping his hands on an apron. "How many went up the mountain yesterday?"

"Five," the old man answered.

"Good! That must be they," I said happily.

"But they weren't going very far," the old man added: "only to the monastery of Ay Dhionýsi."

"Oh?" I tried to sound surprised. "Do you remember if there were two Frenchmen among them?"—launching off on another tangent.

"No. They were all from Komotiní."

The officer turned to me and said, "Where are you from?"

I said "Athens" and trusted to luck. I was on the point of adding that my father came from Northern Epiros, but the officer was eyeing me impassively.

"If you intend to climb the mountain, you must have permission from the major commanding the battalion up at the Stavrós. We haven't had any foreigners here for some months," he said.

"The path leads straight up from here, does it not?" I asked, anxious to be gone.

"Yorgi, take him up to headquarters," he said to the old man. The two of us walked out of the courtyard on to a path that zig-zagged up the face of the bluff.

I said to the old man, "If you see my friends today, tell them I've gone on and shall wait for them at the Alpine Club Hut."

"Do you expect to get to the summit? To the Mýtikas itself?" he asked.

"For years I've been hoping to do this," I said. "I have come a long way for it—all the way from Athens."

"We used to go up when we were boys, chasing the wild goats on to the topmost pinnacle of the Mýtikas itself, but I haven't been there since I was sixty. However, old Khristo down in the village, who's over seventy and climbed it last summer, must have been up and down a hundred times before the foreigners came and made what they called the first ascent. He guided them."

"The Swiss, you mean?"

"Yes, and you'll see the Swiss flag there since they were the first to climb it, as they say. Naturally, there's no Greek flag to say Olympos is a Greek mountain. There are things we take here as a matter of course; when our goats get lost we have to bring them down again . . . Now, I won't take you farther than here; you'll find your way. There are soldiers all over the hillside. See, there and there." He pointed out a band of men building a gun emplacement and another group leading a train of mules laden with planks. "They're busy everywhere," he said.

"So I have seen," said I, looking down the way we had come. The steep slope had lifted us well up over that strip of lowland between mountain and sea: the old invasion route of Persians, Huns, Goths, Slavs and Turks.

"This is the way the Bulgars would come if they marched into Greece," the old man said. "So now they're sealing it off as best they can. Poor Greece, she is never quiet."

We wished each other a good hour and parted.

Then I had an access of anxiety and called to him down the slope, "It doesn't really matter about the permit, does it?"

"The what?"

"The weather," I said, thinking better of it.

"No, certainly not," he called. "It'll hold for several days longer."

Then a soldier with his mule came clattering down the path towards me. "Going up to the Mýtikas, eh?" he said as he brushed by.

"I'm looking for some friends from Komotiní who have gone on to Ay Dhionýsi. You don't happen to have met them on the road?" I asked, still intent on diverting interest away from myself.

"Not a soul," he replied, hurrying after his beast.

It was one o'clock when I came into a thick forest of deciduous trees near the top of the hill. I went off the path a little distance to eat some bread and cheese, then lay down in the soft, luxuriant underbrush and slept. When I awoke, the shadows had moved and the white midday glare given way to the warm yellow of the afternoon; with the weight of heat and weariness off my eyelids I could stretch, yawn and roll about in the fragrant moisture of small-leaved plants.

A voice called through the trees, "If you go to the Mýtikas you'll be alone, poor evil-fated one. Nobody new has passed by the Metókhi." A group of soldiers waved to me and went on up the path.

By now everyone on these hillsides must know someone was on his way to the summit. In half an hour I reached the top of the headland, where huge umbrella pines stood on the grassy lawn, streaked with their shadows in the crystal afternoon. In hammocks between their branches and on the ground soldiers lay about like figures in a *fête champêtre*. Water flowed out of a rock into a hollowed log, and mules wandered over the hilltop, lazily cropping the grasses. I continued walking, not too quickly, into the forest.

I could see the yellow shore a long way down, but already at three o'clock the air was cooler among trees denser and leaves more translucent than the dry, scrawny pines covering the lower slopes with their lanky boughs and sparse, shadeless foliage. I had come to the end of the track up the loose stones of the sun-scorched hillside, and from here on the path levelled out into a broad avenue ten feet wide or more, curving in and out round the ravines and ridges like a contour on a map. At last I could walk erect as in the privacy of some endless terrace, with the steep slope above me and the plunging depth below carpeted red in leaves lying light on the surface but packed down, stuck together and melting underneath into black, sweet-smelling loam. Up and down, before and behind, wherever the eye could reach, the mountainside was held in place by the trunks of grey, enormous beech trees, and slanting sunbeams shone through the masses upon masses of their leaves and the arabesques of their long branches stretching out into the bright, vertical air. The path curved westward, and through the glistening leaves rose the other side of the Litókhoro gorge, cliffs with sun-crisped edges and a haze of blue shadow. At a turn in the path I looked a thousand feet down the ravine's throat and saw a tiny quadrangle of walls glowing peach-coloured in the last rays like a soft jewel sunk in the depth of the forest: the Monastery of Saint Dionysos in Olympos, where I had been told five hundred monks once lived, built so deep in the ravine that the six aged men left to guard its empty halls never see the sun for eight months out of the year.

Now from the shore of the Aegean, evening was slowly flooding up the gorge. It was nearly six when I saw on the path ahead of me two men reclining against a stone.

"Health and happiness! Where is your Worship going?" one of them called, a very old man with a snowy stubble of beard over his jaw. "Sit and rest yourself."

I dropped my pack and the two levered themselves into different positions with the long wild-olive crooks they held under their arms. For the first time that day I spoke the truth about myself and it seemed not to surprise them; while I talked they listened more to the murmur of bells from a herd moving slowly away. I told them I had not expected to find shepherds here.

"Last year, it's true, there were no shepherds on Olympos," said the younger man, who looked forty but might equally have been ten years more or less; his eye had the frosty glint of one who lives close to animals and the weather, and as he talked the breath whistled out through the spaces where several of his teeth had been. "Last year we had to pasture our things in the flat-

land round Litókhoro. It was unsafe to take them any distance
from the village for there were a few Andartes not yet captured.
A party of Athenians came to climb the Mýtikas for the first time
since the war, but they got no farther than where we're sitting.
Three Andartes took all their money, their watches and most of
their clothes."

"And their shoes," added the old shepherd. "The sight of those
rich Athenians limping into the village without shoes!"

"So after that," the other went on, "the army made a final drive
into the mountain and forbade us to come anywhere near. They
captured two of the brigands."

"And the third?" I asked.

"Once they surrounded him, but he got away. They say he
was so hungry he became like a savage. He may still be somewhere on the mountain, but it's more likely people are hiding him
in some town. But Olympos is large, and Ayios Dhiónysos pro-
tects the solitary. Tomorrow you'll go up to the Mýtikas and tonight we shall be all together," he said, rising to his feet with a
push on his crook. "We go now to gather the things. Keep straight
on to the goat-pens at the head of the ravine. Tonight we shall
drink milk. . . ."

As I walked on, they clambered up into the forest, shouting
after their beasts, "Na! Na! Na! NA NA NA NA your Christ, your
Cross, your baptismal tub!"

During the last half-hour of my road I heard a sound below
me like a strong wind growing louder and louder as the floor of
the ravine rose up towards the level of the path, which led out
into a wide area formed by the plunging confluence of two gorges
higher up, the cliffs on three sides echoing to the roar of water
falling high and low. In a corner of the glen was the familiar wall
of branches in the shape of a horseshoe. On the level top of a little cliff over the water another wall of heaped-up branches with
matted goat's hair capes thrown over them formed a semicircle
round a fireplace of boulders and a single cedar with red bark
and thick needles, from whose lower branches hung a few big-

bellied pots blackened and caked with soot. There was a smell of dead ashes in the fireplace and the floor of the shelter was strewn with boughs of fir and cedar. I threw off my rucksack and felt the strange buoyancy that springs up under one's feet at the end of a day's walk laden down. This was the place marked on my map as Priónia, where the old general had said the water was seven degrees above freezing at the height of summer. I looked over the edge to the long, smooth, sliding pools below, overhung with willows and dark green masses of boxwood, then climbed down the rocks to a tiny beach of silver sand where I took off boots and stockings and washed my feet, which straightway became numb. Filled by the waterfall above it, the pool was fifteen feet across and deep enough to stand in to one's shoulders. Walking in the mountains produces the habit of a few overwhelming desires, of which it is not possible to feel more than one at any given time, and the effort of the day now culminated in the need to immerse myself. I undressed hurriedly and dived in head foremost, then with three strokes an unbearable ache seemed frozen into my body. Almost paralysed, I climbed out and dried myself wildly with shirt, trousers and sleeping-bag; half wet still, I put on my clothes, flinging my arms about and dancing up and down to bring life back into my hands and feet.

A small boy sat on top of the rock, gazing down at me without astonishment. "I've lit a fire," he said.

I scampered up the cliff. A pile of branches was snapping and crackling in the fireplace, and I put my hands as close as possible to the flames.

"Was it your father I met back there on the path?" I said.

"Yes. There are three who share this goat-pen."

"Brothers?"

"No. Better than brothers. Nowadays brothers, fathers, sons, all kill each other."

"How old are you?"

"Eleven."

Dusk was filling the glen. The cliffs pointed dark into the high, radiant sky where six thousand feet above us the southern peaks of Olympos still bathed in gentle yellow light like a flight of wings against the blue.

The boy, whose name was Niónios, or Dhionysos, after the patron saint of the mountain, told me how every day one of the children here would take the milk down to Litókhoro, while another child brought the donkey up again in the evening. Then from the far side of the ravine a loud yell carried into the glen, followed by a piercing whistle that bounced back and forth between the rock walls, and through the forest I saw a herd pouring down the steep, a shepherd behind them swinging himself from trunk to trunk, hooting and whistling in his descent. In half an hour the other herd arrived, driven by the two I had met on the path, and the walls of the glen resounded to the flurry of hoofs and bells while several hundred goats were driven through the pen and milked. Then, when it was dark, five of us sat round the fire and dipped our bread into the cauldron of milk between our feet. Words were not necessary since they asked no questions. We fell asleep around the same fire and during the night someone threw a cape over me, the only sign of any particular regard.

The goats were milked again before dawn. Then the herds swept up the mountainside in separate directions and the three men and the boy were gone with barely a salutation, in the shepherd manner.

I climbed up through the cedars and followed the stream to its source under a huge rock in the middle of the gorge—a place which the shepherds had called Palavós, the Babbling Fool. From here on directions should have been unnecessary. I could see the whole upper gorge mounting the eastern face of Olympos; willow, beech and walnut trees gave way to gigantic firs almost black against the white stone, climbing the steepest ridges that led up to the tight-bunched, starry summits of which one never lost sight, though they looked still more remote from here than from the sea. For seven more hours they remained vertiginous and inaccessible, while the path climbed and the gorge grew shallower and then divided into a vast fan of gullies, between two of which, pointing on a high spur, I caught sight of the gable of the Alpine Club Refuge; I reached it at one o'clock. A well-built house of stone was an incongruous thing at six thousand feet, with the precipitous gorge in full view all the way down to the coast, and the white, wide, concave wall of rock with its summits shooting into the air, yet from that same wall the long limbs of the mountain descended with other peaks all round like hospitable arms. I tried the door of the refuge; it was locked, but the weather was fair and I had no need of a roof. On the dry stones under the big, straight, jutting trunks I ate a midday meal and fell asleep. At three that afternoon the fog floated up in small, white puffs like water-lilies through the ravine. Leaving my rucksack under a tree, I set off up the steep ridge for a horizon in the middle of the sky.

The great firs thinned out and the packed boulders of the ridge grew smaller and looser, while the sky became hazy and more and more white clouds floated upward from the sea. The going was steep but so regular that I did not think to scan with any great care the terrain of the main eastern wall to my right. In two hours I reached the top of the Skala peak, not quite three hundred feet lower than the highest summits that rose one beyond the other in a straight line directly to the north. Now at last I was only separated from the top of Olympos by a small col—but in a matter of minutes everything around me was invisible in the dark fog rising from the lower zones of air. There was a swirling wind in the grey-brown light, and then a dim, pyramidal shape loomed through the mist in front of me: another peak called Skolió to the west. It was five; there was a chance the cloud would lift towards sunset and from there I might have a view of all three summits, the Stepháni and the Great and Lesser Mýtikas. So I crossed to the Skolió along the edge of a precipice and there waited for Olympos to reveal itself behind the thick, milky element pouring steadily up the nearest visible brim of the cliff beneath me. Then in the space of a few seconds the rim extended farther and farther out into the fog, and suddenly a dark depth dropped across the air to one long, jagged mass of stone, fissured and split from top to bottom into a series of black points while moment by moment the cloud lifted off them. The whole wall plunged for thousands of feet into a world of menacing, slimy ledges, one beneath the other slanting too steeply for hand or foot, to a point where one could see no more. Down there it was night already; here there was still time to climb higher.

I made my way back along the precipice to the Skala peak, descended into a narrow col, then began to mount up a steep slope while the fog came down again and covered everything but the next handhold and a small circle of brownish-yellow stone tilted up against the surrounding whiteness. At last I could see the edge of the stone circle all round me with nothing beyond.

I had only one desire now: to stay till the fog should clear and I could see the sunset from the summit; somehow or other I would find my way down to the refuge in the dark. The fog did clear after a few minutes, only to show me I had climbed the wrong peak; a few feet higher, a few yards away across another chasm, rose the top of the Great Mýtikas, and now the sun was setting. Under a heavy bank of clouds the last watery rays slanted ever so slightly upward from the other side of Greece. On one side was the vertical drop into that dank, inhuman cirque I had seen from the Skolió, and on the other the eastern wall of the mountain facing the Aegean. I decided to go straight down it, instead of returning to the Skala and descending by the long ridge I had come up in the afternoon. It was growing dark so fast it was hard to see what hazards this might entail, and I started down again, taking a little extra care where to place each foot. Soon I needed my compass with its luminous dial. Seeing nothing but the black outline of the earth around and above me, I could not take one route and avoid another but only keep on in a straight line down the mountain. I realized my stupidity when I reached the edge of an unexpected precipice in the dark. There was no knowing its height; it took an hour to climb to the nearest place where I could traverse to an easier slope. Even then I could only continue in the same straight line, following the compass, and once again before I knew it I was lying on a narrow ledge, feeling with one hand a new cliff falling away on the other side. A few feet off I could just make out the shape of a fir tree, its top level with the ledge; uncertain whether I could climb back again to some other traverse, I stood up and jumped. My outstretched arms clasped a whipping, bending, stinging mass of branches and tightened round the trunk, which only swayed backwards and forwards as I climbed down to another ledge where it grew, and from which I was unable to find an exit for what seemed like a very long time. And so down three thousand feet of precipices, which would have been insignificant by day, during the next four hours.

It was midnight when I reached the slope above the refuge and stumbled in the dark upon the rucksack under the tree.

I woke up next morning thinking of water; the two gullies slanting on either side of the refuge were filled with perpetual snow and ice. Beneath, in the gully to the south, was a spring which flowed with a thin trickle during the morning hours, and here I filled my canteen before setting off again, this time with my rucksack. Higher than this there were no more springs on Olympos, as I remembered many times that morning when I would have given much to drain my canteen of its last drop on the hot stone and little cliffs which last night's descent had made familiar. While the hours wore on, high overhead the Skala and the two peaks of the Mýtikas and the Stepháni next to it preserved, it seemed for ever, that brilliant, sharp remoteness I had first noticed from the shore. It was like climbing a gigantic stair, mounting so slowly I hardly noticed it growing narrower, nor the twisted pinnacles that rose like baroque columns out of the slope, one above the other, closer and closer on either side, until the whole vast eastern wall had become a precipitous couloir between a forest of pinnacles of which the highest was the Mýtikas itself. Now it was like a stair inside a tower. I climbed more and more slowly.

The first moments at the top came less as a surprise than as a sense of something justly fulfilled. The level space around me was only a few feet wide but long enough to lie down on, with several irregular, flat slabs forming, as it were, miniature terraces beneath. I stood on the easternmost edge and all at once my thirst vanished with the cool touch of wind as I breathed the upward rush of tingling air. I ate an apple and needed nothing more during a long afternoon. Once the fog blew up out of the ravine and for some time I was left alone in the middle of the white air with a small Swiss flag painted on a square of metal that swivelled round and round the top of a rod planted permanently and neatly in the rock. While the cloud lightened and moved, there stood forth one by one the Lesser Mýtikas which I had climbed yesterday, and the Skala and Skolió, to the north the Stepháni and Prophit Ilias. The mist withdrew over the sea, soft and blue 9,580 feet below, and the sun came out from the clouds and the intimate sky smiled on the hills of Macedonia and the peaks of the Grammos and the Pindos, on Athos rising across the sea, on Parnassos farther south, and on both sides of the summit the immense, brown, shadowy, undulating uplands of Olympos, spacious and warm and kindly as if fingers of sunlight had formed their shape. There were winds everywhere, but it was possible to take shelter on these narrow but comfortable slabs of stone, still warm under a cloudless sky: for the setting of the sun the Greek uses a verb meaning to reign in splendour.

At half past seven I climbed down to the brown plateau below the Skolió peak. In one corner there was a snowfield near which I installed myself for the night, filling my canteen with snow and melting it against my body in the sleeping-bag.

I slept round the clock and returned to the top at nine next morning. It was a clear day, with haze on the horizon. The hours passed, gentle and slow. During the afternoon I descended the eastern face into fog-filled basins and the zone of fir trees and the beech forests six thousand feet lower to reach the goat-pens of Priónia at nightfall. The shepherds were there with their children and they made a place for me round the fire for the evening's milk. They asked if I had seen the brigand anywhere, but I had forgotten about him long since. After we had eaten, the old shepherd with the white stubble on his face leaned back against the wall of the shelter and said, "The spirit moves me to sing a song." So he began it, and the others joined in.

> Lads of the Morea and you of Roumeli
> By the bread we have eaten together I beseech you
> Go to my country and to my own people.
> But do not go into my village when either the sun or the moon
>   is high,
> Do not let off your guns, do not sing songs
> Lest my mother hear you, and my unhappy sister.
> And if they come and ask you news, do not tell them the
>   first time,
> And if they ask again and yet a third time,
> Do not say I am dead, lest their hearts be made heavy.
> Tell them only that I got married in these parts,
> That I took the gravestone for mother-in-law and the black
>   earth to wife,
> And the little stones for my brethren and cousins.

During the night fell the first heavy rain of winter. We sat huddled together until it grew light around five o'clock. It was still raining while the shepherds milked the goats, and the fire for the morning cauldron flamed bravely against the downpour. An hour later, as I stuffed a sodden sleeping-bag into my rucksack and tightened down the straps, one of the shepherds pointed up through the walls of the glen to where the highest peaks were all turning crimson.

"Still another day of sun," he said; "thanks be to Saint Demetrios."

The others were lashing two barrels full of the night's and the morning's milk to the saddle of a grey, patient, blinking donkey.

One or two of the men called good-bye and the others waved as they ran off after their herds. It was Niónios' turn to take the milk, and I went down with him, reaching the plain at mid-day. We parted at a house on the outskirts of the village. Several women standing in their doorways or looking out of their windows called to me, "So you went up the Mýtikas, eh?" as I walked through the streets, and when I sat down to a full meal outside a cookhouse in the square, a number of people came up to me and asked about my trip up the mountain. Gendarmes greeted me, and an old man who told me he had taken the first Franks up Olympos in 1913 sat down at my table and showed me letters he had received in the course of the years from mountain-eers who had visited Greece, as well as a note of thanks from the Court Chamberlain acknowledging a congratulatory telegram he had sent to the King of the Hellenes on his birthday several years before. Once he called across the square and a thickset girl with a round, sturdy face and a rifle slung over one shoulder strode over and gave me a handshake of alarming strength.

"This is my daughter," said the old man.

"So you're the one?" she said heartily. "Well! I have work to do. I'll see you later."

As she walked off her father said, "That girl has killed many a *kapetánios* of the guerrillas." He gave me a photograph of himself standing on a scrub-covered slope with a coil of rope across his chest and an alpenstock in one hand. He said I must be tired and showed me to a little copse of pines where I could sleep before the Salonika-Athens train came by in the afternoon. His manners were courtly and his bearing dignified; when he said he would come and wake me in an hour and I apologized for the trouble, he said, "It is an honour to do what one can for a foreigner."

Yesterday, I reflected drowsily under the pine trees, I was alone on the summit of Olympos, last night I had been with shepherds who could not read or write, now I was in the custody of a ceremonious old villager, and tonight I would be back in Athens; in a couple of weeks I would be coming into New York harbour. At three that afternoon the train stopped for a few minutes at the little station by the shore: just long enough for me to be helped up the steps by the old man and his goodtempered, muscular daughter, who waved as the train started forward. Now I was in motion. A much longer journey had begun, and a part of me had left Greece already.

The train was crowded with passengers from northern Macedonia and all the racks were full, so I fitted my pack between my knees as I sat down in the only empty seat in the car. It was hot and I drank some of the water I still had from Prióna.

A woman on the seat facing me said, "Have you been on Olympos?" Her voice was quiet and she spoke English clearly.

I asked, "Do you know what time we get to Athens?"

"I think around midnight."

On either side the yellow fields and the blue sea sped past as I sat isolated among my own thoughts.

"I'm coming back from a village near the Serbian frontier where they speak Slavo-Macedonian," she said. "I thought it would be interesting to see how people lived in a region one hears so little about in Athens. It is a military zone and frontiers change—the family I stayed with ate weeds and carob beans, anything short of grass. They gave me their one bed because I was a stranger, and searched far and wide for food to give me."

The train was turning; I saw in daylight the brown eddies of the Peneiós sliding smoothly under the plane trees on the bank.

"They wouldn't take money," she went on, "how can one ever repay such people! I decided to take one of their daughters back with me, take her out of that ghastly life. Her father and mother wouldn't hear of it, but finally last night I prevailed on them. She's fifteen; my family know nothing about it yet. Heaven knows what they'll say. I don't care; I'll give her my bed to sleep in, I can give her my clothes. I'll educate her in some trade and share with her everything I have till she can make her way."

Night fell when we entered the mountains beyond the plain of Thessaly. People wandered up and down the car, striking up acquaintances in the atmosphere of curiosity and good-fellowship I had met so many times in trains and buses. It is easy to come close when there is an end to a journey.

On the two seats next to us were an old man and a boy in his early twenties, father and son. The old man told us he was ninety-six; he had been born in Constantinople and in his youth had gone to Rumania. "I was a baker," he said, "a prosperous man. I have buried three wives, good women all. I made many children; this one is my youngest, the others have gone all over the world. Perhaps my eldest sons are grandfathers themselves now, who knows? This is an age when families are scattered and lose one another. Now in Rumania they do not want foreigners to own shops—one can understand why, perhaps—yet I was always used to finding money when I put my hand in my pocket."

"You who come from America," said the boy, "tell me, is it possible to live there like a human being? Is there a place in the world where one can live like a human being?"—he repeated the phrase bitterly. "We were driven from our home by the new régime. The Greek Government made proclamations saying refugees would be made welcome in Greece, our mother-country as they called it, though our ancestors had been living in Asia Minor since the Byzantine Empire. We came and they put us in the camp for refugees at Lavrion, under the supervision of the police. First, committees of foreigners picked out certain of us for emigration, after that the police decided who should leave. Jobs were promised to the rest but we were never allowed out and at last I managed to get away to Lamia. Someone gave me a donkey and a cart and I went round the villages collecting vegetables and fruit to sell in the streets. Two years ago in Bucharest I was studying to be an architect."

"And wandering about the streets like a beggar he took a girl without a dowry and married her—naked, the fool. That is why I too," said his father, "left the camp at Lavrion and came to Lamia to be with my son and teach him the right path. For months we lived in a pine forest outside the town, then the rains began and the Welfare Bureau allowed us to move into a ruined mosque where the wind blew through the empty doors and we had no blankets. The *vláka*, he married a girl simply to have someone to keep him warm at night! Then he made enemies with the Welfare Bureau and they told the police to chase us out. We went to Saloníki, and the girl went back to live with the others on the streets, just as I said she would. Now the police in Saloníki have told us to leave or they will send us back to the camp. So we go to Lamia again because the fool wishes to find his wife and take her to another city where all our sorrows will begin again. Sorrow lasts as long as life. Life is long; I can never remember a time when I was not alive," he murmured absently. "Periklí, where are those grapes, so that we can offer something to our guests?"

The boy pulled a basket from under the seat and lifted up a bunch of dusty, half-squashed grapes long since gathered off the vine. "Share these with us if you will," he said in a gruff voice with an edge of sarcasm to it, as if to cover up his shame at offering so little.

An hour later they got down from the train at Lamia station, carrying their basket between them, and the old man came round to our window to say good-bye a second time. As we moved out of the town the black shapes of mountains rose again into the darkness that seemed to press in against both sides of the lighted car. The woman from Athens got up and went to the far end to see the girl she was bringing back with her.

Across the aisle sat a young woman in black with a childlike face and huge frightened eyes, with a little boy beside her holding on his lap a bundle wrapped in a tablecloth. Next to them both and on the facing seat three young men, good-looking and well dressed, were busy engaging her attention with jokes and questions. For a long time she answered nothing to their conceited banter, but finally putting one hand to her mouth, said in a muffled voice, "My husband was killed."

One of the young men said, "How old are you?"

"Twenty-three."

"*Po-pó!*" he exclaimed with a look at her son. "That makes how old when you were married?"

The girl for some reason burst out laughing at this remark, which took her by surprise; she had no teeth at all.

"So you're going to Athens, eh?" said one of the young men, who was certainly under twenty-three himself.

The girl nodded.

"*Bá*, you don't really know where you're going. You don't know anything about anything." Being a man, he could behave as he liked towards a widow.

From the far end of the car the woman from Athens came down the aisle, stepped between the girl and the young men and said firmly, "I'm sitting here."

They stood up slowly one after another, looking her up and down. Then they walked off.

Across the aisle I watched the girl's mouth, a dark hole in her face as she talked.

"He died last spring. Two years ago the Andartes took him prisoner and carried him off across the Albanian frontier. He escaped and came home and the police in our village put him in prison because they said his mind was infected by the ideas of the Communists. Finally they let him go; he was called into the army. He was killed on the Bulgarian border, somewhere north of Serres." She glanced down at her son. "It is not easy for a widow to go on living in her own village," she said with a look of supplication at the other woman. "I have a sister in Athens; we're going to her. I shall try to find work."

A man came down the aisle, selling bread and cheese and salami. The woman bought most of the contents of his basket and gave it to the widow and her little boy. Then she turned to me and said, "Won't you join us?"

I moved into the place next to her. The young widow's spirits revived with nourishment, but the boy still looked so miserable that I made a mouse out of my handkerchief which I flicked into his lap; he smiled and his mother, hiding her mouth with her hand, laughed like a child. Soon I fell asleep; many hours had passed since the early downpour at Priónia.

I heard a voice repeating my name over and over again; the woman beside me was trying to wake me up. We had arrived. She and the girl from the Slavo-Macedonian village, and the young widow and her son and I got down from the train together; carrying one another's bundles, we went through the station and all got into a taxi. We stopped at a door of frosted glass and wrought iron with a light burning behind it, in a dark street off Canning Square. To one side was an array of names in little slots, but we looked in vain for the widow's sister.

"I don't know what sort of a house she lives in." The widow looked round her at the concrete pavements and the high buildings echoing to the roar of a late tram on the avenue. "She only told me the number and the street."

"It's an apartment house," the woman said. "We'll find her somehow."

That moment an elderly couple in evening clothes pushed past us and turned a key in the door.

Our companion said, "Do you have the kindness to tell us if Kyria Koula Dhimitriou lives in this building?"

"Is it Koula you want? She lives in the cellar. Press that button," said the man.

He and his wife passed in and closed the door behind them with a clang. We pressed a button beside a slot without a name; the door buzzed and sprang open.

"I think your sister is the caretaker of this building," the woman said gently. "I hear steps inside, may the Panagia be with you."

The widow and the boy went in, each holding a little bundle in one hand, and again the door swung to. We went back to our taxi where the Macedonian girl was waiting. We sped up the long, dark, empty streets, turned a corner and drew to a halt outside my door. I offered her twenty thousand to pay my share of the taxi.

"No, I won't accept it," she said.

So I had to press it into her hand while I jumped out of the car and called "Good-bye."

A small hand reached out from the window of the taxi as it started forward again and vanished in the dark, while a street lamp on the corner illuminated the slow, downward-fluttering motion of a discarded drachmae note on the pavment.

CHAPTER **12**

The Unharvested Sea

I SAILED FOR AMERICA. THE past receded minute by minute as the waves of the wintry Atlantic rose and crested and spread across the water and sank and rose again.

I had grown used to waking before sunrise; one murky December morning I went on deck to look at the docks and warehouses along the Hudson River and the black silhouette of square-topped buildings rising against the sky like tree-trunks lopped and pollarded. That day a taxi carried me over a broadbanked road amid a hundred purring cars winding round the grey basins of Central Park to an apartment in a brownstone house on the East Side, and during the next weeks I met again the friends of my family and the people I had once known in school, in college, in the army. Old associations, friendships, affections had spoiled with absence and the inevitable process of growth and change which always takes one by surprise. There was a strange sensation in still working on the last chapters of my book on fortresses, begun so long ago. While the buses droned and boomed, and the thousand-windowed, straight, square apartment buildings of a billion bricks hid all one might have seen of sky, I must still leaf through ten or fifteen ragged little notebooks in which I had scribbled among those crumbling ruins smelling of thyme and the sun's heat; between their pages I would come upon a blade of grass

254

from Navarino, a thistle-spine from Argos or an insect squashed black from Kalamata.

I went to Washington and every day for a month talked with individuals who sat behind what was called the Greek Desk in this or that branch of a governmental agency whose scope and size baffled the imagination. I would state my qualifications and make my request: a job where it would be possible to make sure that the country people of Greece obtained the greatest benefit from the sums allotted, supposedly, for the purpose by a distant but well-intentioned Congress out of the taxes paid by a hundred-odd million of my fellow-countrymen. From behind the Desk they would ask what I thought of the success of the Truman Doctrine and of the American expenditures in Greece, but my answers were apt to be lengthy; my listeners would suggest I make an appointment with another office on another day.

One morning, before setting forth on my round of government buildings, a letter came to me from Kostandí. His family were well, he said, and the countryside round Sparta smelled sweetly at this season; he had broken the jaw of one of his neighbours, and the *kerata* had put him in prison for two months, but God is first and now he was out again; his eldest brother, Leonídha—did I remember the one they called the Monk?—had been taken to America by the rich cousin who owned the Old Santa Fé restaurant in Ouasigton Di Si, who had once made him blown-up promises but never done anything to help him. I decided to leave the United States Government to its own devices for one day, and found my way instead to a night club called Old Santa Fé on the corner of Alaska Avenue and Z Street. Now the doors of night clubs in the daytime, particularly when it is raining, have a shut, forbidding look somehow intensified by the curtained placards of nude girls in the windows; so that it was with a feeling of vague guilt that I tried the door and found it open. My feet sliding over a deeply carpeted floor, I walked into a long, dark room where the desolate light of the early afternoon fell upon the white squares of tables ready laid and a space of shiny parquet in the middle for the nightly floor-show. A man was polishing the chrome-plated rail of the bar along one side of the room. Did they have, I asked him, a man working here by the name of Leonídha?

"In back," was the laconic reply.

I continued past the bar and up some carpeted steps to the darkest end of the room, through a door into the kitchen. Bright was the electricity burning day and night here from the high ceiling, deep the aprons over the immense, immaculate stoves, loud the clatter of pots and pans as seven or eight white-jacketed men and women dragged them across the floor, filled them from gushing, steaming taps and hauled them up on to the stoves, shouting to each other all the while in a nasal drawl which I did not immediately recognize as Greek: "Where this afternoon is the *Bóssis?* And who makes up tonight the *bilophéri?*"

The bill of fare, the boss—the words dawned on me standing in the kitchen door; that sinuous language could transform even the American idiom to its own pattern. Then a burly figure in a tight, white coat, bending over a sinkful of soapsuds with mountains of plates all round him, turned to face me, and there was Kostandí's brother, who had been the companion of a dance which lasted all one summer's day two years ago in a mountain village on Taygetos.

He dropped a dish into the foaming sink. "Andriko!" he cried.

"How long since anyone has called me by that name," I said as we grasped each other's hand.

"Panagia! It's as if I saw one of my own brothers."

I was introduced to everyone. They were all relatives, like Leonídha, of the Boss, who had brought them over since the war. A chair was brought in for me from the main hall, and I sat down in their midst while they peeled carrots and potatoes and plopped them into the huge vats that were then dragged off to cook upon the stoves. They knew no English, but in two or three years they had already lost the jagged intonations of their native tongue, speaking without gestures, as if these might give away their origins and brand them as foreigners in the eyes of those who some day would be their fellow-citizens. They brought me coffee as they might have done in Greece, but the coffee was not the thick, black Turkish syrup in a tiny cup but a thin brew made instantaneously out of concentrated powder. "Maxwell House Brand. Good stuff, eh?" said one of them, who knew a few words of English, adding with a laugh, "You are the boss in this land of brands."

"And how do you like 'this land of brands'?" I asked. "Is it better than Greece?"

One man pointed to a window opening on a grey courtyard and said, "Where is the sun?"

"The heat is sticky whether the sky is cloudy or bright," another said, pulling down the corners of his mouth and fingering his white jacket with distaste.

"But it's nicer here in America, when all is said and done," said a woman who was peeling carrots and no one contradicted her, so that it was impossible to know whether they were happier here or not. Anyway they all had plump, pink faces.

When I had drunk my coffee, someone brought me a cake, not a baklava or kataïphi but a slab of something frothy with a great deal of whipped cream.

I said to Leonídha, who sat beside me plunged in thought, "You've grown fat here."

He lifted his heavy shoulders in an inexpressive shrug and muttered, "What do you expect? There's nothing to do here but eat."

"Do you like America?"

"One doesn't know the language; one gets bored; there is nowhere to go."

He was earning forty dollars a week, most of which he sent home to his father and mother. He lived in one room costing fifty dollars a month, together with four others whom his cousin had brought over from Mistra a year before. These came in later that afternoon. I recognized their faces from mornings in the coffee-shops round the little square beneath the plane tree and from afternoons on Kleoméni's terrace, but not the saddle shoes they wore nor their wide-brimmed hats and padded shoulders.

Towards evening (as I could only tell by looking at my watch; for night and day and the passage of the seasons had no existence in this brightly-lit kitchen) they pressed me to stay on through the night and see the floor-show. I declined, but they led me out to meet the Boss. This was the cousin to whom I had written a letter at Kostandí's dictation one night in Ay Yanni; Panayiota had said, "A pity for the trouble." He was sitting alone at one of the white tables under the mysterious effulgence of red, green and purple globes: a big, smooth, dark man who looked as if he had any number of young girls under his control and as much to eat as he desired, and as many poor cousins as he needed to work for him. He told me he had been twenty years in America, and when we talked of Mistra and of Kostandí, he said he was planning to bring him over too. Then we talked of Greece in general. "Tourism is what she needs," he said. "Plenty of tourists, plenty of foreign capital. I say the future of Greece lies in hotels. They've got to build lots of nice, big, *de luxe* hotels all over that country. I'm going over next summer to see what I can do about it." He said I could stick around and see the floor-show, but I excused myself and went back to the kitchen to say farewell to Leonídha.

He would not come out into the dining-hall with the deep carpet and coloured light globes, but stood in the kitchen door with the white electricity behind him, looking lost and miserable and rather stupid and constrained in his dish-washer's jacket, and only said, "Good-bye, Andriko . . . just as if I had seen one of my brothers."

So I went out into the grey, wet vistas of Alaska Avenue and a week or so later returned to New York, having lost my temper so often and said so many stupid things among Governmental desks and offices that possibilities of a job in Greece were finally ruled out.

During the next six months I completed my book. From time to time letters would come from friends in Greece. One from Andoni in Megara said: "Do not be desolate, Koumbáre. Some day you will come back and I shall hear you playing *Tou Kítsou i Mána* on your flute and I shall run down the mountainside to meet you, and we shall go down and drink cold water from the spring. Always we talk of you, your Koumbára and your godson Nikolaki and the children and I, your Koumbáros." There were letters from people I knew only slightly, the innkeeper at Monemvasia or one of the shepherds on Olympos, asking me to send a parcel of clothes. I answered, trying to shut out the sound of traffic always in my ears, and once I wrote to Nikiphóros, to whom I had not said good-bye before I left. The day of my departure from Athens I had charged the person who saw me off to visit him if she had time, to take him a present of some book and say good-bye to him from me.

A year went by. Nikiphóros had said once that he would either write me a volume or else nothing; that he wrote nothing was no surprise. Then at last came a letter; I did not recognize the handwriting on the envelope, but the return address on the back was the name of a school of home economics for girls in Athens, and I suddenly remembered Kallirhói, Nikiphóros' friend. Delighted to have news of him, I opened the envelope and drew out a long letter in a slanting, careful hand, and there fell to the floor a few pages torn out of a pocket notebook, covered in hideous scrawl; it looked hard to decipher, so I turned first to Kallirhói's letter:

Our dear Kyrie Andrea,

It is ten months since a letter of yours dated March 22, 1952, filled us all with delight when Nikiphóros read it to us in his family's house in Pangráti, greatly moved that you had written to him. He sat down to answer immediately in case next day his mind should change. I send you the draft of a letter which was found in one of his pockets. However, it was fated to come into your hands unfinished, and after such a long time, and not sent by him but by me and his brothers, who at this moment sit and write you this letter, our hearts overcome. This will inform you that Nikiphóros died six months ago, on July 10.

From the time that he received your letter not many days went by before an aunt of his arrived from America. She took him on a trip to Macedonia, where the climate made his condition worse and he stayed for a long time in bed, far from his family. When he was able to stand on his feet, he desired to come back to Athens. On the outskirts of Komotiní his bus drove over a bridge and crashed into a ravine. Everyone in it was injured, and he was hurt in the kidneys. That was the fatal blow. They took him to hospital. He fought hard with death.

Every time his brothers and I met since then we have talked of writing to you, but we could never bring ourselves to do it. Today we thought we must with great effort do what should have been done a long time ago. . . .

Your company gave Nikiphóros much courage and pride, even though he did not let any expression of it appear in his manner. I had lived near him for years and knew him well. In many people's eyes he seemed wild, strange, solitary, perverse, with an exaggerated pride in himself. And yet he felt all things so strongly, and only out of great bitterness over his joyless life did all of that appear—everything he failed to be in the eyes of others. For he lived always alone, even in people's company, because he always saw death standing beside him while he was still on the threshold of life. His illness humiliated him and hurt his pride, and as time went on all the more distrust and scorn did he feel towards everything. Yet he was a rare human being who might have been outstanding if his fate had let him live and be well.

. . . His last days were tragic. He knew he would die, yet several times he believed even in a miracle. Once he spoke to me about you and his half-finished letter. He tried to suggest I finish it myself and send it to you, but his windpipe was blocked and he could not speak clearly. He told me how ashamed he was that he had perhaps offended you with his uncouth behaviour, and it relieved him to hear me say that you could never have misunderstood him, because you knew him too well.

I stop here my letter because the memory of that time is more than I can bear.

With boundless respect,
Kallirhói.

I put her letter down on a table. The sheaf of pages were sent me from a dead man. It was night and the lamp burned in the silent room; I turned the little pages over and over, trying to find the beginning or the end, but there was neither date nor heading. The handwriting sprawled this way and that, with hardly a word spelt right and in almost every line a savage gash with the nib of his pen where he had scratched out a phrase or a sentence, and there were gaps that seemed to indicate pages missing. It began abruptly:

to write you a letter to justify myself before you and to thank you for your well-chosen present and for your good feelings towards me. I had decided to pass by your school so that they could give me your address if they had it. Several days passed until yesterday morning I got your letter. You cannot imagine the pleasure it gave me. Double joy, one because I learn after so much time news from you yourself, and one because I held in my hands your address and I would now be able to write to you myself, the no-good *keratá* as you call me and in that you are not far wrong. I recognize that many times my behaviour was not what it should have been, that you were much better than me from every point of view. I treated you carelessly and I did not treat you courteously as a foreigner, as a human being, which you showed me. . . .

Another thing: I considered it a great misfortune that I did not see her myself when she came with your present, so that I might have asked her about you, where you are, what you might be doing, etc. But the same moment I thought of your school, I took the telephone and asked for you. They replied that you had left a long time before. Then I understood you had gone back to your country and my distress could not be described that I did not even have your address. . . .

You will put to good use all your labours, and your long and careful studies here will help you to create yourself and distinguish yourself in whatever you undertake. I hope from now on there may await you satisfaction, joy and good fortune in your life because you are educated, young, strong in health and equipped with many things to make your life happy and fortunate. This I pray for you with all my heart.

About things here what shall I write you? Athens and its life are as you left them. Winter is past and we find ourselves in the spring. As you know at this season the Attic earth is in all its beauty. It has put on a festive appearance, everywhere life overflows, and joy to him who can be glad in its beauty because you must know that there exist—I am avoiding something that I think is drowning me, is making me burst and makes my breathing difficult, and I am trying to cast myself out into the light into the air into life that I may hold on to something and control myself and resist and not fall into chaos but stand somewhere still and find tranquillity quiet calm release

The last word was written in the middle of the page, and there was no signature; nor was it possible, while the light burned on in the room and a sharp wind stirred the curtain and the noises of the winter night in the city came through the window, to catch any echo of his voice, or of other voices in that same country across the dark waters of separation.